# Madonna

The
*Rolling Stone*
Files

# Madonna

## The *Rolling Stone* Files

**The Ultimate Compendium of Interviews,
Articles, Facts and Opinions**
*from the Files of*
Rolling Stone

BY

# THE EDITORS

OF

# *Rolling Stone*

INTRODUCTION BY BARBARA O'DAIR

HYPERION

NEW YORK

Library of Congress Cataloging-in-Publication Data
Madonna, the Rolling Stone files: the ultimate compendium of
    interviews, articles, facts and opinions from the files of Rolling
    Stone / by the editors of Rolling Stone; introduction by Barbara
    O'Dair.
        p. cm.
    Includes discography, filmography, and videography.
    ISBN 0-7868-8154-2
    1. Madonna, 1958–
—Criticism and interpretation. I. Rolling Stone (San Francisco, Calif.)
ML420.M1387M27 1997
782.42166′092—dc21
[B]                                           96–46384
                                                  CIP
                                                  MN

Designed by Robert Bull Design

First Edition

10 9 8 7 6 5 4 3 2 1

# CONTENTS

# FOREWORD

T HE RISE OF MADONNA was an intriguing chain of events for us club-going Downtown New Yorkers in the early 1980s. As we watched, she progressed from homeless, down-and-out musician crashing with friends; at the notorious rehearsal hall called the Music Building; to dance-club enfant terrible, performing to tapes on the roof of Danceteria; to star of a film attempting to depict the Lower East Side punk-rock lifestyle (*Desperately Seeking Susan*); to full-blown icon, trend-setter and idol (as well as nemesis) to millions.

From the beginning, ROLLING STONE was as fascinated by Madonna as were its readers. And as the magazine's journalistic relationship with Madonna unfolds, it makes for fascinating reading. Rock critics ponder her art: superficial dance diva or serious artist with a beat? Interviewers struggle to decipher her: manipulative scene stealer or edgy entertainer with a social conscience? It's all here—from Random Notes to Record Reviews to in-depth Q&As. Rounding out the picture are a few pieces from ROLLING STONE's sister publication, *US,* which add that entertainment magazine's take on the world's most famous woman.

Offering her own insights into Madonna's mystique and artistry, former ROLLING STONE senior editor Barbara O'Dair, currently editor of *US,* has contributed an incisive overview and introduction to thirteen years' worth of coverage from ROLLING STONE.

We've had lots of help along the way to complete *Madonna: The* ROLLING STONE *Files.* Thanks to my ROLLING STONE Press staff: associate editor Shawn Dahl and editorial assistants Greg Emmanuel and Ann Abel. We're grateful to Barbara O'Dair and the fine writers whose work is showcased here (including the Random Notes and Notable News scribes: Christopher Connelly, Merle Ginsberg, Sheila Rogers, Chris Mundy, Jancee Dunn, Nilou Panapour, Kim Neely, Jeffrey Ressner and Michael Goldberg). Our appreciation also goes to Hyperion's

Robert Miller, Brian De Fiore, Laurie Abkemeier, Liz Kessler, and Victor Weaver. We couldn't have done it without ROLLING STONE's Jann S. Wenner, Kent Brownridge, John Lagana, Fred Woodward and Amy Goldfarb. Others who helped include Susan Richardson, Lucia Ware, Travis McGee, Leslie Van Buskirk and Mary Wagman, as well as Liz Rosenberg and her staff at Warner Bros. Also essential was our agent Sarah Lazin.

Most of all, our thanks to Madonna for her many groundbreaking achievements and her constantly surprising and changing personae. Who could be a more thought-provoking—and entertaining—subject?

Holly George-Warren
Editor, ROLLING STONE Press
September 1996

# Madonna

The
*Rolling Stone*
Files

## BARBARA O'DAIR

# INTRODUCTION

**M**ADONNA is the most famous woman alive. Simply, she has imprinted, one way or another, not only a generation but the world. Her artistic legacy includes twelve full-length recordings to date; twenty-nine of thirty-three Top Forty hits in the Top Ten; thirty-five, give or take, videos; fifteen or so movies, at least ten in which she had a starring role (the latest, *Evita,* garnered her a Golden Globe Best Actress award); a book of sexual fantasies; various stage roles; a multimedia company with several successful acts (Alanis Morissette, Me'Shell Ndegéocello); and an extraordinary amount of words written about her, a good number of which appeared in ROLLING STONE and are collected in this book.

Her personal life, from her dalliances to the delivery of her child, is tracked, scrutinized and documented as a matter of course. Her inner life is guessed at from lyrics and hypothesized from biographical nuggets such as her motherlessness since age five, and is as much a source of comfort for her fans as its existence is a source of doubt for her foes.

She is a living icon not just for her contrivances and a life lived large, even less for her music or other artistic achievements, but because Madonna as idea, example, archetype exists simultaneously with the real woman, the gap-toothed galpal who inspired a nation of millions to wear their underwear on top of their clothes. And she goes both ways: like a mirror ball from an era she postdated, she spins and we watch, as she reflects us in jagged, shiny pieces. Like a crystal ball that shows the future, she absorbs the world around her and refracts it, returning a progressive revision in the process.

**F**ROM THE FIRST synthesized stutters of "Everybody" to the husky confessions of "I Want You," her recent cover of the Marvin Gaye tune, Madonna's sexual allure has been foremost in her music. Underneath that allure, which occasionally alternates with the brittle and the bratty, is a haunting sadness. Perhaps it's the combination of this tenderness with Madonna's foibles and humor and power stances that has infiltrated the collective subconscious, enough so that a whole book has been dedicated to women's dream testimonials about her. In her introduction to the collection, *I Dream of Madonna, Women's Dreams of the Goddess of Pop,* editor Kay Turner writes, "Interestingly, women don't seem to dream of Madonna as an unapproachable superstar. . . . The theme that widely characterizes the dreams in this collection is that of friendship."

As Mikal Gilmore opined in ROLLING STONE on the occasion of the singer's first worldwide tour, "Little girls across the world seem to recognize a genuine hero when they see one." (Amy Fisher listens to Madonna in prison—the singer tore up a picture of Fisher's lover-betrayer Joey Buttafuoco on national television.) Boys, however, seem to sometimes see something else. In the grand tradition of rock criticism, the early pieces about Madonna were written mostly by men, and exuded a deep if fascinated unease. In the first major feature about Madonna, Christopher Connelly wrote in ROLLING STONE, "This is a woman who saves her sex-bomb act for the times when the meter's running. And don't let her oft-flashed BOY TOY belt buckle fool you. The men who have gotten close to her—tough guys a lot of them—have gotten their hearts broken as often as not. Throughout her life there has been one guiding emotion: ambition."

Connelly was not the only one to suggest that the star slept her way to the top, merely the first. One biographer laid it out quite pointedly: "She used one boyfriend to get a record deal; she used another to obtain a hit sound; she used her husband to ensconce her firmly in Hollywood; and she used Warren Beatty to gain credibility in the film world." Still, it was the rising star's aggressive yet playful fearlessness, of which this creative dating was merely a part, that has encouraged critics to disdain her work over time. "There are still those people," she told Gilmore presciently in 1987, "who, no matter what I do, will always think of me as a little disco tart."

While Madonna continues to both inspire fierce loyalty and provoke hot denunciations, she manages to be nearly irresistible. "I knew I had to be extra special supercharming to get what I wanted," she told ROLLING STONE's Fred Schruers in 1985, " 'cause I grew up with a lot of brothers and sisters, and we had to share everything. I did all I could to really stand out, and that nurtured a lot of confidence and drive and ambition."

S MADONNA HERSELF tells it, hers was a loving, competitive, middle-class Italian-Catholic household. Born August 16, 1958, in Bay City, Michigan, Madonna Louise Ciccone was the third child and eldest daughter (behind Anthony and Martin) of Silvio, a second-generation Italian immigrant and a Chrysler/General Dynamics engineer, and Madonna, a French-Canadian transplant, for whom her daughter was named. (Madonna the younger added the name Veronica at her confirmation.)

Also by her own account, she was the apple of her father's eye. "I was his favorite," she said. "I could get him to do anything." Her parents had three more children (Paula, Christopher and Melanie) in rapid succession before her mother was diagnosed with breast cancer; she died December 1, 1963.

The loss of her mother was the singular event of Madonna's life. "Once you're hurt really bad when you're young," she has said, "nothing can hurt you again." In 1991 she told her interviewer Carrie Fisher in ROLLING STONE, "She's gone, so I've turned my need on to the world and said, 'Okay, I don't have a mother to love me, I'm going to make the world love me.'"

Thus, while just entering grade school, Madonna found herself the female head of household. "There was no woman between [me and my father]," she told Connelly, "no mother." Yet three years later, her father announced that he would marry Joan Gustafson, the woman who had been hired as the family housekeeper and childcare provider. Madonna found it difficult to accept her stepmother's authority. "I hated the fact that my mother was taken away, and I'm sure I took a lot of that out on my stepmother," she said.

Madonna struggled to maintain her autonomy and assert herself in a changing family structure and a growing brood. (Her father went on to have two other children, Jennifer and Mario, in '68 and '69 respectively, with her stepmother.) As early as eighth grade, she appeared in a Super 8 video now known as the one-in-which-an-egg-was-fried-on-her-stomach (though it was actually placed there pre-cooked), and later threw herself into acting and dance at a series of Catholic high schools she attended. One teacher at Rochester Adams, from which Madonna graduated, said, "She never bothered with the whole peer thing, other than, 'I'm going to be somebody.'"

She performed well both academically and outside of class, participating in choir, Latin club, cheerleading and volunteering, and ended up graduating early, in the middle of the 1975–76 school year, with a dance scholarship to the University of Michigan. "She spent her high school years zipping out of here," her school counselor recalled. "I didn't counsel her; she came to me and told me what she was going to do."

At the time Madonna mostly talked about dance. In fact, it was her high school and University of Michigan dance instructor, Christopher Flynn (who died of AIDS in 1990), who would become both her friend and first mentor. He introduced her to a scene outside of her hometowns of Pontiac and Rochester, Michigan, that would later figure prominently in both her aesthetic and her identity. "He used to take me to all the gay discotheques in downtown Detroit," she said of Flynn. "Men were . . . all dressed really well and were more free about themselves than all the blockhead football players I met in high school." A quick study, Madonna understood the value of eclectic subcultures to the pop mainstream, a knack which would serve her well in the future. In Ann Arbor, she stood out in her ballet classes for her unconventional behavior. "I was a real ham," she told Connelly. "I did everything I could to get attention and be the opposite of everyone else."

Then she met Steven Bray, a black waiter at the Blue Frogge, the University of Michigan's preppiest disco. "He was real cute," she said. "Someone all soulful and funky looking you couldn't help but notice. First time in my life I asked a guy to buy me a drink." Bray was a drummer in an R&B band that played local clubs, and Madonna began to attend their gigs. But she was restless.

A FTER FIVE SEMESTERS, Madonna left the University of Michigan (against her father's wishes) for New York, where she won a scholarship with the Alvin Ailey Dance Theater's third-string company. Then, for a short time, she studied dance with Martha Graham protégée Pearl Lang. Despite these stints, she found a natural home in New York's East Village and began to flourish as a downtown dance diva. The New York City club scene of the late Seventies was the most obvious place to practice her moves, and proved to be the easiest avenue by which to get noticed. "I had heard that a lot of A&R people hung out at the clubs," she said, "and I thought trying to go see them at their offices would be a waste of time."

Madonna's origins in dance music, however, contributed to her problems of legitimacy. Disco's physicality, which by extension implicated the burgeoning black, Latino, working-class, and gay dance cultures and female R&B performers, was considered inferior to the hip sneer of smooth California rock and the mind-trip of Euro-rock; disco bashing was a uniquely white mostly middle-class pursuit in the late Seventies, not coincidentally a time when mainstream rock was at a low ebb.

Some rock critics also perceived disco—coming as it did simultaneously with and then successfully upon the heels of punk—as an establishment sellout, and the soulless and nefarious revenge of an industry threatened by punk's anticommercialism. That dance music brought in a far more multitudinous audience was beside the point to those who pledged allegiance to the spike-haired unregenerates laboring a few short years in a limited limelight.

Madonna stepped onto this contested terrain; her antics by night and music-biz studies by day alone seemed suspect: No rebel would be so interested in the rules. So what if punk hadn't offered more than a few roles that made sense for women, and fewer opportunities. Indeed, the party doll and gun moll had combined to make interesting hybrids like tough cookies Debbie Harry and Chrissie Hynde, both of whom Madonna freely admitted to worshipping. They got *their* hits by dabbling in disco and power pop, respectively: Madonna took those cues, put them under a magnifier and made them catch fire.

And lo, she went out into the world, or to Queens, New York, actually, where she hooked up with a guy named Dan Gilroy, who, as Connelly writes, "wasn't drop-dead hip like the other guys she'd known; he was an affable, self-effacing fellow." Gilroy and his brother Ed were both musicians; they'd rented out an abandoned synagogue in Corona, Queens, where they lived and rehearsed. With Madonna on drums, the trio added her fellow dance student Angie Smith on guitar and formed the Breakfast Club in 1979.

Soon enough, Madonna began to clash with the brothers Gilroy, who "had been honing their musical skills for a number of years," Connelly writes. "But simple craft is not the surest way to success in the music business, and Madonna had something that was more useful: moxie. Dan Gilroy recalls it well: 'She'd be up in the morning, a quick cup of coffee, then right to the phones, calling up everybody. Everyone from [a local record dealer] to potential management. Anything and everything.' "

"I was just a lot more goal oriented and commercial minded than they were," Madonna said. "I just took over in the sense that I said 'What do you know? Teach it to me.' "

Madonna inevitably split with the Breakfast Club and returned to

Manhattan to begin her own band, with Steve Bray arriving to play on drums. While the band was short-lived, Bray was "a lifesaver," Madonna said. "I wasn't a good enough musician to be screaming at the band about how badly they were playing." "She was playing really raucous rock & roll, really influenced by the Pretenders and the Police," Bray said. "She used to really belt." When the band broke up, Madonna started shopping around demos on her own to management companies, one of which was picked up by a small outfit that allowed her to move to spacious new digs on New York's Upper West Side.

The early Eighties were an exhilarating time for urban contemporary radio, with the sounds of Teena Marie, Chaka Khan, Kurtis Blow and Grandmaster Flash and the Furious Five, among others, pounding out of boom boxes and car radios all across New York City. Madonna's tastes, honed not least by the rhythm & blues of her near-hometown Detroit's Motown, were reshaped by these new beats. Her managers, however, didn't quite get it. "They weren't used to that kind of stuff," she told Connelly, "and I'd agreed with my manager to do rock, but my heart wasn't really in it."

Bray, however, did get it, and began to write funk songs with Madonna. With a four-track demo containing a raw version of "Everybody," Madonna approached Danceteria club DJ Mark Kamins one night when he was spinning. Kamins immediately worked the song into the club mix, then helped her to snag a deal at Sire by getting her tape to label president Seymour Stein. "Seymour was in the hospital at the time," she told RS. "I got signed while he was lying in bed in his boxer shorts."

The one single that the Sire deal guaranteed would be the moody, hiccuping "Everybody," which Kamins produced. But despite expectations on the parts of both Bray and Kamins that they'd be producing the resulting album, in the end Madonna chose Reggie Lucas, the man responsible for pop vocalist Stephanie Mills. "I wanted someone who'd worked with a lot of female singers," she said. For his part, producer Lucas said, "I wanted to push her in a pop direction. She was a little more oriented toward the disco thing, but I thought she had appeal to a general market."

*Madonna,* released in 1983, was an infectious brew of dance bubble gum and sexy attitude. It took its time charting singles, until Madonna began to make videos (Arthur Pierson directed her breakthrough video for "Lucky Star"; Mary Lambert, in the first of her many Madonna collaborations, "Borderline"), the medium which she would come to dominate, and the one, in fact, that she would become synonymous with in the Eighties. She described to ROLLING STONE the difference she perceived between herself and other musicians: "They say, 'Well, I have to do a video now, and a pop star has to come on sexually, so how do I do that?' instead of being in touch with that part of their self to begin with. I've been in touch with that aspect of my personality since I was five."

Of the eight tracks on *Madonna,* six were released as singles: "Lucky Star," "Borderline," "Burning Up," "Holiday," "Physical Attraction" and "Everybody." Don Shewey's ROLLING STONE review of *Madonna* was ambivalent, but ultimately upbeat: "There are lots of blue-eyed soul belters with more generous voices and more intricate songs," he wrote. "Still, without overstepping the modest ambitions of minimal funk, Madonna issues an irresistible invitation to the dance." The magazine was less kind in its year-end record roundup: "Take away the ravaged-tart trappings and there's nothing else to talk about." The magazine included the fledgling diva in its 1984 Yearbook anyway, with a large Steven Meisel photograph of Madonna draped in satin, a thrift-shop glamour girl indisputably looking forward. Accompanying the picture was a quote from Go-Go drummer Gina Schock: "People like her give people like us a hard way to go. She doesn't help anybody take women seriously. But you know what? I love the record." Schock's quote summed up the befuddlement: They hated to love her, but they loved her still.

Meanwhile, Madonna had taken up with John "Jellybean" Benitez, a rising dance-pop mixmaster (he had produced her biggest hit to date, "Holiday," from her debut) whom she'd met while dancing at New York's Fun House. While still identified in ROLLING STONE as Benitez's "girlfriend, sex-appeal singer Madonna," she began to make a name for herself, doing budding rock-star things like appearing on a panel at 1984's New Music Seminar and attending David Lee Roth's birthday party.

Even while her first record was climbing the charts, Madonna's second record, *Like a Virgin,* was ready for release. This time, Madonna had chosen Nile Rodgers to produce it. In the stores by early 1985, *Like a Virgin* displayed the from-here-on-to-be-known-as Material Girl festooned and plumped in a tatty prom gown with her hair rakishly swept over to one side, her impressive brow prominent over a wicked stare. The frank sexual aggression and teasing bravado on songs like "Material Girl," "Dress You Up" and "Like a Virgin" (which were the three songs that Madonna did not write and that also came to be identified with her in this period) again upset critics and delighted fans, who it appeared appreciated Madonna equally for her sense of humor and her candor.

*Like a Virgin,* on which Rodgers used his former Chic partners Bernard Edwards on bass and Tony Thompson on drums, would ultimately spawn another set of monster hits—the title track, "Material Girl," "Angel" and "Dress You Up"—as well as the bombastic ballad, "Love Don't Live Here Anymore." It would also establish Madonna as both the premiere pop-music sex kitten and heroine of the decade. "Who would have thought the devilishly simple concept of Boy Toy would capture the imagination of so many *female* teenagers?" asked ROLLING STONE in its 1985 "The Year in Records."

As much as it held her open to criticism from rock purists, Madonna's theater and dance background combined with her naturally frolicsome attitude toward gender conventions to create a broad-minded notion of sexuality. In addition, the closeness she shared with her gay brother Christopher, who would go on to stage-design the Blond Ambition and Girlie Show tours as well as her New York apartment and Los Angeles and Florida homes, would intensify her connection with sexual diversity and the socially marginalized. Madonna instinctively moved toward the artistic expression of these dynamics. Later on, she would learn how to articulate them as well.

L EST YOU THINK Madonna allowed herself to have any time on her hands, late in '84 she beat out Melanie Griffith and Jennifer Jason Leigh for the role of Susan in the film *Desperately Seeking Susan* with director Susan Seidelman. (Madonna's first post-school movie was Stephen Jon Lewicki's *A Certain Sacrifice,* a somewhat explicit indie effort for which she earned a hundred dollars and for which the director later earned $59.95 per video.) Says photographer Herb Ritts (her longtime iconographer who would later shoot her video for "Cherish" among other future Madonna projects): "The first time I worked with her was when I was doing the poster for *Desperately Seeking Susan.* She marched in with this little cigar box full of jewels and trinkets that she wanted to wear. She knew exactly how she wanted to look."

Costarring Rosanna Arquette and Aidan Quinn, the screwball farce was nonetheless stolen by Madonna even while she maintained a friendly relationship with both the director and Arquette. "I love her," Arquette told ROLLING STONE. "She's my long-lost sister." Still, tempers flared when Seidelman hastily rewrote a scene to highlight an as-yet-unreleased Madonna tune "Into the Groove," and the press focused on Madonna's performance, widely considered her most compelling thus far.

By the spring of 1985, Madonna had taken up with actor Sean Penn, whom she married in August 1985, seven months after their first date and amid much fanfare, in Malibu.

Right before the nuptials Madonna embarked on the Virgin Tour: thirty-five dates nationwide with the Beastie Boys as openers. Madonna's first full-scale tour showcased her many solid-gold hits along with the novice singer's shortcomings, which were well-documented by critics. Also on display were most of her now-infamous signifiers: bare midriff, scores of rubber bracelets, crucifixes and lacy lingerie. The regalia prompted ROLLING STONE critic Michael Goldberg to sniff, "One doesn't expect musical revelations from Madonna—and one doesn't get any. What Madonna is really about is sex. . . ."

Almost simultaneous with the marriage, *Penthouse* and *Playboy* published nude photographs of Madonna, for which she had posed to make money just after moving to New York. While she held up well under scrutiny, Madonna allowed that the publicity was upsetting. "I think when I first found out about it, the thing that annoyed me most [was] that I felt really out of control," she told Fred Schruers. "For the first time in what I thought to be several years of careful planning and knowing what was going to happen, it took me by surprise."

Madonna and Penn began to look for a project they could make together. In early 1986, she contributed a song, "Live to Tell," to Penn's film *At Close Range;* she and Bray also began to collaborate on her third record, *True Blue*. By spring, she was traveling with Penn to Hong Kong, where they would costar in her first ill-fated venture, the movie *Shanghai Surprise*. Produced by George Harrison's HandMade Films, the movie had a shooting schedule that included forays to the Far East and London, where a media crush threatened to derail the project. "Sean and I set ourselves up for a challenge," she told Schruers. "A lot of people were saying that's a sure way to end a relationship, you'll be divorcing afterward. It was my second movie, and I had all these feelings of insecurity. . . . Strangely enough, we never got along better."

*True Blue* was released in June of 1986. In addition to the moving "Live to Tell," the record included songs such as "Papa Don't Preach," an ode to teenage motherhood, written by someone else, that was widely construed as—and criticized for being—anti-abortion; "Open Your Heart" (the video of which was to be directed by Penn before being taken over by Jean Baptiste Mondino and notoriously set in an "adult-entertainment center"); and "La Isla Bonita," all of which became hits. *True Blue* was Madonna's first-time production as well as cowriting gig (with pop lyricist and tunesmith Patrick Leonard), as ROLLING STONE's 1986 year-end review points out. While also the most "personal" of her records thus far, it is the least exciting of Madonna's first three records, marred by a production that wove together Michael Jackson–like vocal tics and a tinny, synthetic sound.

A personal disappointment was to follow, when MGM-UA released director Jim Goddard's *Shanghai Surprise* in August. In three weeks the film earned just slightly more than $1 million, and most reviews were scathing. In the movie, Madonna plays a missionary who hooks up with Penn, an American fortune hunter she has hired to hunt down a thousand pounds of missing opium. Despite their personal rapport during its making, the couple's first professional foray was a failure.

Madonna returned to her roots with the EP *You Can Dance* in early 1987, which featured dub versions of several of her hits along with "Into the Groove" and a new song, "Spotlight." Yet Hollywood had not seen the last of Madonna. She began work on a comedy, directed by James Foley (who directed the video for "Papa Don't Preach," starring Danny Aiello as Papa) that would be released as *Who's That Girl* in 1987, at which time a soundtrack record, a tour and a new look would also be launched.

In *Who's That Girl,* Madonna plays Nikki Finn, a young woman imprisoned for a crime she didn't commit who enlists a nerdy lawyer (Griffin Dunne) to help avenge her upon her release. Her character sports a short, highly teased and bleached hairdo and talks like Betty Boop. Though the film would prove to be Madonna's second flop in a row, the title song from its soundtrack would hit Number One in midsummer 1987.

Meanwhile, Madonna had become more involved in raising money to fight AIDS after losing her close friend Martin Burgoyne to AIDS at the end of 1986. As part of her Who's That Girl Tour, she performed a concert on July 13, 1987, at New York's Madison Square Garden that raised $400,000 for the American Foundation for AIDS Research.

Mikal Gilmore observed later that summer, when on tour with

Madonna in Japan, that despite her enormous popularity, "there's nothing star conscious or affected in her manner." Rather, he wrote, "Madonna frequently seems indifferent to her own mystique, more bemused than imperious about it." Gilmore also learned of Madonna's concern over the behavior of her famous, and famously pugilistic, husband. Of the several incidents that had occurred during their time together—mainly fisticuffs with the press—Madonna said, "I don't like violence . . . Those were very traumatic experiences for me. I don't think they'll be happening anymore." The pressures of fame appeared to be, if momentarily, taking their toll. "There have been times when I've thought, 'If I'd known it was going to be like this, I wouldn't have tried so hard.' But I feel that what I do affects people in a very positive way. And you can't affect people in a large, grand way without being scrutinized and judged and put under a microscope, and I accept that."

By the end of 1987, Madonna filed for divorce from Sean Penn citing "irreconcilable differences." Two weeks later, she withdrew the papers.

That winter Madonna shot *Bloodhounds of Broadway,* a low-budget Twenties gangster comedy based on Damon Runyon stories and directed by Howard Brookner, in which she played chorus girl Hortense Hathaway. She also began rehearsing the David Mamet play *Speed-the-Plow* with costars Joe Mantegna and Ron Silver. The play began a limited run off-Broadway in March and moved to Broadway later that spring through the summer of 1988. (Madonna had been put through her paces onstage by the same director, Gregory Mosher, two years earlier with Penn in *Goose and Tomtom.*) Later, Madonna would tell ROLLING STONE's Bill Zehme about her experience of playing a troubled Hollywood secretary who is ultimately beaten down: "I hated to love it and I loved to hate it. It was just grueling . . . playing a character who is so unlike me. I didn't have a glamorous or flamboyant part; I was the scapegoat. To continue to fail each night and to walk off that stage crying . . . It just got to me after a while."

Amid reports of a role being created for her in Warren Beatty's movie version of the cartoon classic *Dick Tracy,* Madonna again filed for divorce from Penn, thirteen months after her first effort to do so. This time, she didn't relent: In fact she filed additional assault charges against Penn—which she did later drop. In her interview with Zehme, she addressed the rumors around the marital split. After reviewing the hearsay, which included a story about a supposed night of terror in late December during which a drunken Penn roughed her up, tied her to a chair and threatened her, Zehme asked, "How accurate are the tabloid tales . . . the nine hours in bondage?" "Extremely inaccurate," she replied. "It's been a slow breaking point all the way. I can't say there's anything specific that happened. . . .

"What happened happened," she mused. "I'm sure we learned a great deal from each other . . . Most passionate people are headstrong. [We were] two fires rubbing up against each other. It's exciting and difficult."

The world would hear more about it on Madonna's next record, *Like a Prayer*. Released in April and once again coproduced and cowritten by Madonna, the album was a startling departure from the pop ditties she'd heretofore been known for, with new songs displaying tenderness, grief and exaltation. J.D. Considine wrote in ROLLING STONE, "Madonna doesn't just ask to be taken seriously, she insists on it. Daring in its lyrics, ambitious in its sonics, this is far and away the most self-consciously serious album she's made." On "Till Death Do Us Part," Madonna takes confession to a new level with disturbing revelations in a song appearing to chronicle the demise of her marriage (Madonna told Zehme that Sean "loves [the song], strangely enough. But Sean is very, very keen on being brutally frank in his work.") Her father and mother are addressed in bald terms in "Oh Father" and "Promise to Try," respectively.

A new Madonna mantra was established with the song "Express Yourself," which directed women not to settle for second best. The song reached Number Two on the charts. What might have been saccharine sentimentality in the hands of a lesser artist are taken, in Madonna's words, "to a higher ground." The record also includes "Love Song," a duet with Prince, and the album's tour de force song, "Like a Prayer," which combines gospel fire with heavy funk to create an overwhelmingly powerful statement of transcendent passion.

The album, Madonna said, is more reflective of past musical influences like Sly and the Family Stone ("Keep It Together" and "Express Yourself") and Simon and Garfunkel ("Oh Father") than the more contemporary influences on her earlier records. However, Madonna being Madonna, her nod back didn't ensure an escape from the pull of current events. This time, the "Like a Prayer" video caused an uproar.

Right-wing religious groups denounced the depiction of a black saint who comes alive when Madonna kisses him, the appearance of stigmata on her palms and her dance in front of a row of burning crosses as blasphemy. In March 1989, the crusaders threatened a boy-cott of Pepsi-Cola, which had offered the singer a $5 million sponsor-ship deal. The company abruptly yanked television commercials that Madonna had made for them using "Like a Prayer," even though the ads showed a different scenario than the video. (Madonna got to keep the cash.) The Pope was even moved to rebuke the singer; Oh Father, indeed.

ROLLING STONE put her on the cover of its September 21, 1989, special issue devoted to, among other things, a "Rock & Roll Photo Album." In the issue's introduction, Anthony DeCurtis proposed the importance of the "look" as part of the elemental power of the rock star. The magazine emblematized Madonna to illustrate that point with two Herb Ritts pictures, one on the cover in which Madonna ca-vorts on the beach with a camera and, in the inside shot, points the camera back at us.

Her turn in *Dick Tracy* as Breathless Mahoney was also a piece of work. As conceived by Beatty (who played Dick Tracy, in addition to directing and producing the film), the role suited Madonna, as appar-ently, for a time, did the leading man himself. For once, Madonna didn't have to play dumb in a part, and her natural sultriness could be joined with her sauciness and given center stage. In short, she could summon her inner Marlene Dietrich alongside her Mae West.

But it was the Madonna-Beatty romance that would stand out most from the making of *Dick Tracy,* though it would take *Truth or Dare,* Madonna's upcoming road documentary, to actually prove that the unlikely duo were ever even an item.

Madonna's Blond Ambition Tour was a true picture of synergy, designed to kick off in May 1990, prior to the release of *Dick Tracy,* and at the same time as the release of a new album, *I'm Breathless.* "In-spired" by the movie, the album is an odd set of faux-period tunes with titles like "Hanky Panky" and "I'm Going Bananas," three swanky tunes written for her Dick Tracy gig by Stephen Sondheim and a curi-ous duet with Beatty ("Now I'm Following You") followed by a ver-sion of the same song by the same name remade as a sampled dance track. But easily the stand-out cut on the disc was the house-music rave "Vogue," one of the most thrilling songs Madonna has ever recorded.

A salute to the black and Latino cross-dressing and transsexual sub-cultures that flourished in the Bronx and Harlem in the late Eighties (as also chronicled by Jennie Livingston's documentary *Paris Is Burning*), "Vogue" moves Madonna's fertile obsession with exhibitionism, posing and the fluidity of gender and identity another notch. This vision was fully realized on Blond Ambition. As documented by director Alek Keshishian on Madonna's invitation, the tour, her most theatrical spectacle to date, leaped over a series of hurdles including torrential rainstorms (Japan), law enforcement officials irate over onstage simulated masturbation in "Like a Virgin" (Canada), and parental bewilderment (Detroit). All in all, Blond Ambition was a great success, as yet another edition of the star was propelled into the public sphere, and with enough eye-catching imagery and affecting tunes to sate all but her harshest critics.

In the midst of all this, *Dick Tracy* was released mid-summer. ROLLING STONE film critic Peter Travers called it a "great big beautiful bore." But Madonna still kind of gets her man: "It's . . . hard to tell if Madonna is an actress," Travers writes, "but she is a definite presence," a point driven home later that fall when ROLLING STONE chose Madonna as the "Image of the Eighties." This photo portfolio shot by Herb Ritts showcased a Weimar-style Madonna along with a collage of shots of her various guises over the decade. As Paul Evans wrote in a short accompaniment to the pictures, "She is a conglomerate of images, a one-woman bonfire of the vanities . . . True to form for the work-mad Eighties, she has dripped big sweat for her celebrity, her Greek-marble thighs the product of militant aerobics, her multimillionaire's wages won with entrepreneurial cunning." Later, he adds, "Madonna is our Postmodern Goddess—her every gesture is a shadow of some past vogue: the platinum blaze of Jean Harlow's hair; the hot boyishness of Louise Brooks; the dark, smoldering earth angels of Italian films. . . . Her look is a crucial medium of her message."

To cap the decade, Sire released *The Immaculate Collection,* a seventeen-song collection of Madonna's greatest hits from "Holiday" to "Vogue" and including the first-time release of "Crazy for You" plus two new songs, "Justify My Love" and "Rescue Me." The collection, dedicated to the Pope, lingered on *Billboard*'s album charts for more than two years.

Further contouring the mood conjured in Blond Ambition, "Justify My Love" is a sensual, mysterious, slightly sinister and hypnotic trance dance with a hooky bass line and beat, over which Madonna moans suggestively (a technique later used on *Erotica*). The video, which shortly accompanied the collection's release, is a depiction of an elaborate sex dream, in which its protagonist (Madonna, toting a suitcase/bag of tricks) enters a hotel and, room by room, explores her fantasies. Shot in black and white by Jean Baptiste Mondino in Paris, "Justify" features a sylphlike male spirit, a butch lesbian in spit curls, a couple of identical boys and a sneering, muscled dude (Tony Ward, male model and Madonna squeeze) who convincingly humps the gartered girly, and is then transformed into a woman, who commences to soul kiss Madonna.

Once again, the video caused consternation in conservative circles and titillated fans with its edgy sexuality. For the first time, Madonna was actually banned from MTV—a ridiculous call on the network's part but one that scored a major publicity coup for the singer. The whole thing was enough to get her on *Nightline*.

In March, ROLLING STONE reported that Madonna had won its 1990 readers poll for best single ("Vogue"), best video ("Vogue"), best tour (Blond Ambition) and had come in second for best female singer and artist of the year, after Sinéad O'Connor. In addition, ROLLING STONE's critics poll picked "Justify My Love" as best video and Blond Ambition as best tour, while also characterizing the "Justify" controversy as hype of the year. Either way, 1990 was Madonna's.

Then everything changed.

WAS IT *TRUTH OR DARE* coming on the heels of "Justify My Love" and Blond Ambition? Was it the drama that preceded the arrival of her porn book, *Sex*? Was it the timing of *Sex* with her next album, *Erotica*? Was it all just too much—too much sex, too much publicity, too much M-M-M-M-Madonna? Or was it simply a turn of the calendar page, the advent of a new decade, and with it the need to bury the old, if only for the time being?

Beatty's whiny complaint—and somewhat disingenuous remark— in *Truth or Dare*, that Madonna "doesn't want to live off-camera," was a sign of the mood to come. While on-camera with Madonna, Hollywood's aging Lothario, no slouch himself in times past at outcharming the charmers, appears slightly out of his depth and awkward. Other viewers sympathized with Beatty as the hen-pecked partner trying to satisfy the whims of his domineering girlfriend. No one asks, however, *what was he thinking?!*

When *Truth or Dare* was released in May 1991, the chronicle of her world tour was received with glee and outrage. Travers wrote, "It's the most revealing and outrageously funny piece of pop demythologizing since D.A. Pennebaker blew the hype off Bob Dylan. . . ." Her pre-show candlelit massage was one of the only things off limits to director Keshishian. Cynics saw the film as massive hype that was "scripted intimacy of the first order," as Peter Wilkinson wrote in an interview with Keshishian concurrent with the movie's release. But even her own brother Christopher, upon seeing the film, remarked, "It is Madonna as I know her."

*Truth or Dare* displays a Madonna who is high-handed, outrageous, self-centered, admirably focused, wackily fun, loving, selfish and a bit strange, if only for the life she has chosen. It is also strangely empowering, and surprisingly layered. Viewers get plenty of concert footage from shows all over the world, shot in color, and black-and-white scenarios involving Madonna's visit to her mother's gravesite, horsing around and/or lecturing her young and feckless dancers, a backstage chat with dad and stepmom, a makeup session, an argument with Beatty, a reality check from her dozen-year manager Freddy De-Mann, a reunion with a childhood best friend and a tête-à-tête with (former) buddy Sandra Bernhard. Now infamous are her fellatio demonstration on an Evian bottle (one of the dares in a game of *Truth or Dare*) and her gag attack after a backstage visit by Kevin Costner, who has the misfortune of calling her show "neat" to her face.

In June of '91, ROLLING STONE ran a new portfolio of sexually charged images of Madonna. Shot by Steven Meisel and titled "Flesh and Fantasy," page after page showcased the entertainer in suggestive poses: Madonna in crimped hair lounging with two other women; Madonna in male drag grabbing the buttocks of a woman with whom she dances; Madonna as contortionist drinking from a glass raised between her feet; Madonna again in drag surrounded by men in women's underwear; and so forth. Madonna, in the grips of a fruitful fixation, had found her perfect collaborator in Meisel; who knew that in this fresh and tantalizing project were shades of her undoing?

This issue also featured the first of a two-part conversation between Madonna and actress-writer Carrie Fisher, one of the more inspired pairings in journalistic history. The discussion ranged over topics large and small, from height to preferred sexual practices, from menstruation and breasts to finding men to date and lesbianism. Sample— Madonna: "I don't like blow jobs." Fisher: "What do you like?" Madonna: "Getting head." Fisher: "For how long?" Madonna: "A day and a half." The second Fisher-Madonna go-round included a chat about how Madonna's father handled her fame and a discussion of friends dying of AIDS, and concluded with what to look for in a man.

Sample—Fisher: "So you just have to have someone who is really confident." Madonna: "Confident, smells good, smart." Fisher: "Is that the order?" Madonna: "No. Smart, confident, smells good, sense of humor, likes to write letters, likes antique jewelry."

The first half of 1992 was promising enough: In April, Madonna and Time-Warner (Sire's holding company) announced a $60 million deal that had been in the works since the previous summer. The new contract would put her at the head of her own multimedia entertainment company, and rivaled the blockbuster contracts of superstars Michael and Janet Jackson. It would permit Madonna to launch a record label and produce books, movies and TV shows under the company name Maverick, and collect a staggering 20 percent royalty rate.

In the summer of '92, the Penny Marshall–directed baseball romp *A League of Their Own* was released, starring Geena Davis and Tom Hanks with Madonna in a supporting role. The movie knocked *Batman Returns* out of first place, and grossed more than $104 million. A spirited camaraderie characterized the making of the film, about an all-women's baseball league in the Forties, as well as the final product. Madonna scored another Number One, "This Used to Be My Playground," even though the song wasn't included on the soundtrack album, and made a dear friend from the cast in Rosie O'Donnell.

In October of that year came Maverick's first venture: *Sex*. This book of Madonna's highly orchestrated sexual fantasies, photographed by Steven Meisel, edited by Glenn O'Brien and designed by Fabien Baron, introduced a narrator called Dita (after the early screen actress, Dita Parlo): "My name is Dita / I'll be your mistress tonight" begin the first lines of the book as well as the song, "Erotica," the title track of the album released shortly after the book. "Give it up / Do as I say," the text goes on, "Give it up and let me have my way / I'll give you love / I'll hit you like a truck / I'll give you love / I'll teach you how to fuck."

Talk about striking a pose. Dita accompanies the reader through a series of pictures starring such luminaries as Naomi Campbell, Big Daddy Kane, Vanilla Ice, Isabella Rossellini and relative unknowns such as the seemingly ubiquitous Ingrid Casaras, the rich Floridian who was former girlfriend to Sandra Bernhard and who would become Madonna's consort for a while. From bisexual trysts to nude hitchhiking to a lewd snuggle with an old gent, *Sex* showcases Madonna in extreme situations and startling explicitness. It is unlike any depiction of a major star in the history of modern entertainment. And bold and wild as it was (though most definitively unromantic), it would sadly prove to be too much.

Still, published simultaneously in America, Britain, France and Germany, the book went on to sell 1.5 million copies worldwide—150,000 copies in the United States in its first day. Even though the singer had been clear to state in her introduction that the book's content was straight from her imagination, it was marketed as nonfiction.

The backlash was immediate. *Sex* was slammed as amateurish, silly and shoddy (its aluminum covers created difficulty in page-turning), and Madonna was blamed for indulging in everything from cynical commercialism to perversion. Time-Warner took some heat as well.

Nevertheless, *Sex*'s launch party was an event. In a four-floor photo studio, Industria, in New York's Far West Village, the bash included a naked lady in a bathtub of popcorn, dominance and submission scenes, and a tattoo booth, around which milled some 800 guests and Madonna, as Dita in braids and a fräulein smock.

Meanwhile, the synergist at work released *Erotica,* her sixth full-length studio album, in October 1992. Designed to complement *Sex* (the CD single enclosed in the book was titled "Erotic"), the record was a deep treatment of sexual subjects with Dita once again at the helm. Arion Berger wrote in her ROLLING STONE review, "*Erotica* is everything Madonna has been denounced for being—meticulous, calculated, domineering and artificial. It accepts those charges and answers with a brilliant record to prove them." Including the tantalizing title track, on which Madonna drops an octave or two to a seductive growl, the disco swirl of "Deeper and Deeper" and the moving ballad "Rain," *Erotica* showcases the magnificent production work of Shep Pettibone, Madonna's latest collaborator ("Vogue") and her finest to date.

Alas, *Erotica* in all its chilly power was more or less forgotten in the *Sex* imbroglio; it would not be the only time that Madonna's best work was overlooked.

Nineteen ninety-three saw Madonna attempt once again to conquer Hollywood, this time in a couple of projects that held more promise than they delivered to her, and her audience. An admirer of the work of director Uli Edel *(Last Exit to Brooklyn),* Madonna signed on to his next film, *Body of Evidence,* in which she stars as a femme fatale who seduces her lawyer, played by Willem Dafoe. Released in January of 1993, the movie caused much unintentional hilarity not least due to the fact that Madonna's character is accused of literally using her body to kill. (Peter Travers wrote, "Hell, Sharon Stone needed an ice pick to dispatch her bedmates.") Produced by Maverick, *Dangerous Game* paired the singer with art-film director Abel Ferrara; dismayed by the final product, Madonna accused the filmmaker of "sabotaging" her part.

For a while it seemed everything she touched went awry: A seemingly spontaneous expletive fest on *Late Show With David Letterman* in March 1994, prompted boos from the studio audience and a two-day media melee; Madonna later said that her appearance had been misunderstood and that their on-air banter had been rehearsed—perhaps somebody forgot to remind Dave. The two did make up a few months later when they presented Artist of the Year together at the televised MTV Video Awards.

After the Letterman debacle, writer Norman Mailer gallantly defended Madonna in the press and ended up scoring an interview with her for *Esquire* magazine. It was a match that seemed destined; in fact, Carrie Fisher had quite pointedly huffed in her ROLLING STONE interview with Madonna that the magazine had asked Mailer first. Nevertheless, in *Esquire,* Madonna came off cool and level-headed with the entertaining if slightly dotty Mailer. While his musings, for instance, about the "insanity" of safe sex seemed hopelessly out of date next to Madonna (and her work), their conversation did lead to some inspired thoughts on the nature of love, lust, power, men and women. At the end of the piece, Mailer grandly proclaims, "I want to leave you with an idea. I've come to the conclusion that you are a great artist. It's on record now." Madonna: "Okay." Mailer: "That's going to be the theme of this piece, that what we have among us is our greatest living female artist." Madonna: "Thank you."

In September of that year, Madonna embarked on the Girlie Show, another world tour that was even more stagey than the last. This time, Madonna's bell-bottomed, bewigged persona clowned through songs from *Erotica* and her past hits; Thom Duffy's ROLLING STONE review suggested the show was more like a Broadway musical, though allowed that Madonna brought "humor and warmth" to the proceedings.

After the Girlie Show wrapped at year's end, Madonna retreated again to her Coconut Grove, Florida, manse, with only occasional trips to Manhattan. It was rumored she had put her Los Angeles mansion on the market, which seemed to signal that she'd had it with Hol-

lywood. And while licking the wounds she'd received in the fallout over
*Sex,* she was also rebounding from soured friendships and failed affairs.

The (ill) winds of change helped her produce *Bedtime Stories* (released in October) on which Madonna addresses her critics with the
song "Human Nature," toys with techno with the Björk-penned "Sanctuary," tackles taboos with "Secret" and "Forbidden Love" and ponders lost love on "Inside of Me" (which she has said is a tribute to her
mother) and "Love Tried to Welcome Me." While the record's lush
pop ballad "Take a Bow" would take the cake (due in no small part
to a magnificent video made in Spain replete with a handsome bullfighter), the album, produced by a variety of R&B notables including
Nellee Hooper, Babyface Edmonds and Dallas Austin, otherwise failed
to reach the masses. *Bedtime Stories,* in short, made little impact creatively.

It did, however, restore Madonna to the health and happiness
club; she lobbied for, got the lead in and began rehearsals and singing
lessons for the film version of the musical *Evita* (directed by Alan
Parker, costarring Antonio Banderas and Jonathan Pryce), a role she
had contemplated for years under several different directors. At the end
of 1995, when the film finally went into production, her presence in
Argentina caused a ruckus—crowds swarmed threateningly and officials resented the hubbub. She was also accused of sullying the name
of Eva Perón with what was presumed would be a lurid portrayal of
Evita. Undaunted, Madonna proceeded with her scenes in South America, breaking only occasionally, on one trip returning to Los Angeles
to testify at the trial of a stalker who had been caught on her property
in the Hollywood Hills. Found guilty of stalking and harassment in
February 1996, the intruder was sentenced to ten years in prison.

During shooting abroad, Madonna also made a trip to the States
to attend the first annual VH1 Fashion Awards, at which she received
the Most Stylish Artist Award, presented—surprise!—by Mr. Sean
Penn, at the time estranged from his longtime girlfriend and mother of
their two children, actress Robin Wright. (Shortly thereafter, Penn and
Wright married.)

The filming of *Evita* took Madonna and the rest of the cast and
crew from Buenos Aires to Budapest then London throughout the winter and spring of 1996. In March Madonna discovered she was pregnant. Her longtime publicist Liz Rosenberg announced the news to the
press via Liz Smith's syndicated column, a safe space usually for

Madonna news. The father was Carlos Leon, a Cuban-born, New York–bred fitness trainer whom Madonna had been dating for several months; the couple had no plans to marry. The baby had not been "planned," Madonna mentioned later in an *US* interview with Mim Udovitch, but was very much wanted.

After *Evita* wrapped, Madonna repaired to a new homestead in Los Angeles to prepare for the birth of her baby. Her publicists, on the other hand, began to prepare a media onslaught. After an October *Vogue* cover story, in which Madonna dished Penn and ex-fling exhibitionist basketball player Dennis Rodman (who had lied in his book, she said, about details of their affair) and others (on publication she claimed her quotes had been distorted), four more cover stories with major magazines (*Vanity Fair, People, US* and *Redbook*) appeared. Timed both around her daughter's birth as well as to the year-end release of *Evita,* the covers kept on coming, while the woman herself lay low, making next to no public appearances or proclamations.

Lourdes Maria Ciccone Leon was born at 4 P.M., October 14, 1996, at Good Samaritan Hospital in Los Angeles. The attending pediatrician was Heidi Fleiss's father, Paul. Later, Madonna would tell Oprah Winfrey in her first televised interview since the birth, and directly before *Evita* was to open, that Lourdes was named for a small town in southern France considered the home of miracles. She also said that when she looked into her daughter's eyes she felt healed of the pain of growing up without a mother.

The double-CD *Evita* soundtrack arrived before the film, and Madonna's rendering of "Don't Cry for Me, Argentina" was considered a lusty and convincing effort. A new song, "You Must Love Me," written by the composer-lyricist team Andrew Lloyd Webber and Tim Rice, upon whose hit musical the film was based, got Madonna a modest hit. But while it was touted as one of the year's biggest entertainment events, the film received mixed critical notices. Madonna was rarely singled out as the problem (director Alan Parker and Lloyd Webber–Rice shared that distinction), but she was also given scant praise. Many critics called *Evita* an oversized music video, and remote to boot, with a point of view that remained elusive despite its subject's photogenicality. Still, Madonna maintained (and Oprah concurred) that Eva Perón was the role Madonna was born to play.

Whether Evita was in fact the *best* role for Madonna to play is another matter. She sings and dances with skill and flair, and the dramatic life of dictator Juan Perón's star wife in some ways seems uniquely suited to Madonna—she, too, moved to the big city, dyed her hair blonde, danced in dives, married a famous man, knew her way around the dressmakers and entertained the masses (though Madonna's childhood was hardly one of squalor, as the story might have it). Yet not only do the filmmakers squander the opportunity to make something more of the Evita myth than a straightforward telling, or singing (and the inherent tackiness of Lloyd Webber–Rice is at the sticky heart of it), but Madonna has given up her sense of humor to play it straight. Intended perhaps to forever prove her ability to carry a film, her role's very self-seriousness undermines her best qualities, not least of which is Madonna's unerring instinct for toppling stereotypes with street-smart sass.

Still, rest assured, this is not Madonna's final act. *Something to Remember,* her collection of ballads released in 1995, pointed toward a direction for the diva that showcases her soulful turn and asserts her as a mature singer for the nineties.

And if her music gets less attention today than in her heyday at the turn of the decade—if nothing else, witness the dwindling number of stories about her in ROLLING STONE since 1992; consider, too, that she had half as many hits from 1991 to 1996 than in the six years previous to '91—it's partially because the work has gotten better. While *Erotica* supplied surface charge in sexually explicit material, both that album and *Bedtime Stories,* her last two recordings of new material, are fuller and display more emotive range, embodied not least in the lower register she often sings in today. (Critic Mim Udovitch has suggested that Madonna's voice might have been electronically speeded up on her early recordings, lending them the caramel-coated chirp we have come to associate with boy-toy Madonna.) They're also, frankly, more transgressive. Ironically, the very thing that distinguishes Madonna's current music from her earlier work is what her critics claimed was missing during her ascent, and at the height of her hit-making power, namely, depth.

## DON SHEWEY

# *MADONNA* ALBUM REVIEW

★ ★ ★

MADONNA, who crashed onto the dance charts last year with "Everybody," has a voice that takes some getting used to. At first, it doesn't sound like much at all. Then you notice its one distinguishing feature, a girlish hiccup that the singer uses over and over until it's irritating as hell. Finally, you get hooked, and you start looking forward to that silly little catch in her voice. It helps that she writes good tunes—catchy and bare to the bone. It helps even more that her album is pristinely produced by Reggie Lucas. Electric keyboards have the clarity of finger chimes. The bass slaps the backbeat like shoes on pavement. Mind you, it's simple stuff: "I'm burnin' up/Burnin' up for your love," or "Holiday/Celebrate." But it's clever at times, too. "Physical Attraction" is practically a capsule history of high-school proms, with its sly references to the Association's "Cherish" and Olivia Newton-John's "Physical."

There are lots of blue-eyed soul belters with more generous voices and more intricate songs—Teena Marie comes quickly to mind. Still, without overstepping the modest ambitions of minimal funk, Madonna issues an irresistible invitation to the dance.

■ **RANDOM NOTES** (July 5, 1984)

"Borderline" vocalist Madonna has a second album, *Like a Virgin*, ready for release, but what's the rush? After more than forty weeks, the first album from the ex–Alvin Ailey dancer is still climbing up the charts.

■ **RANDOM NOTES** (September 13, 1984)

The theme was Olympic—thus David Lee Roth's red-and-white sweat suit. But the bash—a "birthday party" for the Van Halen lead singer held at Manhattan's Area club last month—was strictly a stunt, since the real day is in October. Nevertheless, he graciously accepted best wishes and mingled with such celebs as Edgar Winter, B-52's vocalist Fred Schneider, dance-pop mixmaster Jellybean Benitez and his girlfriend, sex-appeal singer Madonna.

■ **RANDOM NOTES** (September 27, 1984)

The Jacksons tour was a hot topic of discussion on the artists' panel at last month's New Music Seminar in New York. "I don't agree with the ticket price," James Brown said of the thirty-dollar tariff, but he nonetheless vigorously defended Michael and his family. "They're good boys," he said as Peter Wolf, Madonna, George Clinton and Lou Reed looked on. "You don't know how much control they had over this thing."

## CHRISTOPHER CONNELLY

# MADONNA GOES ALL THE WAY

MADONNA AND I are face to face at a corner table at Evelyne's, a cacophonous but spiffily appointed French restaurant in the heart of New York's most newly gentrified neighborhood, the East Village. Things are changing rapidly in this part of town. Its Ukrainian meeting halls and no-frills eateries are under siege from the upscale crowd invading with their asparagus ferns and health-club memberships. Although in transition, many of the neighborhood's blocks still have the same seediness they had when the teenaged Madonna Ciccone first plopped herself down in her own digs.

"The first apartment I ever had all by myself," she recalls between sips of Campari, "was on Fourth Street and Avenue B, and it was my pride and joy, because it was the worst possible neighborhood I could ever live in." Back then she was a struggling dancer, the girl from the University of Michigan who was "dying for attention—but the right kind, you know?"

She has gotten it. Her sirenlike voice and ultrasultry video presence have yanked her from downtown obscurity. She has notched two Top Ten singles, "Borderline" and "Lucky Star," and her album, *Madonna*, has gone platinum and is still high on the charts after a more than forty-week run, postponing the release of the already recorded follow-up LP, *Like a Virgin*, itself as chock-full of hits as its predecessor.

Consider Madonna, though, and it's easy to drift away from her songs and prattle instead about her videos. They have practically re-discovered what it means to project raw sex appeal: feverish tugging on her dress in "Burning Up," as if she couldn't wait to tear the garment off her body; her pouty-lipped antics for "Borderline"; and the upfront eroticism of "Lucky Star," her breasts and bottom thrust at the camera, index finger teasingly tucked into her mouth. Still, her most important bodily part has been her naked tummy, exposed by her two-piece outfits, the curve of it oscillating through male minds everywhere.

Now Madonna has a spacious loft in even-tonier SoHo, a movie deal (she's currently making *Desperately Seeking Susan* for Orion Pictures), and an expanse of money and stardom winging her way. Which is why she can glance out the window of this restaurant and say, "Feels great to come back to this neighborhood and know I'm not as poor as everyone else."

That rub you the wrong way? Too bad—that's her style. She's in the same sans-midriff getup featured in her videos, but in person, she doesn't adopt the coyly fetching approach you might anticipate. This is a woman who saves her sex-bomb act for the times when the meter's running. And don't let her oft-flashed BOY TOY belt buckle fool you. The men who have gotten close to her—tough guys a lot of them— have gotten their hearts broken as often as not. Throughout her life, there has been one guiding emotion: ambition. "I think most people who meet me know that that's the kind of person I am," she says. "It comes down to doing what you have to do for your career. I think most people who are attracted to me understand that, and they just have to take that under consideration."

Some have; some haven't and have lived to regret it. "You'd think that if you went out with someone in the music business that they'd be more understanding," she says, "but people are the same wherever you go. Everybody wants to be paid more attention to."

**M**ADONNA LOUISE CICCONE—she was named after her mother—had plenty of attention early in her life. Born in Bay City, Michigan, twenty-four years ago to a Chrysler engineer and his wife, she was the eldest daughter in a family of six: Daddy's little girl. But her world shattered when she was five, as her mother succumbed to a long bout with cancer. The tragedy brought her yet closer to her father, and there have been few women in her life ever since. "I really felt like I was the main female of the house," she remembers. "There was no woman between us, no mother."

Her little world altered just as dramatically when Madonna was eight, on the night her father announced to the family that he was going to marry the woman who had been the family's housekeeper. Madonna was shocked. "It was hard to accept her as an authority figure and also accept her as being the new number-one female in my father's life. My father wanted us to call her Mom, not her first name. I remember it being really hard for me to get the word *mother* out of my mouth. It was really painful.

"I hated the fact that my mother was taken away, and I'm sure I took a lot of that out on my stepmother." Perhaps smarting from what she took for rejection by her father, Madonna threw herself into the world of the fantastic. In eighth grade, she appeared in her first movie, a Super-8 project directed by a classmate, in which an egg was fried on her stomach (even then he knew). She watched old movies at revival houses. She acted in plays at the series of Catholic high schools that she attended. She danced to Motown hits in backyards. Indeed it was dance that became the consuming passion of her adolescent life. She'd take all her classes early so she could leave school and head into the big city to take yet more classes. She saw world-famous companies whenever they came through town. And her ballet teacher became what she calls "my introduction to glamour and sophistication." He showed his charge a world she didn't know existed. "He used to take me to all the gay discotheques in downtown Detroit. Men were doing poppers and going crazy. They were all dressed really well and were more free about themselves than all the blockhead football players I met in high school."

Rigid, but with a sense of humor, he became Madonna's first mentor. "He made me push myself," she says. By all accounts, she was a wonderfully talented terpsichorean, and he thought she could make it big. "He was constantly putting all that stuff about New York in my ear. I was hesitant, and my father and everyone was against it, but he really said, 'Go for it.' "

Boasting a solid grade-point average in addition to her dancing skills, Madonna graduated from Rochester Adams High School in 1976 and won herself a scholarship to the University of Michigan dance department. Once there, the seventeen-year-old Madonna—no less luscious in a short, spiky, black hairdo—pored through poems by Anne Sexton and Sylvia Plath ("any really depressed women") and attempted to wreak all manner of havoc in her hoity-toity ballet classes.

One former classmate of Madonna's recalls a grim plié exercise—deep knee bends with the stomach held in and the posture perfect—that dissolved when Madonna emitted a huge belch. Or the hot day when the lissome lass moaned what a *drag* it was to have to take class in leotards, and *why* couldn't she just wear a bra? "I was a real ham," she says, chortling. "I did everything I could to get attention and be the opposite of everyone else. I'd rip my leotards and wear teeny little safety pins. And I'd run my tights. I could have gone to a nightclub right after class."

That's exactly where she wound up one night: the Blue Frogge, the U of M's pastiest preppie disco. She was dancing away—engulfed in tight-assed white boys doing their John Travolta imitations—when around the corner came this black waiter.

"He was real cute," she recalls. "Someone all soulful and funky looking you couldn't help but notice. First time in my life I asked a guy to buy me a drink." And he did. The guy she'd picked up was a musician named Steve Bray, and he would eventually change her life. Bray—witty, sophisticated, cool—was a drummer in an R&B band that did the lounge circuit. Madonna became a regular fixture at their gigs.

"She wasn't really a musician back then; she was just dancing," says Bray today. Aside from her beauty, Bray recalls being captivated by the veritable *aura* around this feisty, footloose female. It was un-mistakably the aura of ambition. "She stood out, quite. Her energy was really apparent. What direction she should put that energy *in* hadn't been settled, but it was definitely there."

"Those were good days," Madonna recalls. "But I knew my stay at Michigan was short-term. To me, I was just fine-tuning my tech-nique." After five semesters, she turned her back on her four-year free ride and headed for New York City. Steve? Oh, yeah. "Looking back, I think that I probably did make him feel kind of bad, but I was really insensitive in those days. I was totally self-absorbed." It wouldn't be the last time.

Every item ever written about Madonna touts her membership in the Alvin Ailey American Dance Theater. Not so. Soon after her ar-rival in New York, she apparently won a work-study scholarship and was later asked to take classes with the troupe's third company, which is a little like getting a tryout for the sub-junior-varsity team. Still, it was her first encounter with people who were as driven as she. "I thought I was in a production of *Fame,*" she giggles. "Everyone was Hispanic or black, and *everyone* wanted to be a star."

Madonna was not to the minors born. She left Ailey after a few months and hooked up with Pearl Lang, a former Martha Graham star whose style Madonna describes as "a lot of pain and *angst.*" This was not a match made in heaven, and she left the company soon after.

Living a hand-to-mouth existence in the city and continuing to ig-nore the pleas of her father that she cease this silly business and finish college, Madonna started scanning the trades for less limiting work:

parts where she would not only dance but sing. And that's when she met Dan Gilroy.

He wasn't drop-dead hip like the other guys she'd known; he was an affable, self-effacing fellow from Queens. He and his brother, Ed, were both musicians and had rented out an abandoned synagogue in Corona, Queens, where they lived and rehearsed.

Madonna and Dan met at a party and hit it off—she spent a couple of nights at the synagogue. "He stuck a guitar in my hand and tuned it to an open chord so that I could strum," she remembers. "That really clicked something off in my brain." She cut back to only one dance class a day.

While the relationship was still in its infancy, however, Madonna was given what seemed like the chance of a lifetime: to go to Paris and do background singing and dancing for Patrick Hernandez, a disco lunk who had lucked into a "worldwide hit" with the forgettable "Born to Be Alive." She would be given a beautiful apartment, a maid, a voice coach, people to guide her career. "I was in seventh heaven," she remembers. "I kept thinking, 'I can't believe it. Somebody *noticed* me.' "

In Paris, everything was as promised, but she wasn't happy. "I was like the poor little rich girl," she recalls. The guidance was a joke. No one would talk to her in English. They said they wanted to turn her into the next Edith Piaf, but how could they if she hadn't written anything? She felt lonely, miserable and confined. "Once again I was forced into the role of *enfant terrible*. All I wanted to do was make trouble, because they stuck me in an environment that didn't allow me to be free." So she'd order three desserts in a fancy restaurant and skip the entree. She took up with a Vietnamese kid with a motorcycle. She went to Tunisia with the Hernandez tour, club-hopped with some lively locals and went swimming in a one-piece body stocking. You see, she just wanted to be *noticed*.

Of course, there was still this guy in Queens, batting out letters to his loved one. "He was my saving grace," she says. "His letters were so funny. He'd paint a picture of an American flag and write over it, like it was from the president, 'We miss you. You must return to America.' He really made me feel good." A walloping case of pneumonia persuaded her to come back. As soon as she hit stateside, she rang the synagogue.

She spent the better part of a year there, writing songs for the first time and learning how to play a variety of instruments. "My intensive musical training," she says with a sigh. "It was one of the happiest times of my life. I really felt loved. Sometimes I'd write sad songs and he'd sit there and cry. Very sweet."

In that nurturing atmosphere, Madonna and the brothers Gilroy started a band called the Breakfast Club, with fellow ex-dancer Angie Smit on bass and Madonna on drums. They would rehearse every day there; Madonna had yet to move in with her beau. "I stayed there so much, but I hadn't really moved there yet, and I remember when I said, 'Can I just live here, Dan?' And he said, 'Well, we have to ask Ed.' And I said, 'Ed! You have to ask *Ed?*' "

The Gilroys had been honing their musical skills for a number of years, but simple craft is not the surest way to success in the music business, and Madonna had something that was more useful: moxie. Dan Gilroy recalls it well. "She'd be up in the morning, a quick cup of coffee, then right to the phones, calling up everybody—everybody. Everyone from [local record dealer] Bleecker Bob's to potential management. Anything and everything."

"I was just a lot more goal oriented and commercial minded than they were," says Madonna. "I just took over in the sense that I said, 'What do you know? Teach it to me.' I took advantage of the situation. I wanted to know everything they knew, because I knew I could make it work to my benefit." Cold words? Perhaps.

She knew what to do. "Immediately, when I started working with them, I started thinking record deals, making records and doing shows and stuff like that. And, of course, most of the people you have to deal with are men, and I think I just was naturally more charming to these horny old businessmen than Dan and Ed Gilroy." As Madonna herself realizes, Dan Gilroy "had created a monster. I was always thinking in my mind, 'I want to be a singer in this group, too.' And they didn't need another singer."

Dan found himself torn between his girlfriend—who wanted to sing more, who wanted the band to use her songs—and his brother, Ed. After a year, Madonna announced her intention to return to Manhattan and pursue a singing career. The romance—and the instructional period—were over. "I knew that with that kind of drive and devotion to getting ahead something had to happen," Gilroy says. Was she more talented than her confreres? "No, she didn't strike me as . . . well, she was *fun,* you know? She'd be working at this design thing that I was doing and she would kind of break into a dance in the middle of the day. An incredible attention getter. So that's got to tell you something."

Yes, but given the tensions, was Dan glad to see her go? "Well, no," he says. "I missed her very much." He had taken her in and had taught her the skills she needed, and now she was leaving him. Most of the time she hadn't even had to work a day job. "Ah, well, I was doing a job anyway, so having her there was just a bonus," says Dan. "It was fun. It was a good year. And besides," he jokes, "I have a palimony suit now, you know? Marvin Mitchelson, where are you? Of course, he doesn't *win* too many of those, does he?"

BACK IN THE BIG CITY once more, Madonna quickly summoned a ragtag band around her. Good fortune struck in the form of a telephone call from her old Michigan boyfriend, drummer Steve Bray—he was coming to New York. "I found out that, oddly enough, she needed a drummer," he recalls. "So I said, 'Fine, I'll be there next week.' "

"He was a lifesaver," says Madonna. "I wasn't a good enough musician to be screaming at the band about how badly they were playing."

Times were very lean as they began working together, playing and writing songs. They moved themselves, their equipment and personal belongings into the Music Building, a garment-center structure that had been converted into twelve floors of rehearsal rooms. It housed the cream—if you can call it that—of the post–New Wave scene in New York. Nervus Rex was there, and so were the Dance and the System. "I thought they were all lazy," says Madonna of that scene. "I felt a lot of affection for them, but I thought that only a handful of people were going to get out of that building to any success."

Bray notes that Madonna was not exactly the most popular person on the scene. "I think there was a lot of resentment of someone who's obviously got that special something. There are so many musicians out there, but there are only a few who really have that charisma. The community out there kind of, I think, frowned on her about that. She had trouble making friends."

It didn't matter much to Madonna, who felt that most of the groups there wanted only to hit it big among their pals. She wanted to be big nationwide, and the scene didn't approve of such a desire. "It was like living in a commune," agrees Bray, "very close-minded thinking—if you're good in New York, if you can get regular jobs at CBGB's or at Danceteria, that's fine, you've made it. And that's definitely not the case."

Her band changed names like socks: first they were the Million-aires, then Modern Dance and finally Emmy, after a nickname that Dan Gilroy had given Madonna. ("I wanted just Madonna," says she. "Steve thought that was disgusting.") By any name, it was a hard-rocking outfit that was continually beset by snafus, especially when it came to guitarists. "She was playing really raucous rock & roll, really influenced by the Pretenders and the Police," says Bray with a sigh. "She used to really belt. If we'd found that right guitar player, I think that's when things would have taken off . . . but there are so many horrible guitar players in New York, and we seemed to get them all."

The money was too short, and the band finally split up. Meanwhile, a manager heard a demo that Madonna had put together (it was an early version of "Burning Up") and signed her up. As part of the deal, she was put on salary and moved out of the Music Building, ending up in spacious digs on New York's Upper West Side. Madonna was quick to pull Bray onto the gravy train. Her new band—called Madonna—started playing the circuit yet again.

Madonna's notion of music, however, was starting to change. It was the heyday of urban contemporary radio in New York, and Madonna was captivated by the funky sounds emanating from boomboxes all over town. She started writing material in that vein, but the band and her manager hated it. "They weren't used to that kind of stuff, and I'd agreed with my manager to do rock, but my heart wasn't really in it."

She would rehearse rock & roll with her band, then stay behind with Bray and record funkier stuff. There were fights, arguments, the band was pissed off. She'd come so far; how could she turn back now? But . . . "I finally said, 'Forget it, I can't do this anymore. I'm going to have to start all over.'"

And so she did, with the loyal Bray once more at her side. During the day, she and Bray would write songs; at night, she'd hit the clubs: Friday night at the Roxy; other nights at Danceteria, the offical home for white hipsters with itchy feet and a sense of humor. It was fun, sure, but it was also a way to press the flesh, to work the room, to bounce up into the DJ's booth, lay a cozy rap on him and slap a tape into his hand.

At Danceteria, she caught the eye of Mark Kamins, a widely re-spected club DJ with ties to record companies. "She was one of my dancers, you could say," says Kamins. "There was a crowd out there that came every Saturday night to dance." Did he know she had other ambitions? "Hey, everybody does at a nightclub, but she was special."

He was impressed enough with what he saw to hit on the young woman now and then. She gave him a copy of her vaunted funk demo, a recording she and Bray had made that included a song called "Everybody." "I was flirting with him," she admits. Kamins and she started dating. He listened to the record and liked it. He put the song on at the club—just a four-track demo!—and people danced to it. He went into the studio with her and produced an improved version. And he went to Sire Records and single-handedly got her signed to a deal.

Bray was jubilant—at last he'd get to produce Madonna for real. What he didn't know was that Madonna had promised Kamins that in exchange for his work on her behalf *he* would get to produce her debut album. Executives at Sire and its parent company, Warner Bros., had already given their okay.

Madonna, however, had a surprise for them both. Neither Kamins nor Bray would be producing Madonna. The job instead fell to former Stephanie Mills producer Reggie Lucas. Why?

"I was really scared," she says. "I thought I had been given a golden egg. In my mind, I thought, 'Okay, Mark can produce the album and Steve can play the instruments.' " Uh-uh—Steve wanted to produce. "It was really awful, but I just didn't trust him enough." The pair had a bitter falling out. "Steve didn't believe in the ethics of the situation."

"It was very hard to accept," he says today.

And what about Kamins? "Similarly, I didn't think that Mark was ready to do a whole album." Kamins got the word, not from the woman who had promised him, but from Sire. "Sure, I was hurt," he says gruffly. "But I still had a royalty coming from the record."

Madonna was still performing, but not with a band. Instead she'd hop onstage at dance clubs and sing to backing tracks or lip-sync, enlivening her performances with the sort of lusty dancing that has now become her trademark. That's where Lucas—unaware of the intrigue that had preceded him—first saw his newest act.

"I wanted to push her in a pop direction," he recalls. "She was a little more oriented toward the disco thing, but I thought she had appeal to a general market. It's funny about that thing with Kamins. The same thing that happened to him pretty much happened to me on her second record, when they had Nile Rodgers."

And the rest was history, though it was a history that was a long time in the making. The LP's first single, "Holiday," was not an immediate success, but Madonna was content. "All I said was, 'I know this record is good, and one of these days Warner Bros. and the rest of them are going to figure it out.' "

It's likely that her videos were the breakthrough, as Madonna perfectly merged her dance training with her knowledge of the randier things in life. How did she manage to put across such seething sexuality where so many have tried and failed? "I think that has to do with them not being in touch with that aspect of their personality. They say, 'Well, I have to do a video now, and a pop star has to come on sexually, so how do I do that?' instead of being in touch with that part of their self to begin with. I've been in touch with that aspect of my personality since I was five."

Keeping her in touch with that side of her personality off the set these days is master mixer John "Jellybean" Benitez. The pair met during one of Madonna's stints at the Fun House, the disco where Jellybean first earned his reputation. They have stayed together for the past year and a half, but Madonna flinches at the suggestion that this is her most stable relationship.

"Why does it seem like *that*?" she queries before giving a throaty laugh. "We've had our ups and downs, let's not fool anybody." Still, the relationship was serious enough for Madonna to bring him home and meet her parents. Why has Jellybean held on where so many have fallen by the wayside? Would you believe ambition?

"We both started to move at the same pace," says Jellybean. "My career has exploded within the industry, and hers has exploded on a consumer basis. We're both very career oriented, very goal oriented." Which may mean that the relationship is safe . . . at least for the time being.

OUR DINNER IS FINISHED. Along the way, Madonna has coolly sussed out the room for us: Yes, that's Rudolf of Danceteria in the corner with his girlfriend, Diane Brill. You know, she usually seems like she's strapped in her clothes, don't you think? Madonna's been all but unnoticed, but that's okay. In your hometown, coolness is its own reward. Elsewhere her influence is becoming pervasive. The Madonna clones are ratting their hair, putting on rosaries and baring their bellies from coast to coast.

It is an indication of the peculiar state of pop stardom these days that Madonna has gotten only the most fleeting glimpses of her own fame. She hasn't toured—won't, in fact, until next year—hasn't performed live in a long time. She hasn't even left New York a lot. She can count on one hand the numbers of times she's been mobbed.

For now, the buzz of recognition is still easily dealt with, even on a trip uptown to Danceteria. "It's like going back to my high school," she coos in the cab, and her arrival does bring out that exact mix of admiration, excess cordiality and what-are-you-doing-here puzzlement. She gets a hug from graffiti artist Keith Haring and is kissed on the mouth by a nearly endless series of hepcats. ("Gotta be careful who you kiss on the mouth these days," she says, wiping her lips.) There's no gawking, no crush of unknowns, no autographs requested, but her presence clearly delights everyone else who's there.

She's an unqualified success. But did she exploit people to get there? "I think that a lot of people do feel exploited by her," says Dan Gilroy. "But then again everyone's got so many expectations about a relationship with her. She's very intense immediately with somebody, very friendly. Perhaps people feel, 'This is what our relationship is about,' and then if there is any cooling of that, it's taken to be a rejection."

And what's the final tally? In addition to reaping a chunk of royalties from *Madonna* and for the one song he produced on it, Mark Kamins says that his affiliation with her has given his career a shot in the arm. Reggie Lucas is inundated with projects. Steve Bray eventually patched it up with Madonna—"the relationship's too old to have something like that stand in its way"—and shares writing credit with her on four of her new album's songs. And Dan and Ed Gilroy of the Breakfast Club (whose first LP is due early next year) were able to find a new drummer to replace Madonna: Steve Bray, who has the final word on those whom Madonna has touched.

"Exploited? People say that, but that's resentment of someone who's got the drive. It seems like you're leaving people behind or you're stepping on them, and the fact is that you're moving and they're not. She doesn't try to be that polite. She doesn't care if she ruffles someone's feathers."

True, Madonna? She smiles. *"C'est vrai."*

## KURT LODER

# *MADONNA*
# YEAR-END ALBUM REVIEW

**M**ADONNA'S BARE-BELLIED, fondle-my-bra image is strictly bimbo city, and of course it sells—this debut album was one of the year's longest-running hits. Her voice is thin and not consistently successful in its search for the proper pitch, and her songs . . . well, she's still searching there, too. "Borderline" isn't a bad tune, but it was written by Reggie Lucas, one of her producers. The LP has a pristine sound, but the arrangements are awfully light—more lawn-party disco than dance-floor funk—and they lack anything resembling punch. Madonna's whole act—a sort of *Interview* magazine wet dream of what's hip and happening in glittery Manhattan—seems custom-designed to gag feminists of both sexes, as well as anyone with even a vestigial interest in rock, funk, soul, you name it. Take away the ravaged-tart trappings and there's nothing else to talk about. Maybe she'll move on to movies—although anywhere will do.

■ **YEAR-END RANDOM NOTES** GREAT FACES OF 1984 (December 20, 1984) "People like Madonna give people like us a hard way to go. She doesn't help anybody take women seriously. But you know what? I love the record."
—Gina Schock of the Go-Go's

## DEBBY BULL

# *LIKE A VIRGIN*
# ALBUM REVIEW
★ ★ ★1/2

IN THE EARLY SIXTIES, when girls were first carving their niche in rock & roll, the Crystals were singing about how it didn't matter that the boy they loved didn't drive a Cadillac car, wasn't some big movie star: He wasn't the boy they'd been dreaming of, but so what? Madonna is a more, well, practical girl. In her new song, "Material Girl," she claims, "the boy with the cold hard cash is always Mr. Right/'Cause we're living in a material world/And I am a material girl." When she finds a boy she likes, it's for his "satin sheets/And luxuries so fine" ("Dress You Up"). Despite her little-girl voice, there's an undercurrent of ambition that makes her more than the latest Betty Boop. When she chirps, "You made me feel/Shiny and new/Like a virgin," in her terrific new single, you know she's after something.

Nile Rodgers produced *Like a Virgin,* Madonna's second LP; he also played guitar on much of it and brought in ex-Chic partners Bernard Edwards on bass and Tony Thompson on drums. Rodgers wisely supplies the kind of muscle Madonna's sassy lyrics demand. Her light voice bobs over the heavy rhythm and synth tracks like a kid on a carnival ride. On the hit title song, Madonna is all squeals, bubbling over the bass line from the Four Tops' "I Can't Help Myself." She doesn't have the power or range of, say, Cyndi Lauper, but she knows what works on the dance floor.

Still, some of the new tracks don't add up. Her torchy ballad "Love Don't Live Here Anymore" is awful. The role of the rejected lover just doesn't suit her. Madonna's a lot more interesting as a conniving cookie, flirting her way to the top, than as a bummed-out adult.

■ **RANDOM NOTES** (January 17, 1985)

*Persona* revisited? In their costarring movie, *Desperately Seeking Susan* (due in March), Rosanna Arquette takes on aspects of Madonna's personality—but who's borrowing *whose* style here?

Well, both say they recognized similarities in each other *right* away. "We're like sisters—we've got lots of miseries in common, and boyfriend problems," says Madonna of her friend. "I love her," reciprocates Rosanna. "She's my long-lost sister."

Now that they've found each other, the two intend to share social lives as much as possible. But in the meantime, *Desperately Seeking Susan* has wrapped up shooting, and the lucky stars miss each other terribly—yet are equally busy capitalizing on their respective glittering constellations.

Madonna's shooting a new video with Grace Jones svengali Jean-Paul Goude, and getting ready for her first-ever national tour this spring.

Rosanna's shooting a western, *Silverado*, with Lawrence Kasdan *(The Big Chill)* in New Mexico. She's also featured in two other upcoming pictures: George Miller's *The Aviator* and Martin Scorsese's *After Hours.*

Though like a virgin to the film world, Madonna will get her own movie next fall—it's being developed for her now. Meanwhile, the experienced chartbuster also hopes to enter the realm of soundtracks—she's penned several songs for *Desperately Seeking Susan,* which are under consideration.

■ **RANDOM NOTES** (March 14, 1985)

Madonna's major-screen debut takes place next month in the already mega-hyped *Desperately Seeking Susan,* but her scantily hyped minor-screen career actually began in 1979, when she made an odd little New York underground film entitled, appropriately enough, *A Certain Sacrifice.* "There was an ad in the trades saying this director needed a sort of quirky, offbeat girl," said Madonna, "and I was just dancing at the time, and thought, 'Oh, great, I'm going to be a movie star.' " The "quirky girl" turned out to be a a quasi dominatrix who has three sex slaves, then a boyfriend. She's raped—by yet *another* admirer—and coerces an entire coven of weirdos to avenge the act. Our Material Girl isn't thoroughly pleased with the results. "It's long and dreadfully boring. By the time I got into the middle of the movie I was throwing temper tantrums, because I didn't want to be involved. It's embarrassing for me to watch." Virgin director Stephen Jon Lewicki, however, sees its value as "prehistoric Madonna" and plans to release it soon to clubs and TV, and as a home videocassette. Well, it may not be hard-core porn—in fact, it's mostly just *weird*—but a lot more than the familiar bellybutton is bared.

## ■ RANDOM NOTES (March 28, 1985)

Madonna and new beau Sean Penn were declared an item when spied smooching in the corner at a party in Manhattan for comedienne Whoopi Goldberg. Sean didn't care to dance, so Madonna pranced around with her girlfriends instead. Ah, but shed no tears for Madonna's latest ex, DJ Jellybean Benitez. He was spotted drowning his sorrows at the prehistoric Studio 54 with Phoebe Cates, lissome star of TV's ultracampy *Lace* (and its sequel, *Lace II*). Seems he's mixing Cates' debut album.

## ■ RANDOM NOTES (April 11, 1985)

Forget the Grammy Awards. They're about as relevant to contemporary music as *Hullabaloo*. The *real* show took place throughout the week at two Hollywood hotels, the Sunset Marquis and Le Mondrian. Madonna and Sean Penn were holed up at Le Mondrian, while over at the Sunset, it was all *Lifestyles of the Rich and Famous,* with Huey Lewis, Cyndi Lauper, Peter Wolf and Corey Hart lounging around the pool with their entourages. Bruce Springsteen, Annie Lennox, Dave Edmunds and Jellybean Benitez were only slightly less conspicuous, as they lunched on mozzarella-and-tomato salads and the like.

## ■ NOTABLE NEWS (April 25, 1985)

Word is the main concept for the next Prince movie is a *West Side Story* plot featuring two Minneapolis bands: the Family (with Jerome, formerly of the Time) and Mazarati. Right now we hear Prince won't be in it, but he might direct or produce. . . . Speaking of His Majesty, word around L.A. is he and Madonna have been spotted eating sushi together. Isn't she afraid Sean Penn will find out?

## FRED SCHRUERS

# LUCKY STARS

How Rosanna Arquette, Madonna, and Director
Susan Seidelman Lost Tempers and Found Each
Other Through *Desperately Seeking Susan*

ROSANNA ARQUETTE opens a leather wallet as big and thick as a hotel Bible and shuffles through credit cards, vital jottings and snapshots to pluck out a blurry Polaroid taken during the last few days of shooting on *Desperately Seeking Susan*. She holds it up: "We're really tight." There they stand, Rosanna and Madonna, all sassy grins and Harpo-and-Chico goofball camaraderie, two full-figured and comely young women whose only real-life money problem is where to spend and store it. They wear identical hats, just-bought porkpie jobs in black leather. "I never met anyone who has such a focus," she says of her costar. "She goes right for it and she gets what she wants. I admire that a lot. But I think behind all that is a little tiny girl inside."

Our ostensible subject is *Desperately Seeking Susan,* the bargain-budgeted ($5 million) little film, directed by Susan Seidelman, that went from being an oddball artistes' showcase to Orion Pictures' rush-release entry for the Easter-season box office. Though the picture breaks many rules, both artistic and commercial, the result is one of the fresher entertainments to make it through the Hollywood bottleneck in these formulaic times.

Part screwball comedy, part satire, part set designer's equivalent to "out" jazz, *Susan* turns on mistaken identity. Arquette's bored housewife, Roberta, follows the trail of Madonna's gutterball schemer, Susan, into a slapdash murder mystery that scrambles suburbanites and hipsters into something between farce and dreamy fable. Early on,

Roberta gets a knock on the head that gives her amnesia, and the two undergo an identity switch, setting up a skein of sardonic jokes that bounce off the wall at unexpected angles.

Madonna owned a platinum LP when she signed on to the project and has since earned a second one. The consensus, even among industry skeptics, is that the singer has the goods onscreen, too. What clearly has Arquette cutting conversational wheelies, though, is Orion's promotion of the film, in which she seems to play background to Madonna's phosphorescent pop icon.

"Can you blame them?" she says. "A studio sees a hot commodity and they immediately capitalize on it. It's a little misleading, because it's not a teen movie. I know the preview has been playing before *The Purple Rose of Cairo,* and it's been booed. The audience was people who love Susan Seidelman and who would go to see me, and that's sad."

There are precious few young actresses who can give Rosanna a power outage, onscreen or off. From a speck on the horizon, hitchhiking cross-country and arriving in Los Angeles at age seventeen, she's built a career mostly on the kind of quicksilver expressiveness she showed in *Baby, It's You* and in TV's *The Executioner's Song;* at twenty-five, she's in the front rank of actresses arriving at stardom. Today she drove in to Hollywood from her new house an hour up in the Topanga Canyon hills, leaving a coating of ocher dust behind the back tires of her otherwise gleaming Saab Turbo. Her silky, silvery dress is a bit of a war whoop among all the cut glass and linen of this Beverly Boulevard restaurant's cool, mirrored spaces, yet there's something more fundamental out of place. It's as if her heart were thudding audibly, even visibly, while she charges forward and back in a virtual self-interview.

"I've never been like this. I'm a wreck. I get hurt very easily. I don't have a tough shell. That's why I'm so freaked out. I'm so insecure. I'm really insecure. It's pretty stupid for me to be in this business, isn't it?"

Rosanna pauses, then gives a little tadpole wriggle with her right hand to signal that she's not really waiting for an answer. She glances once more at the Polaroid and tucks it away. She can't stifle these complaints, yet she can't stand voicing them. "We're great friends," she concludes in her trigger-burst style. "All these things I said to her. I think her performance is really good. All I'm saying is, 'Let her be an actress.' "

"**I** HAD A FEW SCENES where I was really shittin' bricks," says the twenty-four-year-old refugee from Pontiac, Michigan. "A few times I was so nervous I opened my mouth and nothing came out." Madonna is anything but mute tonight, as she takes a break from the Los Angeles rehearsal sessions for her first tour, and though she pauses occasionally to punctuate a phrase with a Mae West-ian secret smile, she lets you into the conversation only edgewise. "I think I surprised everybody, though, by being one of the calmest people on the set at all times. I think that had to do with the fact that I was in total wonderment: I was gonna soak everything up."

One keeps waiting for the brittle bitch, the self-absorbed bombshell who's supposed to lurk under her winking, vamping, wriggling electronic image, but the Madonna who sits talking over coffee comes on disarmingly humble.

Rosanna has expressed resentment over the insertion into the movie of a Madonna song backing a quickly rewritten scene in which the Susan character gyrates around a New York club. A video clip using the unreleased tune, "Into the Groove," spotlights Madonna. "It does take things out of context a bit," says Madonna, "kinda calls attention to another facet, but . . ." What that "but" means is, it sells tickets, chump. Still, it's become an issue. . . .

"Yeah, really?" says Madonna. "Who's it become an issue with—besides Rosanna?" Her laugh is quick and not unkind. Insiders say the song found its way into the film on its own virtues. "Susan Seidelman was not out to make a pandering rock & roll movie," says executive producer Michael Peyser, thirty-one, who worked on *Susan* after serving as associate producer on Woody Allen's film *The Purple Rose of Cairo*. One of the music coordinators, Danny Goldberg, had no time to compile a soundtrack LP when the film's release date was pushed up, but in talks with MTV execs, he paved the way for "Into the Groove" to air, even though the song might never show up on vinyl.

Madonna is not naive about the studio's gambit: "I have a big audience of kids for my music, and you know how they use soundtracks to push movies—I think they're using me in the same way, and it's really a drag, because I'm trying to establish myself as an actress, not as a singer making movies. But I'll be happy if it becomes a commercial success, simply because it's a different kind of movie than most of what's out now. There are a few formulas people have been using the past five years, with *Flashdance* and *Breakin'* and all that stuff; this movie is like a return to those simple, straightforward caper comedies

Claudette Colbert and Carole Lombard made in the Thirties. They give you a taste of real life, some poignance, and leave you feeling up at the end—none of that adolescent-fantasy bullshit."

IF MADONNA IS A FAN of screwball comedy, Susan Seidelman is more intent on spray-painting her own signature on the canvas of the blank generation she grew up with. "I think I'm a little bit of a satirist," she says. "I grew up in the epitome of Sixties suburbia. You know, Dunkin' Donuts shops, TV dinners. We had canned vegetables at home because we thought it was more modern than having fresh vegetables. So that pop–Andy Warhol–whatever aesthetic is something I took for granted.

"Inside that, I wanted to make a fable about identity and appearances. But this film isn't an essay. I dislike movies in which the theme becomes the plot, where everything is like an essay on Loneliness or Frustrated Housewives or Sexual Whatever. If you look at movies like *Some Like It Hot* or *Tootsie,* you could probably write a lot about sexual roles, but the films don't get bogged down in their message. To be able to show something rather than tell it is much more interesting, and the best devices are the ones that work most invisibly. I mean, if Rosanna's character is torn between her husband and another guy, and we see her in a magician's box being sawed in half—that works great if you think about it, but it's gotta work on an immediate level, too. To me, a script is a skeleton that I liked enough to—well, hang my skin on."

The skeleton of *Desperately Seeking Susan* had been rattling around Hollywood for five years before finding its skin, and it would be there still were it not for a coming together of inspired amateurs who—not incidentally in this male-run industry—are mostly women. The script was the debut effort for Leora Barish, thirty-six, who had quit life as a sometime saxophonist in Manhattan's East Village and moved to California seven years ago. She brought it to a close friend, Sarah Pillsbury (who indeed is from the Minnesota cake-mix clan her name evokes), who went from Yale to producing documentaries, including a 1979 Oscar winner. Teamed with friend Midge Sanford, savvy in the Byzantine ways of Hollywood development deals, Pillsbury optioned Barish's script as their first project. It floated through studio limbo, gathering praise from many women and indifference from most men, but it refused to die. "We reconceived it as a lower-budget, up-and-coming-star kind of movie, as opposed to using the older, established actresses we'd been talking about," says Sanford, and finally Orion took up the option. Sanford and Pillsbury sent Arquette's agent the script, and a week later, in June of last year, she signed up. The producers had been fans of independent filmmaker Susan Seidelman's critically lauded debut film, *Smithereens,* and they tapped the director for *Susan* early on.

Seidelman, thirty-two, had come out of the split-level Philadelphia suburb of Abington, studied fashion design at Drexel University and clerked for a few months at a local TV station before applying to film schools; New York University "shocked" her with an acceptance. She moved to the Lower East Side in 1974, when St. Mark's Place was a strip of shuttered hippie boutiques. She gravitated toward directing in the three-year course and began piling up awards with her twenty-eight-minute debut, "And You Act Like One, Too," about a too-married woman. *Smithereens,* begun in 1980 with $10,000 from her grandmother's will, became the surprise hit of the 1982 Cannes Film Festival. ("I think they wanted to make a statement about mainstream American films," she says diffidently.) In it, young actress Susan Berman played Wren, a sort of punk-rock groupie living by her wits against the harsh and indifferent backdrop of the Lower East Side and its punk rajah, Richard Hell. Shooting was delayed when Berman, racing along a row of loft windows, ran out of fire escape ("like some horrible Road Runner cartoon," recalls Seidelman) and broke a leg. Still, Seidelman brought it in for $80,000, and it earned plenty more— enough to buy her a SoHo loft whose spotless varnished-wood floors and sparse, Sixties-gauche furnishings hardly mirror the unkempt world of her films.

So messy and wheedling are her heroines that Seidelman's films seem to have at least one foot in the genre pundits are calling "slob comedies." Madonna's Susan is an empress of trash, a libidinous but untouchable she-wolf who washes down cheese puffs with vintage wine, cadges triple tequila sunrises and steals other people's goods and services with an amiable, Pigpen-ish air.

Madonna admits that when she arrived in New York in 1978, she, like Susan, "relied on the kindness of strangers." When Seidelman heard of the singer's interest in the part, she invited her over: "She was nervous and vulnerable and not at all arrogant—sweet, but intelligent and verbal, with a sense of humor. I just started seeing her as Susan." The chiefs at Orion were skeptical—some 200 actresses had read or been videotaped for the part—so Madonna was given a screen test.

"She had this presence you couldn't get rid of," says Sanford. "No matter how good the other people were, we kept going back to that screen test."

"Susan is conniving, an opportunist," says Madonna, "but she really did care about [Roberta's husband] Gary Glass and her boyfriend, Jim, and all these people." Part of her cockeyed charm is a warmth underlying her aloof facade: "Anybody who goes around acting like nobody matters obviously is protecting themselves and hiding what they really feel. So I always wanted to have that little bit underneath there."

What's underneath may be the "little tiny girl" Arquette is sure she sees in Madonna—perhaps the girl whose mother died when she was five. "I knew I had to be extra special supercharming to get what I wanted, 'cause I grew up with a lot of brothers and sisters [she was the third of eight children], and we had to share everything. I did all I could to really stand out, and that nurtured a lot of confidence and drive and ambition."

Poet Edward Field wrote that Mae West "comes on drenched in a perfume called Self-Satisfaction," and it's a knack Madonna shares. She and Seidelman had a decent rapport, but conflicts between the young director and three precocious pros—Arquette, Laurie Metcalf (as Roberta's vituperative sister-in-law) and Aidan Quinn (as Roberta's love interest)—were frequent. Production veteran Michael Peyser often picked up the pieces. "Susan has a wonderful quality; she's guileless, totally honest," he says, but he pegs her as a Hitchcock-style director: "She comes from *filmmaking,* as opposed to directing. She was working with some excellent people, like Laurie and Aidan, who are and will be major stage actors of their generation; they're used to a little more stroking."

"I really do like actors," says Seidelman. "I'm not manipulative, at which Hitchcock prided himself. I'm not good at hiding what I feel. I can't say, 'Oh, brilliant'; when I'm unhappy, it's written on my forehead."

Amid the production's turmoil, Madonna took consolation from Mark Blum (so likably obtuse onscreen as Roberta's husband, Gary). "If I'd get upset, he'd take me aside and tell me a joke or make an analogy about the situation, chill me out."

Rosanna, fresh from her dream collaboration with director Martin Scorsese on his forthcoming *After Hours,* was not to be chilled out. She and Seidelman staged tense debates over the degree of Roberta's amnesia, and during one twenty-hour day, an angry Rosanna burst into tears. Stalled and frustrated, Seidelman cried too. "You could say it was cathartic," says Seidelman. "You scream, cry, get it out and go on."

"**O**UR WHOLE SOULS were in it," says Rosanna now, "but any film I've ever made was hard. By the second month, she would look at me and I would know what she wanted. It's just that I had never worked with a director who needed complete control of me. See, I never rehearse my lines exactly how I'll say them. I just memorize them and know my character." While making *After Hours,* she points out, Scorsese was "never negative. In one situation he came up to me and said, 'Do you think you should laugh in this scene?' and I said, 'Oh, no, Marty. I can't see where she'd laugh in this scene.' He said, 'Oh, yeah. You're right. You're right. Forget I ever said anything.' And he walks away. That's what he does, very subtly. It's like he planted the seed, watered it and split. And as I was doing the scene, I don't know where it came from, but I just started laughing."

Arquette also had few problems making Lawrence Kasdan's next film, *Silverado.* "I'm just a pioneer woman heading west who has a very strong vision. And she wants to work her land." She's completed two other projects, a public-television play, *Survival Guide* ("It's just a very bizarre half-hour comedy"), and the recent disaster *The Aviator,* which prompted *At the Movies* reviewer Gene Siskel to say, "This is garbage," while Roger Ebert confirmed, "Transcendentally bad." Rosanna's one-time boyfriend, Toto drummer Steve Porcaro, had been so upset at the love scenes in *The Executioner's Song* that she says she made *The Aviator* partly because "it didn't have any nudity, it was safe—one of those all-American kind of movies." Her eventual breakup with Porcaro spurred her recent spate of work.

Now Arquette is with L.A.–based record producer James Newton Howard, and things seem . . . serious: "We work hard on our relationship. We have an incredible therapist. Our guy's name is Don, and he's great. We're gonna work out all the shit in our relationship before we make a giant decision like getting married.

"I don't want to talk about my relationship with Steve Porcaro anymore," she says, with some heat. "We're very good friends. But everybody's gotta ask me, 'Well, you're the Rosanna in the song,' and blah-blah. Isn't it boring? Say this: 'I am *so bored* talking about my relationship with Steve Porcaro.' "

She made another change around the time of the breakup. "I had gone to a drug program with a friend. That was another thing [reported in the media], that I was the one with a drug problem. I did take drugs. I smoked a lot of pot. I don't think I was an addict." (These days, Rosanna will not touch drink or drugs, and her choice for lunch is a spinach-and-avocado salad and mineral water.)

"Life is wonderful. Why do you guys have to look for the shit? 'Cause it's bad karma for you to do that, do you know that? It's not proper journalism."

It has become clear that Rosanna just had a crash course in this subject: "I did nine interviews yesterday." The actress and her publicists seem determined to blow back the Madonna promo machine by filibuster. The problem is that the quick-draw dramatics that are a blessing in front of the camera make her emotional dynamometer shudder ominously during what should be a simple talk.

"I grew up pretty fast," she says of her gypsylike upbringing on the artsy-hippie circuit traveled by her actor father and writer mother. "I think I was nineteen when I was fifteen. And now I'm fifteen. Madonna taught me a good lesson, because she just laughs off the bad press. They think they're hurting her, and she just laughs: 'Ah, that's bullshit.' But I still get hurt."

She's balancing her promo chores with acting class: three times a week, she joins a group of about fifteen (Nicolas Cage among them) for four-to-five-hour sessions with Sandra Seacat. "She's also Jessica Lange's coach," says Rosanna. "She's a very spiritual, highly realized being, a guru."

Her list of professional heroines includes Lange, Christie, Hawn, Winger and Spacek, but hovering above them all is Natalie Wood. The cat who shares Rosanna's hillside retreat is named Natalie, and when Arquette was being costumed for her character in *Baby, It's You,* she balked at a pageboy haircut until someone reminded her it recalled Natalie.

Wood is an interesting point of reference for Arquette—two beauties whose acting carries a seemingly artless transparency. Right now, Rosanna is a capital-A Actress, and as a result she's in many ways a considerable snob. But for the last three pictures she shot, she took pay cuts that left her with perhaps half of her real price. She's pouring her life into her work, and that leaves rough edges. She's a walking contradiction in terms, a Topanga Canyon firecracker.

Rosanna abruptly jumps up and reaches into her coat pocket, fetching a plastic bag of sizable vitamins in assorted colors. She counts out a handful, recounts and downs them with water: "Stress depletes your body of vitamins B and C." As an afterthought, she pops one more. The ritual seems to take the pedal off the floor, and she looks across the table apologetically, coat over her arm. "This is who I am, just hyper and emotional. I always have been. My emotions have always been right there."

■ **RANDOM NOTES** (May 23, 1985)
The Beastie Boys, currently opening on Madonna's Virgin Tour, are the only white rap group on record—and they've got big plans. Like getting a major-label deal, starring in an upcoming rap movie and making Madonna a "Beastie Boy Toy." Says member King Ad-Rock (who's the son of playwright Israel Horovitz): "If I go out on thirty-five dates with Madonna, I know I'm gonna get *something*."

## MICHAEL GOLDBERG

# PERFORMANCE REVIEW
# MADONNA SEDUCES SEATTLE

### Her first show features all the hits and more

JUST HOW SUCCESSFUL Madonna's first full-fledged concert was depends on how much you like to look at a pretty girl. Kicking off her U.S. tour in front of nearly 3000 screaming teenyboppers at Seattle's ornate Paramount Theatre, Madonna was a sweaty pinup girl come to life. She wiggled her tummy and shook her ass. She smiled lasciviously and stuck out her tongue. She rolled around on the stage and got down on her knees in front of a guitarist. And when she raised her arms, her scanty see-through blouse also rose, revealing her purple brassiere. Oh yeah, she also sang.

Musically, the seventy-minute, thirteen-song performance was a satisfying, if unspectacular, re-creation of Madonna's records. She sang the hits ("Lucky Star," "Holiday," "Borderline," "Like a Virgin," "Crazy for You," "Material Girl"), soundtrack songs ("Gambler," from *Vision Quest*, "Into the Groove," from *Desperately Seeking Susan*) and hot album cuts ("Burning Up," "Everybody") in the same thin, sometimes squeaky and always tempting voice that by now you either love or hate. And her recently assembled band—a drummer, two guitarists, three synthesizer players—faithfully reproduced the exquisite disco sound of her records. One doesn't expect musical revelations from Madonna—and one doesn't get any.

What Madonna is really about is sex, and there was plenty of that. The show began with glamorous close-ups of her projected onto five large screens that hung behind the band. Madonna then made her appropriately melodramatic entrance: a pink silhouette of her appeared on one of the screens, which rose, revealing the star, who descended a white staircase to the front of the stage, belting out "Dress You Up." Wearing a kind of neopsychedelic outfit—a coat embroidered with yellow-and-green and white-and-orange designs, a turquoise micro-miniskirt, a lace top, purple tights and black high-heeled boots—she looked like Susan, the character she plays in *Desperately Seeking Susan.*

Madonna's clumsy dance steps, funky costumes and camped-up come-ons made her appealing and—surprise!—likable. She's not some perfect, unattainable sexual icon; she's a real person, like her fans. (At least 80 percent of the girls in the crowd had done their damnedest to mimic their idol's looks, from bleaching and tousling their hair to wearing such Madonna-associated items as see-through blouses, fingerless gloves and crucifix earrings, which were on sale for twenty dollars in the lobby.)

"Will you marry me?" Madonna asked the enthusiastic crowd when she returned for the encore. As the audience screamed "Yes!" she sang a spirited version of "Like a Virgin" that included a bar or two of "Beat It" stuck in the middle.

Afterward, at a small celebration in her manager's hotel suite, Madonna was aglow. Sipping champagne, laughing about some writer who'd written that she has set women back thirty years, she looked like a very happy star. "I was excited," she said of her first concert. "Excited and nervous."

■ **RANDOM NOTES** (June 6, 1985)
Elizabeth Daily, 22, and Jellybean Benitez, 27, are about to make waves. Daily's an actress who costarred in *Valley Girl* and *Streets of Fire,* and will appear in *Pee-Wee's Big Adventure* this summer. She's also a singer, "a white Tina Turner," she claims. She used to do vocals for Giorgio Moroder's demos, but now she's making her own LP, with board brain Jellybean helping out. Though he started as a DJ-remixer, Benitez has gone on to produce his old flame, Madonna, and "good friends" like Jane Wiedlin and Phoebe Cates. Now he's so hot that a film based on Jellybean is in the works. Meanwhile, he's making a how-to video on deejaying, producing the soundtrack for a rock version of *Oliver Twist* called *Street Smart* and spinning discs at Steve Rubell and Ian Schrager's Palladium.

■ **RANDOM NOTES** (June 20, 1985)

Long before he became Mr. *Miami Vice,* Don Johnson was a struggling singer/song-writer who penned some tunes for the Allman Brothers. Well, *Vice* may be nice, but he hasn't kicked his musical habit. Last March, Johnson got a taste of rock & roll glory when he joined Prince onstage at the Orange Bowl in Miami. "Prince kinda looked up and went, What is this? I winked at him and shook my butt," he says. Then, while filming the miniseries *The Long Hot Summer* (based on works by William Faulkner) in New Orleans, Don and pals Jimmy Buffett and Dan Fogelberg went to see the Neville Brothers at the jazz festival. When Charmaine Neville handed Don a tambourine, he chimed in on "Amazing Grace." Now he's going to record his own album, on which he says he'll sing "whatever I want to." Meanwhile, the heat's still on with *Miami Vice.* "There are so many rumors about this show," says Don. "I heard *I* was Madonna's new lover. It's true she wants to meet me and get an autographed *Miami Vice* jacket. When she played here, I sent her flowers and wrote, 'With major lust, Don Johnson.' " Major lust, indeed.

■ **NOTABLE NEWS** (July 4, 1985)

*Yes,* Madonna is reading lots of film scripts, and *yes,* she'll star in another film. But she hasn't settled on anything yet.

■ **RANDOM NOTES** (August 29, 1985)

Backstage at Live Aid in Philadelphia, in between all the peace and love, the buzz was biz. Robert Plant said he had collected enough songs for a follow-up Honey-drippers LP. . . . Tina Turner said she is soliciting songs for her next LP. . . . Rick Ocasek said he had nearly completed his second solo album, due out around Christmas. . . . That inseparable couple, Madonna and Sean Penn, were burning up backstage, making the already unbearable temperature even hotter. Observed Sire Records' prez, Seymour Stein, "She's so in love she's radiating it."

■ **NOTABLE NEWS** (September 12, 1985)

The semiporn film Madonna tried to keep out of circulation—*A Certain Sacrifice*—will be released after all, as a home video, on October 1.

■ **NOTABLE NEWS** (September 26, 1985)

Prince should start shooting his second movie, titled *Under the Cherry Moon,* this month in Nice, France. He plays a piano player. Directing is Mary Lambert (the videos for Madonna's "Like a Virgin" and "Material Girl") in black and white (no purple).

■ **NOTABLE NEWS** (October 24, 1985)

Madonna will be interviewed by brat-pack mentor Harry Dean Stanton for *Interview* magazine.

■ **NOTABLE NEWS** (November 7, 1985)

Madonna will *not* star in *The Ruthless People*, contrary to what Disney Studios has announced. Now she is seeking a film she could star in with hubby Sean Penn.

■ **RANDOM NOTES** (November 7, 1985)

Just a few paltry months after the honeymoon, and here's Sean Penn frolicking with a woman in lingerie *other* than his wife. She's Mary Stuart Masterson, his girlfriend in *At Close Range*, which, although due for general release in February, may appear for a brief run in December. For a change, Sean plays the good guy; Christopher Walken (as his father) plays the bad guy. Director James Foley *(Reckless)* worked at *very* close range with his star. "Sean and I were simpatico from day one in every aspect—rewriting, casting. It came out of a shared sense of the story. His sense of dramatic integrity is similar to mine. If he wasn't in the movie, I might well have turned to him anyway. We complement each other." The thirty-one-year-old Foley now wants to team up with *the* team, Sean and Madonna, and is reading scripts with them. Meanwhile, of his own rumored teaming with Diane Keaton, he shyly told us: "I love her in a major way. I love her fucking guts!"

■ **RANDOM NOTES** (November 21, 1985)

How about this for a movie? A cast made up of most of the so-called Brat Pack (Demi Moore, Emilio Estevez, Rob Lowe, Melissa Gilbert and Ally Sheedy), Rosanna Arquette and Madonna, Jeff Goldblum, Malcolm McDowell and Mary Steenburgen, Brat Dad Martin Sheen and a thousand extras—and directed by Nicholas Meyer, who made *The Day After* and *Volunteers*. Too bad for Hollywood it's not a movie, but a thirty-second public-service announcement for the organization Pro-Peace, which advocates global nuclear disarmament. It's calling for volunteers for the Great Peace March, from March to November 1986, in which 5000 well-shod people will walk from Los Angeles (no one walks *in* L.A., of course) to Washington, D.C., fifteen miles a day for 255 days. The stars of the commercial said they would go *if* they had time open. Meanwhile, Emilio and Demi are engaged, Rob and Melissa are back together, and where was Sean Penn? Maybe he doesn't advocate nonviolence.

**■ RANDOM NOTES** (December 5, 1985)

Billy Idol, hard at work in New York on his next album, *Whiplash Smile*, is planning to show a side of himself that may surprise you. The new emotion surfacing in his lyrics? "Vulnerability." That *is* a new one. "When you're hurt," Idol says, not sneering for a change, "it's hard to write about it. But you have to be able to show in your songs the person you are. I want to get my exact emotions down, get them in songs, then give them a twist." Meanwhile, the platinum Idol managed to sneak into New York's Ritz recently, disguised in a beret, to debut some songs from the album. Idol leaped onstage with Psychedelic Furs sax player Mars Williams, and they tested out Billy's version of the old classic "Love Don't Live Here Anymore" (also covered by Madonna on *Like a Virgin*) and a new tune, "World's Forgotten Boy." That could describe Idol himself if he doesn't hurry up with those new tracks.

**■ NOTABLE NEWS** (December 5, 1985)

Madonna has started work on her third LP, in Los Angeles.

■ **YEAR-END RANDOM NOTES–THE BIGGEST** (December 19, 1985)

"During the Sixties and Seventies, everybody was so pure and dedicated to causes other than themselves. It was a rough time for me because I am a materialistic girl. Well, along comes this girl with this great hit record 'Material Girl,' and that charmed me; I thought, 'At last!' She looks fantastic, she's a good actress, and I love her clothes. She also has a great body, which you can actually see some of. I know women who have lovely bosoms, thirty-six-inch bosoms, and you wouldn't even know because they wear turtleneck sweaters. If you have such a lovely body, why not make the most of it? I was not the least bit appalled by her pictures in Penthouse. She never pretended to be Miss America. Another thing I love about her is she seems to love men; she has made some men happy, and they have made her happy. Madonna has done a little living."

—Helen Gurley Brown

### FRED SCHRUERS

# *LIKE A VIRGIN*
# YEAR-END ALBUM REVIEW

**M**ADONNA'S SECOND ALBUM neatly pirouettes around the sophomore jinx that might have snared her after the massive success of her first LP. She's aimed once more for hits, and producer Nile Rodgers is slicker and surer than a spring-loaded ammo clip. The droning male chorus and Mr. Machine synth riff behind "Material Girl" strike just the right note of snickering wit; that song and the whipped-cream tastiness of the title cut guaranteed at least two hits and a very, very clever, er, repositioning of Madonna's image. Who would have thought the devilishly simple concept of Boy Toy would capture the imagination of so many *female* teenagers? Go ahead and print the lyrics on the cover—the girl has an ear for expertly inexplicit lyrics, so she's got Tipper Gore by the short hairs. Maybe there's still a chance that dance-hall sex, not violence, will usher this decade out.

■ **NOTABLE NEWS** (January 16, 1986)
Madonna is attempting to get the gig writing the title track of her hubby's next flick, *At Close Range*. She is also attempting to produce her third album herself, without employing the help of Nile Rodgers, who's none too happy about losing the material wealth—oops, *girl*.

**■ NOTABLE NEWS** (February 27, 1986)

Madonna and collaborator Steve Bray are working toward a spring release for her third record, which will include "Live to Tell," from the movie *At Close Range;* "Poppa Don't Preach," about a girl who gets pregnant; and "Spotlight."

**■ RANDOM NOTES** (March 27, 1986)

Even in Hong Kong, they recognize Madonna. For her role in *Shanghai Surprise,* she's made up and dressed down as a missionary. But when the little Chinese girls see her, they still scream—*politely.* It's business as usual, then, for the world's most conspicuous couple. Sean Penn and the little woman arrive at the set at 6:00 A.M., depart at 9 P.M. and find life in Hong Kong a bit boring. In fact, Madonna really misses 7-Elevens and cheese popcorn. Even under the stress of acting together, Sean and Madonna's honeymoon continues—according to sources on the set, the effect of Cupid's arrows hasn't worn off, which should come in handy when they have to portray lovers. And they're getting a little coaching on how to handle fame from someone who knows—the movie's executive producer, George Harrison. He visited the set with a film crew from London (led by Bob Geldof's girlfriend, Paula Yates) that's making a film on the making of the film. Harrison's written a song for the soundtrack called—surprise—"Shanghai Surprise" and will probably record it himself.

**■ RANDOM NOTES** (April 24, 1986)

Okay, so Sean Penn and Madonna were the werewolves of London during a few weeks of shooting on *Shanghai Surprise* in England: Madonna's Mercedes ran over photographer Dave Hogan's foot when he tried to snap her, and the relentless Fleet Street newshounds came to regard the couple with such bitterness that they tagged them the Poison Penns. But all's well that ends well. A news conference was called, and the film's producer, George Harrison, emerged from media seclusion after nearly twelve years, rallying to Madonna's defense in front of seventy-five reporters. And they all finally got the photo they wanted.

## FRED SCHRUERS

# CAN'T STOP THE GIRL

H ERE WE ARE on a nice drive down Cahuenga Boulevard—the journalist's rental wreck following Madonna's forty-plus-grand midnight-blue Mercedes sports coupe—and the journalist is thinking that if there's one reliable fact in the weed patch of speculation, infotainment and infrared-scope surveillance surrounding Madonna over the past thirty-six months of precipitate celebrity, it's that after intensive lessons she's had her license for little more than a year, and some California cracker of a driving instructor in a string tie no doubt told her how important prudence is to any driver, especially one who represents such a ghastly big pile of future income as she . . . *it's a red light—*

Well, dress me up in a winding sheet. We just ripped across some Hollywood boulevard shortly after 11:00 P.M. with twin herds of Porsches getting big in the side windows. A shouted apology comes back on the wind: "I didn't mean to do that!"

This is not to imply that five months short of her twenty-eighth birthday as well as her first wedding anniversary—and little more than two months before the release of what's almost certain to be her third multiplatinum album—the girl is reckless. But if you're gonna follow her from North Hollywood to Sunset Boulevard, wear boxer shorts the nurses won't laugh at.

We've just come from a playback of the album (title: *True Blue*), which is due out June 15th, and her jauntiness does seem to be in order. She's coproduced it as a classy garage sale of pop styles ranging from the dance-floor hits that brought her here, to a pair of Sixties-radio replicants so cleverly candied they make your teeth ache ("Jimmy Jimmy" and "True Blue"), to the album's heartfelt bookends—"Papa Don't Preach," about a young girl in trouble, and "Open Your Heart," which is slated to be accompanied by husband Sean Penn's debut as a video-clip director. That's not to mention "Live to Tell," the ballad that serves as both the theme of Sean's movie *At Close Range* and the lead-off hit single from her album. Some pundits had predicted such a somber ballad would crash and burn deep in the charts, but that theory was so wrong that when someone asked to hear it during the album playback, Madonna's reply was an almost resigned shrug: "Well, just get in your car."

Did any celebrity bear a longer and harder public scrutiny in the past year? Mounting the first tour of her life, watching her nude image slapped across dueling spreads in the September 1985 issues of *Playboy* and *Penthouse,* seeing the hasty release of her sleazy 1981 film debut *(A Certain Sacrifice)* and being penned in hotel rooms from Tennessee to Hong Kong with the choice of hiding from the paparazzi or facing the pack alongside a hot-tempered husband who was allegedly prone to pounding on them with rocks—it would have sent anybody else back to the beach house on a diet of Stoli and barbiturates.

But here, tonight, she blithely guns her Mercedes down Sunset— this woman who says she's "never had more than two drinks at a time"—and nips into the parking lot of a restaurant where they keep a defensible corner reserved for just such visitors. The hottest name in town this week is Muammar, and we talk about him right after ordering drinks. "I hope my record gets out before the world blows up," she says. "When [the bombing of Libya] happened, I think everybody looked up from what they were laboring on. . . ."

Our waiter interrupts with a phone call ("See?" she says, "I am important"), and when she returns, Madonna announces that Sean is on his way with Chrissie Kerr, a.k.a. Hynde. They've been watching her husband, Jim, front Simple Minds in concert at the Greek Theatre. The two couples met at Live Aid last August (Sean being an ardent fan of "Don't You [Forget About Me]," Madonna a longtime Hynde admirer) and renewed their acquaintance when shooting on Sean and Madonna's *Shanghai Surprise* moved to London this past February. Since then Chrissie's been recording in Los Angeles, minding her two daughters (Natalie, three, by Ray Davies, and Yasmin, thirteen months, by Jim) and waiting for Simple Minds' yearlong tour to bring Jim to town.

Sean's imminent arrival was clearly the best sort of news for Madonna, who decided to back up her Caesar salad (she eschews meat and fish) with a baked potato as she talked about her record. She'd produced about half of it with ex-boyfriend and continuing collaborator ("Angel," "Over and Over") Steve Bray, the rest with Patrick Leonard,

who emerged from L.A. keyboard session work to be the music director for the Jacksons' Victory Tour, then Madonna's Virgin Tour. She is
saying "I wrote 'Love Makes the World Go Round' " at the precise moment Sean arrives table side. "Hi! Come over here and sit next to me."

Sean, wearing the leather jacket he's been known to convert into
a portable pup tent when the flashbulbs ignite, gives an easy greeting.
"He is such a gent," says Chrissie. "It's like walking around with a
cop." They wedge into the alcove, black-haired Chrissie and blonded
Madonna looking like good and bad angels. Madonna quickly talks
Chrissie into ordering a strawberry daiquiri, which gets rejected after
one sip—a little trigger that propels Chrissie into the sardonic vein that,
for her, carries both warmth and acrimony. By the time her white wine
arrives—alas, too cold—the Ohioan, with her husky, transatlantic-
inflected voice, and the Michigander, with her tintinnabulating alto,
have begun trading little jabs. Sean, asked by Chrissie how to warm
the wine up, suggests she breathe on it.

"No, I mean really warm it up."

"Sit on it," essays Madonna.

Missed me, Chrissie's smile says. "It's no wonder people think
you're a bitch, ya know."

"It was you I looked up to, Chrissie."

They modulate into the neutral subject of rabid fans, in particular
one girl who's been tracking Madonna from her exercise class to a local
recording studio and back out to the gate of her and Sean's place in
Malibu's Carbon Canyon, where the girl leaves roses and sometimes
lingers, hoping to be let in the gate.

"Today," Madonna says, "I had just gotten away from the paparazzi—they nailed me, incidentally . . ."

"Did you look good?" injects Chrissie.

"Devastating," says Madonna, tucking it quickly into her sentence, "and I hear this car honking, and she's got her window open,
and she goes"—Madonna, to good comic effect, approximates a bari-
tone—" 'Hey! Hey! Like the roses?' "

Sean's grin wrinkles like the tilde over *señor,* and he fixes it on his
bride till he's sure he's got her attention. Then he asks, "You know
when you leave—in the morning?"

"Yeah?"

"I wake up, buzz her up, and she makes me my breakfast."

"Oh, honey. Oh, well. That's good, because I don't go to class in
the morning," she says, pausing for effect, "but I do work up a sweat."

Sean looks fixedly at his salad, as if he'd seen Dr. Livingstone and a file of native bearers marching through it. He is applying his considerable actor's will to not smiling, or at least not laughing out loud, while the rest of the table grins moronically, because these two are so conspicuously in love with love that everybody present couldn't feel any sappier, or happier, if they had been caught making mud pies.

"I love you," she says in a small voice that goes one, two, three, up the scale. "Honey, you're blushing—your ear's blushing—was your salad good?"

Then, to restore sobriety, she instructs everybody to hold their breath and count to ten, promises to see them the next evening at the première of *At Close Range* and says goodnight. Sean, who'll head home separately in the pickup truck he drove into town, walks her to her car and returns to finish his drink. He is induced to recite a poem of his own composing, albeit with a heavy debt to the scabrous style of Charles Bukowski, about some whores in a sushi bar. Now Chrissie takes another poke.

"Who wears the pants in this family?" she wants to know. There's barely a pause before the notorious Penn eyebrows waggle.

"I take off the pants in this family," he says. "Who wears them, it doesn't make much difference to me."

"BEING REALLY COLD had a lot to do with it," Madonna is saying, talking about the eeriness of her arrival in the mainland China city of Shanghai with Sean in January. "We arrived in the middle of the night and lost a day. We were supposed to go to sleep, but we couldn't sleep, and we ended up just walking around in the streets on this steel-cold morning. It was still dark out, and the streets were filled with people doing tai chi. So dreamlike—you saw all these hands moving. They hang their wash out—put a stick out the window and put their clothes on the stick, and they're frozen in the air. When it gets light out, people are traveling around with buckets, a huge chunk of meat and a head of cabbage, their food for the day."

Was she—recognized? "No, they didn't know who I was. Blond hair . . . I'm like from outer space to them. A Martian. I loved that. That was great."

Shanghai 1986 was not the sin-festering port it was when Marlene Dietrich's Shanghai Lily returned there ("To buy a new hat," she said) in 1932's *Shanghai Express*. It's a place made austere by Peking's bureaucracy, too full of cement walls to stand in for the opium-ridden, whore-stalked, rickshaw-trafficked 1938 metropolis of Sean and Madonna's *Shanghai Surprise*. So they drank in what local color they could, as planned, and moved on to the capitalistic frenzy of Hong Kong.

The place was hardly the liberating retreat they'd imagined when they put this movie deal together (they were given implicit approval of the script—of the whole creative endeavor, in fact, just as Sean had had in the making of *At Close Range*). Hordes of photographers and reporters from the city's English-speaking dailies—and not a few imported from Great Britain—crowded close to their street locations, chanting, "We want Madonna!" And the very spots that could stand in for teeming 1938 Shanghai were the slums controlled by Chinese gangsters, people who were not easily reasoned with or threatened, who blocked them at every turn with escalating demands for payoffs. Unusual locations made the company fair game for local extortionists. "We were at this one location for eighteen hours," Madonna says, "and there was only one little road to it. They blocked it off. So, it's two o'clock in the morning, it's cold, we're tired, we have to get up the next morning at six, and we couldn't get out of there because this guy was parked, and he wanted fifty thousand dollars. That went on every day. And nobody would help us.

"There were big black rats underneath our trailers. . . . I kept saying, 'I can't wait till I can look back on this, I can't wait. . . .' It was a survival test. I know I can get through anything now, because I think we had a lot of odds against us.

"First of all, I think Sean and I set ourselves up for a challenge, being married and working together. A lot of people were saying that's a sure way to end a relationship, you'll be divorcing afterward. It was my second movie, and I had all these feelings of insecurity and being inadequate—'I'll be a terrible actress, he won't love me anymore'—all that stuff.

"But I've seen Sean work with other people, and—a lot of people have said it—he's a very giving actor. He would never make you feel like you weren't adding up in a scene. That's his main thing when he's making a movie, making it work for whoever's in the scene with him.

"Strangely enough, we never got along better. We took turns being strong and not letting it really affect us. There was a time when I was so overtaken by it, and I was crying, and he said, 'Don't worry, baby, we'll make it work—we'll make it work despite all the problems.'

"Then in two weeks, he'd be miserable, and he couldn't stand it, and I'd be holding him up, saying, 'We'll get through this, you're really good in it, and that's all that matters.' "

In *Shanghai Surprise*, which HandMade Films hopes to have ready for release this August, Penn's Mr. Wade is a petty grifter wandering the Orient, while Madonna's Gloria is a staid Massachusetts girl who's fled the prospect of a safe marriage to do missionary work. He's virtually flung at her feet, and a mutually reluctant courtship begins, similar to that between Bogart and Hepburn in *The African Queen.*

It wasn't the collective inexperience of the filmmakers that kept it from being a lark (director Jim Goddard came out of the hybrid known as long-form television and was recommended to Sean by Martin Sheen after the *Kennedy* miniseries). Most distractions came from the voracious press. The worst confrontation was on the island of Macao, when the couple were brought to their suite in the Hotel Oriental, having been told the entire place had been swept clean of peepers, "and there was a guy in the doorway of our hotel room."

This turned out to be a good way to get famous for having a camera strap twisted around your neck, and the heat this enterprising gentleman (actually the head of an English-language daily) brought down on the production caused much consternation. Coproducer and Hand-Made Films principal George Harrison flew in to mend fences. By the time the production moved to London—not without a calamitous airport scene in which a photographer bounced off Madonna's limo and injured himself—the flames had been fanned so high (SPOILT BRAT WHO RULES MADONNA blared *The Sun*) that a press conference was held to defuse the situation. Madonna and the forty-three-year-old ex-Beatle ("He's a sweet sort of hapless character," Madonna says, "who doesn't have a mean bone in his body") faced the press on March 6th. The *New Musical Express*'s reporter said Madonna "was as quick-witted, self-possessed and beautiful as I'd hoped she would be" but noted the tabloids had painted her again as "the same old surly she-cat."

"I have nothing to apologize for," she said and woke up the next day to hear a local radio station playing the phrase repeatedly on a tape loop. But for the remainder of her London stay, she was able to step out her door unmolested for a daily jog in Holland Park.

It was the second media gantlet she'd run in six months. It says a good deal about Madonna that her instinct is to wade into the thick of the fray—which is what she did when the skin mags printed nude studies of her that dated from 1978 to 1980. All three photographers involved were artsy types, as the magazines laboriously pointed out, but the net effect seemed to be a tarnishing rather like the one that temporary Miss America Vanessa Williams suffered when her far spicier pictures were pulled out of the drawer. Added to the impending release of the ineptly erotic *A Certain Sacrifice,* it made for a jolt.

"I can't say I wasn't devastated by the experience," Madonna allows. "Sean kept saying, 'Look, this is all going to blow over,' but nobody wants their skeletons to come out of the closet. I think when I first found out about it, the thing that annoyed me most wasn't so much that they were nude photographs but that I felt really out of control—for the first time in what I thought to be several years of careful planning and knowing what was going to happen. It took me by surprise.

"I think all the pictures have gotten out, but if they forgot one or two that do come out, it's not gonna blow me away," she says. "I don't even think about it anymore. It's like when you have a terrible thing you think is the end of the world—like in fifth grade when my mother told me I couldn't wear these sheer white stockings everybody in my school was wearing, I cried for hours, thought I wouldn't live through the next day. You think it's the end of the world, and then one day it's not."

But the day she was scheduled to appear, as part of the Live Aid extravaganza, before 90,000 people in Philadelphia's JFK Stadium and countless more on TV, she had her doubts. "It was the first time since the pictures came out that I was making a public appearance. Part of me felt about *this* big," she says, gesturing, "and another part of me was saying, 'I'll be damned if I'm gonna let that make me feel down. I'm gonna get out there and kick ass, get this dark cloud out from over my head.' " She came up with socko deliveries of "Holiday," "Into the Groove" and the debut performance of "Love Makes the World Go Round," shrugged off Bette Midler's sarcastic intro ("A woman who pulled herself up by her bra straps and who has been known to let them down occasionally") and managed a quip as she sweated through the show in a long, heavy and obviously hot brocade coat: "I ain't takin' shit off today—you might hold it against me in ten years." That performance exorcised most of the grinning demons. To those on the inside, she remained the unswerving trouper. "That whole week," remembers Pat Leonard, "was full of rehearsals, flying around and being nuts, getting ready for the show—she only said one thing in reference to those photos. We were out to dinner at a restaurant in Philadelphia, and I was making fun of her about something, and she said, 'Aw, Lenny, get off my back. I've had a rough week.' That's all she said."

CHANNEL RECORDERS is a humble enough one-story building tucked into a quiet street off a broad Burbank boulevard, and in a control room crowded with racks of synthesizers, Madonna, Steve Bray, Pat Leonard and engineer Michael Verdick have been locked in

a comically abusive struggle for about two months now, involving endless rude jokes, imitations of the Elephant Man and arguments over
tape snippets, with Madonna cracking the whip. "If you just talk in
the hallway for more than twenty seconds," says Bray, "you hear, 'You
guys! Get in here.' "

The star, who was stuck at a photo shoot, was skipping this session, at which her three collaborators—pop technocrats in sneakers and
sweat pants—were bearing down on a drum pattern.

"She's been here for every note until now—and she's already called
twice in the hour we've been here," says Pat Leonard. They learned
her byword—"Time is money, and the money is mine"—early on, and
they also learned Madonna doesn't like rules.

"We'll do something," he adds, "and I'll say, 'Let's go to the next
chorus and repeat it,' and she goes, 'Why? Where do these rules come
from? Who made up these rules?' "

"It'd be different if she wasn't right," says Bray.

"I found out after the first song or so," says Leonard, "that if you
listen to what she says, it instantly becomes a 'Madonna' record—her
instincts just turn it into that, no matter what producer she's working
with. She likes bells, and that's a good call, because that kind of high-
end information is very important to the ear. It's appealing, without
stepping on anything. And she's adamant about bass parts—that's her
key to the song. So put those two elements together with her voice in
the middle, and you've got the spectrum covered."

"It's weird," says Verdick, who recently coproduced human dy-
namo Ted Nugent's new album, " 'cause she's the hardest-working person I've ever met."

"When she came back to town after doing her movie," says
Leonard, "we figured she'd want to take a day off—after the whole
thing of going from China to London to New York. But the only reason we didn't start work the day she came home was that she had meetings about a new movie [Blind Date, which would have put her opposite Moonlighting's Bruce Willis, but it was nixed because it would
have interfered with mixing sessions for her LP].

"In the tour video," says Leonard, who played keyboards in the
road band, "there's an example of her concentration—when she stops
'Holiday' and talks. The video is edited, but she went on quite a bit
longer, saying hi to her grandmother—the whole thing. She's crying,
and the band was getting choked up—three years before, she probably couldn't have afforded a ticket to this place [Cobo Hall, in her home

town of Detroit], and after she talked for five minutes, she sings 'Holiday . . .' to bring us back in—and it's perfectly in pitch. We all went, 'Now how the fuck did she do that?' "

Steve Bray's most memorable moment as a tour spectator came at the Madison Square Garden date, when she told the audience, "There's a place across the street. . . . I used to look out the window at the Garden and say, 'I wonder if I'll ever get in there.' "

And, Bray says, "she did live literally across the street, on Thirtieth between Eighth and Ninth, in one of those little rooming houses where you'd walk in and it would smell so shitty I'd say, 'I'm not coming here to visit you again.' Then she was living for a while between Avenues A and B, and I always thought I was gonna be killed by junkies—that was just three years ago."

"When I started working with her," says Leonard, his studious look giving way to a squint, "I used to get so burned, man, so pissed, when people would say, 'How can you work with her?' I'd say, 'What are you saying? What do you know that I don't know?' " He ticks off a litany with emphatic flicks of his hand: "She's a nice person. She's smart. She's dedicated. She's fucking talented as hell. She's prolific. She's compassionate. She's not this person everybody thinks she is."

"It's delicate," notes Bray. "There's a single-mindedness to her that doesn't really leave a lot of space for—you can read it the wrong way if you're expecting her to give you something she really don't have time to."

"Steve would know this better," says Leonard, "but I've seen her change a lot in the last two years. She fought so hard, and when it first all turned up, she kept fighting to make sure it didn't go away. Now there's a lot more trusting. She doesn't think it's gonna go away."

THE WORLD PREMIÈRE of *At Close Range* at the Bruin Theater in Los Angeles was attended by the usual swiveling searchlights, considerable accumulations of star watchers gathered behind ropes and not a few paparazzi. As Pat Leonard had predicted to his wife, Susan, before they went in, Madonna laughed loudly at the part she always laughs at—when a demonic Christopher Walken offers Sean's beleaguered screen girlfriend some cornflakes. Afterward, the star and his bride managed to clear out with minimal interference from the photographers (although it took what looked like a phalanx of wrathful Hitler Youth seemingly jacked up on atropine and PCP to keep it that way).

The celebrity guests then went by car to a nut-crushingly hip nightspot called Helena's for a little party, where Cher sat with Aztecan aplomb, Sean's parents occupied a sociable little table with Charles Bukowski himself, and Don Johnson asked Madonna (without getting a definitive reply) if she'd like to duet with him on an Otis Redding song on his forthcoming record album. Harry Dean Stanton and his date Michelle Phillips came by, and Michelle leaned toward Madonna, who looked especially swell in her new, classic gamin look, and fondly said, "Pretty little bad girl."

Everybody had hoped Sean wouldn't clout any photographers, and he didn't. "He will fight for that privacy," Madonna had said a few days before, "and even if they get a picture of him with his coat over his head, or whatever, he didn't give it to them. They didn't get his eyes. They'll get tired of picking on him, and us. They will. He wants to protect me—he sees a lot of people being, in his eyes, disrespectful to me—or wanting to start rumors or say bad things, to create an untrue image of me. As inefficient as his methods might be, he has a way of thinking, an integrity, and he sticks with what he believes in, no matter what. There's not many people who do that.

"When you're an actor, you do your work and you go home, and people deal with what's up on the screen. When you're a singer, obviously it's you. That's what music is all about. It's a lot more accessible. You're saying, 'This is me,' so people know you intimately. They see you onstage, being vulnerable, sweating, singing, crying, dancing, whatever it is. Or just standing still. But it's a statement: 'This is me. And here I am for all you people.' "

The concert-closing scene on the Virgin Tour featured a bittersweet dialogue between Madonna and a resonant 'Daddy' voice, calling her offstage. Her actual daddy, Tony Ciccone, was to come out in Detroit to fetch his third-born child at concert's end, and she prepped him. "I said, 'Dad, when you come onstage, think back to those days when you were really mad at me—like the talent show I did in seventh grade.' I had on a bikini bathing suit, and I had painted fluorescent paisleys and flowers all over my body, and I danced under a black light, with a strobe light blinking, to 'Baba O'Reilly' by the Who.

"He was mortified. I said, 'Think of that, and how you wanted to yank me off the stage.' And he did, boy—he just about dismembered me. When I came offstage, I was so hysterical I just collapsed laughing. That was a total release. Because I felt like my father was finally seeing what I do for a living."

## DAVITT SIGERSON

# MADONNA: HER AIM IS TRUE

### *True Blue* Album Review

O F ALL CURRENT SUPERSTARS, none has manipulated the apparatus of fame more astutely than Madonna. Like Prince, she recognized the virtue of a one-word name and demonstrated the truth of an old adage—sex sells. She has played America's public morals like a virtuoso, building from starlet to mega-slut to bad girl with a heart of gold to New Honest Woman.

Cynics and idealists can agree: A conquest this perfect requires both luck and smarts. Up comes a good-looking, good-singing doll who parlays great ambition and market sense into a lowbrow dance album that becomes an international hit. She completes the transition from genre diva to mass-media wet dream brandishing a BOY TOY belt buckle under her bared bellybutton (for all convent girls to admire and feminists to loathe), then turns it around in a show of humor and pluck. But Madonna's march takes her to the brink of overexposure.

Then, out come the *Penthouse* and *Playboy* spreads. How do a couple of four-year-old portfolios just happen to make it into the hands of two fiercely competitive publications at the same exact ideal-for-Madonna moment? If it isn't a fix, then clearly God likes bad Catholic girls. And what could be better? That this bathroom consummation of BOY TOY love should be followed immediately by ritual purification at the altar of real love. Madonna marries Sean Penn and at long last hits the matrimonial sack.

And she did it all in less time than it has taken Ronald Reagan to send millions below the poverty line. Like Jimmy Cagney, to whom she dedicates "White Heat," Madonna is a lovable punk: cynical, street smart, funky, sexy, fundamentally idealistic, indestructibly self-respecting. Like Cagney, she's a national icon—but first and always, a patron saint of parochial-school America.

It is for the prokie that *True Blue* is written. Singing better than ever, Madonna stakes her claim as the pop poet of lower-middle-class America. On "Where's the Party," she presents a concise manifesto for the straphanging classes: "Couldn't wait to get older/Thought I'd have so much fun/Guess I'm one of the grown-ups/Now I have to get the job done." But Madonna isn't sad about her responsibilities. Full of immigrant-stock hustle, she's going to "find a way to make the good times last." On "Jimmy Jimmy," she laughs at her breathless boyfriend. "You say you're gonna be the king of Las Vegas. . . . You're just a boy who comes from bad places." But it's a loving laugh—and, surprise, Jimmy really does leave to make a better life. The story ends sadly, but the song is so happy that we can't doubt Madonna's pride in her guy or that she'll find a way to follow.

In "Love Makes the World Go Round," the happiest anthem for this age of uplift, Madonna scores at least as many points as "We Are the World" with lines like "It's easy to forget/If you don't hear the sound/Of pain and prejudice/Love makes the world go round" and "We're all so quick to look away/'Cause it's the easy thing to do."

Produced by Madonna with Pat Leonard and Stephen Bray, the sound of *True Blue* is yet another canny move. Armed with the success of "Into the Groove" (an unretouched eight-track demo by Bray and Madonna that is dance-pop perfection), M. resisted any temptation to reach for the kind of tour de force production Nile Rodgers achieved on *Like a Virgin*. Instead, we have a clean, accessible record assembled by a singer and songwriters to showcase material and performances. And (excepting the "Both Sides Now" rewrite "Live to Tell") it's true blue to Madonna's disco roots.

If there is a problem with Madonna's proke-rock testament, it's the lack of outstanding songs. Only the magnificent "Papa Don't Preach"—Madonna's "Billie Jean"—has the high-profile hook to match "Like a Virgin," "Dress You Up" and "Material Girl." Not coincidentally, all of the above were written by outside contributors. "White Heat," "Jimmy Jimmy" and "World Go Round" are excellent within their aspirations (though not quite up to "Into the Groove" or "Lucky Star"). But none has the feel of a pop event. "Party" starts well but doesn't ignite, and "True Blue," a cross between "Heaven Must Have Sent You" and "Chapel of Love," squanders a classic beat and an immensely promising title.

In commercial terms, it may not matter. "Live to Tell" hit Number One on career momentum, and "Papa Don't Preach" is great enough to carry several of *True Blue*'s solid contenders home. In a clever double-entendre, M.—no longer anything like a virgin—pleads for her father's approval of the decision to keep an unborn child. Given Madonna's conscientiousness and ambition, it's not likely *True Blue*'s dearth of career records was intentional. But its integrity and very freedom from attention seeking may turn out to be yet another piece of great timing in a remarkable career.

Madonna's sturdy, dependable, lovable new album remains faithful to her past while shamelessly rising above it. *True Blue* may generate fewer sales and less attention than *Like a Virgin,* but it sets her up as an artist for the long run. And like every other brainy move from this best of all possible pop madonnas, it sounds as if it comes from the heart.

■ **RANDOM NOTES** (September 11, 1986)
The video for "Open Your Heart" must have been an eye-opener for Madonna. Filmed in Los Angeles seedy Echo Park district, the clip shows Madonna performing at a local adult-entertainment center. Then she encounters a lad named Felix Howard and, well, we'll leave the rest to your imagination.

■ **NOTABLE NEWS** (October 9, 1986)
Madonna and collaborator Stephen Bray have cowritten and are set to coproduce a debut record for British model Nick Kamen. This is the first time Madonna has produced a record for somebody else.

## LAUREN SPENCER

# MADONNA'S FIRST FLOP: *SHANGHAI SURPRISE* A BONA FIDE BUST

*S*HANGHAI SURPRISE, Madonna and Sean Penn's first film together, is dying a quick and oddly quiet death at box offices around the country.

On August 29th, MGM-UA opened the romantic adventure-comedy (produced by ex-Beatle George Harrison's HandMade Films) at 400 theaters in medium-sized cities across the United States. By the end of its third week of release, the film had earned just slightly more than $1 million in total ticket sales and was averaging less than $1000 a week per theater. "That's awful," said *Variety*'s James Greenberg of the response to the film. "I've rarely seen a worse opening."

The studio chose to delay the opening of *Shanghai Surprise* in such media centers as New York and Los Angeles. People in those cities had to wait until September 19th, when, in its second wave of release, the film opened in another 400 locations. A source within MGM-UA indicated that one reason for the film's unusual release pattern was that the company hoped to delay the expected bad press for as long as possible. And with good reason—reviews of the film have been, almost without exception, extremely negative. *Variety* called *Shanghai Surprise* a "silly little trifle," and *USA Today* described the film as a "dull, hopelessly muddled mess."

Critical comment out in the heartland was scarcely more positive: In Cleveland, The *Plain Dealer* critic Roxanne T. Mueller wrote that *Shanghai Surprise* "is awesome in its awfulness, momentous in its ineptness and shattering in its stupidity." (Mueller reports that when she saw the film at a regular matinee showing at a Cleveland theater, she was the only person in the audience.) Douglas D. Armstrong of the *Mil-*

*waukee Journal* wrote that Madonna, who plays a missionary working in Shanghai in 1938, "acts and emotes with all the conviction of a guest in a sketch on a Bob Hope special." Betsy Light of the *Indianapolis Star* noted that Penn seemed miscast as the American fortune hunter who becomes involved with Madonna's character when she hires him to hunt down 1000 pounds of missing opium. She also wrote that first-time director Jim Goddard's work was "mundane" and "incredibly slow."

One dissenting voice amid all this naysaying was Joe Pollack of the *St. Louis Post-Dispatch,* who called *Shanghai Surprise* "a very proper piece of late-summer entertainment."

Theater owners expressed disappointment at the sparse turnout for *Shanghai Surprise,* and some had their own theories as to the reason for its failure. According to Ed Deblin, manager of the Fleur Four in Des Moines, Iowa, "When we showed *Desperately Seeking Susan,* people came dressed up like Madonna, but that's not happening with this movie. Maybe it's because she changed her look?"

■ **NOTABLE NEWS** (November 20, 1986)
Early next year, Madonna will release an EP called *You Can Dance.* Along with five remixes, it'll contain "Spotlight," a new song.

## ■ YEAR-END RANDOM NOTES 1986 HOT SHOTS

(December 18, 1986–January 7, 1987)

To think that we once thought her less than a lady. Madonna risked respectability by getting hitched last year and fallibility by starring, with her new hub, in this year's calamitous Shanghai Surprise. But as demonstrated by "Papa Don't Preach"—a politically incorrect anthem for Catholic girls everywhere—she remains a lovably subversive pop presence. "She's warm, thoughtful, dedicated, full of humor, vegetarian, intelligent, great looking and has a voice that reflects all of the above. And one day she'll be president."

—Chrissie Hynde

# *TRUE BLUE* YEAR-END ALBUM REVIEW

B Y CONVENTIONAL RECKONING, *True Blue* didn't live up to the standard of its multiplatinum predecessor, *Like a Virgin.* The album lacks boffo tracks of the sort Nile Rodgers confected for *Virgin,* and it seems muted. But on *True Blue,* for the first time, Madonna produced herself (in partnership with songwriters Stephen Bray and Patrick Leonard), and she had a hand in writing all nine songs. And while it's not as splashy as her past work—and not quite as much fun—the result is more personal. There is a compelling intimacy in "Live to Tell," the sinuous hit ballad, that she's never achieved before. And with "White Heat," she delivers a veritable anthem for the wised-up woman of the Eighties. *True Blue* is a less lustrous achievement than Madonna's two prior albums, but that may have been inevitable. If the past is any indication, she'll continue to shed images—and critical assessments—in the future. She seems, more than ever, unstoppable.

■ **RANDOM NOTES** (February 26, 1987)
Madonna is working on her next film, a comedy called *Slammer,* alongside New York musician Coati Mundi (from Kid Creole and the Coconuts). He's the bad guy, and Madonna's the good guy—well, sort of. She plays a young woman who's been imprisoned for a crime she didn't commit. Upon her release, she enlists a nerdy, workaholic lawyer (played by Griffin Dunne) and a 158-pound cougar named Murray (playing himself) to help win back her reputation. Due out this summer, *Slammer* is directed by James Foley, whose credits include the "Papa Don't Preach" video and the underrated movie *At Close Range.* Reportedly, Madonna is also writing some songs for the *Slammer* soundtrack—in between takes on the set. Whistle while you work?

■ **NOTABLE NEWS** (April 23, 1987)

Bryan Ferry has written some songs with Smiths guitarist Johnny Marr for Ferry's new album, which will feature backing vocals from Madonna on at least one cut.

■ **NOTABLE NEWS** (August 13, 1987)

Madonna's July 13 concert at Madison Square Garden was a benefit for the American Foundation for AIDS Research.

■ **RANDOM NOTES** (August 13, 1987)

"I was very lucky," says Michael Davidson. "Doors opened up like it was *The Twilight Zone.*" Having your debut single ("Turn It Up") appear on Madonna's *Who's That Girl* soundtrack *is* a lucky stroke, but this twenty-four-year-old singer's life seems charmed. What else do you call it when a pair of women you meet on the beach turn out to be successful French disco producers who *insist* on recording your first sessions? Or when a friend of a friend introduces you to Andy Warhol in Paris, and he thinks your tapes sound "great"? "He talked about the pop market," Michael says of the late artist. "He had all these ideas. When I came to New York, he sent me around to meet people." In no time, Michael found himself signing with Sire Records and talking to Steve Bray, the Breakfast Club's drummer and Madonna's frequent collaborator. "He said he couldn't do anything," says Michael, " 'cause he was working on *Who's That Girl* . . . but could we include 'Turn It Up' on the soundtrack?" That soundtrack also features songs by Scritti Politti and Coati Mundi. "Mine was one of the very first chosen, other than Madonna's songs," Michael says. "I was very lucky."

## VINCE ALETTI

# PERFORMANCE REVIEW

Madison Square Garden

New York City

July 13th, 1987

IN CALLING her current series of concerts the Who's That Girl Tour, Madonna is doing more than making a convenient commercial tie-in to her latest movie and hit single. Changing costumes, roles and attitudes throughout her show, Madonna turns the question into a playful, provocative examination of identity. She makes the most of our curiosity, even our skepticism; without pinning down the "real" Madonna, she parades enough personas across the stage to impress us with the impossibility of choosing just one.

At Madison Square Garden, Madonna came out as the professional seductress from her "Open Your Heart" video, dressed in a black bustier and working the stage from one end to the other. Looking sluttish but perfectly coiffed, she sang, "I'll make you love me," then pumped out a solid ninety minutes to fulfill that promise. But first she stopped to talk about the occasion—a sold-out benefit with a $100 top ticket price that raised about $400,000 for the American Foundation for AIDS Research (AMFAR). "I don't want to turn this into a morbid event," she said, "but AIDS is a painful and mysterious disease that continues to elude us." After expressing hope that the money being raised for AMFAR might speed a cure, Madonna switched back to her party-girl mode and went right into "Lucky Star."

Performing on a sleekly designed set with a moving floor, a flight of steps, several levels and panels for videos and other projected images, Madonna managed to dominate the theatrics even when she was miniaturized by the special effects. The staging got rather out of hand with "Papa Don't Preach," during which the panels filled with a succession of images that included photos of a church, the pope, a doctor, the White House, Ronald Reagan and a happy child and ended with the words SAFE SEX. "White Heat," which followed, turned into another production number; the stage sprouted with huge cutouts of gangsters, which Madonna shot down one by one.

But even this conceptual overkill didn't overshadow Madonna's singing. Madonna, whose image was always more powerful than her voice, now sounds strong enough to belt out her most demanding material and keep going. Without losing the graininess that gives her vocals character, she's developed a rich fullness that delivers an emotional punch previously missing in her shows.

Madonna has also gotten savvy enough to spoof herself. For "Dress You Up," she donned a silly hat, crazy glasses and a garish dress with eyes springing out from the breasts. She kept this outfit on for "Material Girl," undermining the song's message and playing against the Marilyn Monroe iconography of its video. The tacky trappings came off during "Like a Virgin," which Madonna nonetheless refused to take seriously, chirping it in a Cyndi Lauper–like New York accent.

The sendups and production numbers were buoyed by Madonna's energetic, eccentric dancing. And it was all balanced by emotional knockouts like "Live to Tell," which ended with Madonna stretched out on the stage, and "Who's That Girl," which closed the show's first encore. "Girl" ended dramatically: Madonna came to the front of the darkened stage and sang, "Who's that girl," over and over in a sad chant that became increasingly self-absorbed and haunting. Throwing the question back at the audience, Madonna prompted us to search for an answer that's expansive enough to fit this brilliant, chameleonlike performance.

## MIKAL GILMORE

# THE MADONNA MYSTIQUE

IT IS A SEVERE, wind-swept Saturday night in the teeming city of Tokyo, and Madonna—the most notorious living blonde in the modern world—sits tucked into the corner of a crowded limousine, glaring at the rain that is lashing steadily against the windows. "We never had to cancel a show before," she says in a low, doleful voice. "Never, never, never." With her upswept hairdo, her cardinal-red lips and her pearly skin, she looks picture perfect lovely—and also utterly glum.

Madonna has come to Japan to launch the biggest pop shebang of the summer, the worldwide Who's That Girl Tour, and since arriving at Narita Airport several days ago, she's been causing an enormous commotion. By all accounts, the twenty-eight-year-old singer, dancer, film star and lollapalooza has been fawned over, feted, followed and photographed more than any visiting pop sensation since the Beatles way back in 1966. All this hubbub is nothing new. In America, Madonna has attracted intense scrutiny throughout her career: from fans, inspired by her alluring manner; from critics, incensed by what they perceive as her vapid tawdriness; and from snoopers of all sorts, curious about the state of her marriage to the gifted and often combative actor Sean Penn. But in Japan—where she enjoys a popularity that has lately eclipsed even that of Michael Jackson and Bruce Springsteen—Madonna is something a bit better than another hot or controversial celebrity: She is an icon of Western fixations.

Tonight, though, Madonna's popularity in the Far East may have suffered something of a setback. Just a couple of hours ago, after spending a difficult day trying to wait out a minityphoon, Madonna and her management were forced to cancel the opening date of a three-night stand at Tokyo's Korakuen Stadium. It was a necessary decision, but it was also immediately unpopular: fans had traveled from all over the nation to attend these shows, and the late cancellation was seen by some media commentators as an affront. Now, as Madonna sits in the back seat of a car en route to a dinner that she has arranged as a morale booster for her band and crew (many of whom worked the entire day in the rain), things get worse. The show's cancellation, she learns, sparked riots when many of the 35,000 fans refused to vacate the concert site. In fact, some admirers are reportedly staying in the stadium, chanting prayers for the rain to go away and pleading for Madonna to appear. For the woman who has always told her audience, "Dreams come true," this is proving a disillusioning day.

A BIT LATER, seated at the middle of a long dining table in an elegant Italian restaurant, Madonna pokes at a salad and sips halfheartedly at a liqueur as various members of her team, among them musical director and keyboardist Pat Leonard, choreographer Shabba Doo, drummer Jonathan Moffett and thirteen-year-old dancer Chris Finch, offer their support.

Then, suddenly and quietly, a Japanese girl is standing at the end of the table, staring hard at Madonna. The girl—who appears to be about fifteen—is clutching an armful of Madonna souvenir programs to her breast and looks as if she'd been out in the rain for several hours. Apparently, she was among the many fans who spent the afternoon waiting at Korakuen, and though nobody can figure how she has come to know that Madonna is in this restaurant, the girl is nonetheless standing here, her face quivering with adoration and disappointment. Madonna meets her gaze, and the room fixes on their silent exchange.

"Please, please, so sorry, so sorry," the girl says in broken English, bowing deeply several times. There is something in her manner that says that she is deeply embarrassed about how she is presenting herself, but it seems she can't help doing it. A waiter rushes over to remove her, but Madonna signals him to stay back. "Let her stay," she says, still meeting the girl's eyes. The girl holds forth her souvenir books with a pleading look, indicating she would like Madonna to sign them, and Madonna nods. Watching the singer sign the programs, the girl begins to sob uncontrollably, and watching the girl cry, several people in the band and crew also give way to tears.

When Madonna is finished signing the books, the girl again apologizes profusely and signals that she would like to come closer. Gingerly, the girl moves down the length of the table until she is standing across from the singer. Then, reaching out gently, she clasps Madonna's hands and kneels before her, bowing her head, tears falling from her eyes and landing on the tablecloth in widening pools.

After a few moments, the girl stands, gathers her books and, bowing deeply a few more times, backs out of the room, to applause from the band and crew. A half-hour later, when it is time for Madonna to leave, a few dozen photographers have gathered outside the restaurant. It's the typical shoot-the-celebrity scene, and Madonna strides through it all wearing an exemplary mask of poised unconcern. But off to one side stands the Japanese girl, still clutching her treasures, still crying, and for her, Madonna saves her lone smile.

"WHEN PEOPLE MAKE THEMSELVES that vulnerable," says Madonna of the Japanese girl, "they always endear themselves to me. I mean, I was touched by it. She was obviously acting that way because she gets some kind of joy out of what I have to offer. And yet there was something so servile about it, all that bowing and stuff. Sometimes it makes you feel like you're enslaving somebody, and that's a creepy feeling."

It is the day after the canceled performance, and yesterday's bitter weather has given way to clear skies and a mild, warm wind. Madonna sits at the dining table in her hotel penthouse, wearing a tailored black suit with dark-gray stripes and munching steadily on some sort of greenish health nuts. She says she did not sleep much the night before—perhaps because 300 Japanese fans kept an all-night vigil outside the hotel, occasionally chanting her name—and in an hour, she is scheduled to leave for Korakuen Stadium to begin the sound check for this evening's concert. For the moment, though, she sits picking through her health kernels and tries to account for her intense appeal to the Japanese.

"I think I stand for a lot of things in their minds," she says. "You know, a lot of kinds of stereotypes, like the whole sex-goddess image and the blond thing. But mainly I think they feel that most of my music is really, really positive, and I think they appreciate that, particularly the women. I think I stand for everything that they're really taught to *not* be, so maybe I provide them with a little bit of encouragement."

Madonna runs her fingers through her blond tufts and smiles. For a person who hasn't slept much, she looks radiant. Indeed, the star quality that was so transfixing the night before at the restaurant is just as evident in casual circumstances. There's nothing star conscious or affected in her manner. If anything, Madonna frequently seems indifferent to her own mystique, more bemused than imperious about it. Those who come in close contact with her not only have to adjust to the resonance of her beauty and fame—which can be considerable—

but also to all those past images that her beauty echoes. There are moments when Madonna can recall Marilyn Monroe, Marlene Dietrich or Jean Harlow—blond legends with whom she clearly shares a bit of aura and purpose.

In any event, to observe Madonna is clearly to consider a star of the times, a star, in fact, who seems to be growing bigger with every move. In four years, she's had more than a dozen smash singles. And by the end of the Who's That Girl Tour, she will have performed before nearly 2 million spectators on three continents, in what may well be the most elaborately staged large-scale pop revue to date—and reportedly for more money per show (perhaps as much as $500,000) than any other entertainer in show-business history.

"I swore after my last tour I wasn't going to do another," she says. "That whole living-out-of-a-suitcase business—I don't know how Bruce Springsteen does it; I could never go on tour for a year. I told my manager the only way I would do the tour is if I could make it interesting for myself. Because that was the challenge: being able to make a show interesting in a stadium, where you're not *supposed* to be interesting, where it's like just this big mega-show, real impersonal. I wanted to make it really personal, even though people would be sitting really far away from me. And I think that's what we've managed to do."

Besides the tour, Madonna is currently appearing in her third feature film, a neo-screwball romp titled (what else?) *Who's That Girl*. It borrows heavily from the spirit and plots of some of the singer's favorite classic comedies, principally Howard Hawks's *Bringing Up Baby* and Preston Sturges's *The Lady Eve*. The film may be a bit too modern-manic to live up to its sources, but as Nikki Finn—a streetwise woman wrongly convicted of murder and hellbent on vindication—Madonna turns in a cunningly dizzy, often affecting portrayal that not only works as a homage to her favorite actress, Judy Holliday ("She could really come off as being dumb," Madonna says, "but she knew exactly what was going on"), but also has inspired speculation in Hollywood that Madonna may become one of the most bankable new actresses of the decade.

"The project," she says, "was brought to me by Jamie Foley, who directed it and who knew I'd wanted to do a comedy for a long time. The script needed some work, but there was just something about the character—the contrasts in her nature, how she was tough on one side and vulnerable on the other—that I thought I could take and make my own."

Beyond *Who's That Girl*, Madonna is set to star in an updated remake of the Marlene Dietrich film *The Blue Angel* (to be produced by Diane Keaton and directed by Alan Parker). Beyond that, she is currently considering producing several other movies, including an Alfred Hitchcock–style thriller and a film version of Lorrie Moore's novel *Anagrams*. All this activity has led some observers to wonder how deeply committed Madonna is to her singing career. Madonna, though, sees a similarity in what she's doing with her two careers.

"Acting is fun for me," she says, "because, well . . . for most people, music is a very personal statement, but I've always liked to have different characters that I project. I feel that I projected a very specific character for *Like a Virgin* and that whole business and then created a much different character for my third album. The problem is, in the public's mind, you are your image, your musical image, and I think that those characters are only extensions of me. There's a little bit of you in every character that you do. I think I had something in common with Susan in *Desperately Seeking Susan,* and I think I have a lot in common with Nikki Finn in *Who's That Girl,* but it's not me. Still, I wouldn't have been attracted to her if we didn't have something in common."

What is it that she and Nikki Finn have in common?

"Nikki? Um, she's courageous, and manipulative." Madonna pauses and giggles. "And she's funny, and sweet. That's enough." She laughs again, running her hand through her hair.

Isn't Nikki also terribly misjudged?

"Yes," says Madonna, with a nod and a smile. "Yes, she is, but she clears her name in the end, and that's always good to do. Clear your name in the end. But I think I'm continuously doing that with the public."

Has that ever been a hurtful process—for example, weathering all those unflattering characterizations around the time of "Like a Virgin"?

"At first it was," she says. "I mean, I was surprised with how people reacted to 'Like a Virgin,' because when I did the song, to me, I was singing about how something made me feel a certain way—brand-new and fresh—and everyone else interpreted it as 'I don't want to be a virgin anymore. Fuck my brains out!' That's not what I sang at all."

Madonna pauses and glances for a moment at her reflection in the tabletop. "People have this idea," she says, "that if you're sexual and beautiful and provocative, then there's nothing else you could possibly offer. People have *always* had that image about women. And while it might have seemed like I was behaving in a stereotypical way, at the same time, I was also masterminding it. I was in control of everything

I was doing, and I think that when people realized that, it confused them. It's not like I was saying, 'Don't pay attention to the clothes—to the lingerie—I'm wearing.' Actually, the fact that I was wearing those clothes was meant to drive home the point that you *can* be sexy and strong at the same time. In a way, it was necessary to wear the clothes."

So is it feminism she's offering or a denial of it?

She considers the notion, then shrugs. "I don't think about the work I do in terms of feminism. I certainly feel that I give women strength and hope, particularly young women. So in that respect, I feel my behavior is feminist, or my art is feminist. But I'm certainly not militant about it, nor do I exactly premeditate it.

"And when women didn't like me, I just chalked it up to the reason women *always* have a problem with me: I think that women who are strong, or women who wanted to be strong or be respected, were taught this thing that they had to behave like men, or *not* be sexy or feminine or something, and I think it pissed them off that I was doing that. Also, I think for the most part men have always been the aggressors sexually. Through time immemorial they've always been in control. So I think sex is equated with power in a way, and that's scary in a way. It's scary for men that women would have that power, and I think it's scary for women to have that power—or to have that power and be sexy at the same time."

Is that why so many critics seemed perfectly comfortable with male rock stars' sexuality but were incensed by Madonna's displays?

"Well, yeah! *I* thought about that, certainly. I'd think, 'Why aren't they letting all this stand in the way of appreciating Prince's music?' He was certainly just as sexually provocative, if not more than I was. I wasn't talking about giving *head*. He was much more specific than I was."

There's a knock at the door of her suite, a reminder that it's time to head over to the stadium. "Actually, I can't complain," Madonna says, getting ready to leave. "Plenty of people are getting my message. I'm not going to change the world in a day. I don't know, maybe it never will be where men and women will be equal. They're too different. I mean, it just seems like as long as women are the ones that give birth to children, it'll never really change. I'm not saying that in a sad way. I think more and more women will be able to have more freedom to do whatever they want, and they won't have so many prejudices thrown at them, but I think it would be much too idealistic to say that one day we will never be discriminated against because we're women.

"I don't know, am I too cynical?"

SEVERAL HOURS LATER, Madonna stands onstage before 35,000 fans at Korakuen Stadium—outfitted in a brazen corset-bustier, executing fast, sure pirouettes and striking starkly bawdy poses that recall the cocky femmes of *Cabaret* and *The Blue Angel*. It rapidly becomes apparent that all Madonna's talk about sexual pride was hardly trifling. Indeed, although it may come as a major surprise to many of her critics, there has probably never been a more imaginative or forceful showcase for the feminine sensibility in pop than Madonna's current concert tour. In part, that's because Madonna is simply the first female entertainer who has ever starred in a show of this scope—a fusion of Broadway-style choreography and post-disco song and dance that tops the standards set by previous live concert firebrands like Prince and Michael Jackson.

But there is more to the show than mere theatrical savvy. Actually, a majority of Madonna's new song-and-dance routines amount to stirring statements about dignity and triumph. Some of these are simply fun—for example, the skit in "True Blue," where the singer gets charmed and then used by a muscle-bound lady-killer (played slyly by the show's choreographer, master break dancer Shabba Doo) but then wins the cad back. Other moments are both fun and serious, such as "Open Your Heart," in which Madonna pulls off some eye-busting stripper-style moves that are not only enticing but also defiant and smart. And yet still other moments come off as unabashedly serious, particularly a rendition of "Papa Don't Preach" that takes sharp aim at some of the current batch of male authority figures (including the pope and the president) who would presume to have the power to make key decisions regarding a woman's control of her own body. ("Ronald Reagan," Madonna says later, "is one papa who shouldn't preach.")

But it is in "Live to Tell" that Madonna makes her most forceful comment on feminine spirit. For the most part, the song is Madonna's least theatrical performance. She sings her ballad of battered hope while standing stockstill at the front of the stage, under a giant projected photo of herself that strongly resembles Marilyn Monroe. At the song's end, as the photo turns dark and deathly, Madonna slumps to the floor, in a pose that suggests surrender and desolation, and then gradually forces herself back to her feet, as if recovering her strength and courage through an act of titanic will. It's a moment that could be seen as a mourning of Monroe's gloomy end or as a refusal of the very sort of despair that was the fate of the actress.

It's also a moment that makes plain a link between the stars: Like Monroe, Madonna is bent on epitomizing and championing a certain vision of female sexuality, and also like Monroe, she is often damned and dismissed as an artist for doing so. Whether this connection is apparent to the audience gathered here in Tokyo is hard to say, though this much is sure. In that instant in "Live to Tell" when Madonna rises from the floor and stands with her head erect, a decidedly feminine yowl—in fact, the loudest roar of the evening—greets the motion. It is an acclamation that will be repeated on several other nights in the weeks ahead, as the tour makes its way around America. Madonna will still have her detractors, but somehow little girls across the world seem to recognize a genuine hero when they see one.

THE NEXT EVENING, aboard a plane en route to Los Angeles, Madonna seems surprised, even a tad miffed, to learn that her performance of "Live to Tell" may be seen as a commentary on Marilyn Monroe. Apparently, she never intended for the portrait that accompanies the song onstage to bear such a striking resemblance to Monroe.

"Actually," she says, "I think 'Live to Tell' is about something very different. It's about being strong, and questioning whether you can be that strong, but ultimately surviving."

But she's aware, isn't she, that many people see certain similarities between her and Monroe? After all, she was the one who deliberately evoked Marilyn in the "Material Girl" video. And both artists inspire arguments about sexual values and share a certain allure.

"Oh, sure," she says. "I mean, at first I enjoyed the comparisons between me and her. I saw it all as a compliment: She was very sexy—*extremely* sexy—and she had blond hair, and so on and so forth. Then it started to annoy me, because nobody wants to be continuously compared to someone else. You want people to see that you have a statement of your own to make.

"But yes, I *do* feel something for Marilyn Monroe. A sympathy. Because in those days, you were really a slave to the whole Hollywood machinery, and unless you had the strength to pull yourself out of it, you were just trapped. I think she really didn't know what she was getting herself into and simply made herself vulnerable, and I feel a bond with that. I've certainly felt that at times—I've felt an invasion of privacy and all that—but I'm determined never to let it get me down. Marilyn Monroe was a victim, and I'm not. That's why there's really no comparison."

But has she, like Marilyn, ever had times of wondering . . .

Madonna anticipates where the question is headed. "Of wondering, 'Oh, God, what have I created?' Oh yes. Like when *Desperately Seeking Susan* came out, and I was going with a well-known actor, then I announced my marriage, *then* the *Playboy* and *Penthouse* pictures came out—everything sort of happened at once, one big explosion of publicity. No matter how successful you want to be, you could never ever anticipate that kind of attention—the grand scale of it all.

"And at first the *Playboy* photos were very hurtful to me, and I wasn't sure how I felt about them. Now I look back at them and I feel silly that I ever got upset, but I *did* want to keep some things private. It was like when you're a little girl at school and some nun comes and lifts your dress up in front of everybody and you get really embarrassed. It's not really a terrible thing in the end, but you're not ready for it, and it seems so awful, and you seem so exposed. Also, *Penthouse* did something really nasty: They like sent copies of the magazine to Sean." Madonna pauses and shakes her head, as if trying to dispel the memory.

"That whole time was almost too much," she says after a moment. "I mean, I didn't think I was going to be getting married with thirteen helicopters flying over my head. It turned into a circus. In the end, I was laughing. At first I was outraged, and then I was laughing. You couldn't have written it in a movie. No one would have believed it. It was better than anything like that, it was just so incredible. It was like a Busby Berkeley musical. Or something that somebody would stage to generate a lot of publicity for one of their stars."

Why does she think she and Sean Penn have attracted so much scrutiny? After all, other celebrity couples manage to avoid that much brouhaha.

"But they don't love each other as much as we do!" she says, then lets go with a nice, loud, goofy laugh. "Maybe people sense that. I don't know. We're both very intense people. Plus, he had a sort of rebellious-bad-boy image in Hollywood, and I had the same one, only, you know, for a girl, and I think the press really wanted to seize on that opportunity of that combination."

Does she ever get the feeling that people want her marriage to fail?

"Oh yes, from the time we got married. They couldn't make up their mind: They wanted me to be pregnant, or they wanted us to get a divorce. That put a lot of strain on our relationship, too, after a while. It's been a character-building experience, and a test of love to get through all of it." She falls silent for a time, studying the darkening sky outside the window. "A lot of the times," she says, "the press would make up the most awful things that we had never done, fights that we never had. Then sometimes we *would* have a fight, and we'd read about it, and it would be almost spooky, like they'd predicted it or they'd bugged our phones or they were *listening* in our bedroom. It can be very scary if you let it get to you."

Wouldn't it be easier if she and Sean just accommodated the press?

"Well," she says, "I can never speak for Sean. He will always deal with the press in his own way. For myself, I *have* accommodated the press a great deal. I've done numerous press conferences, numerous interviews. But I'm a lot more outgoing and verbal that way than Sean is. Also, in the beginning of my career I invited controversy and press and publicity, and I don't think he did at all. He was a very serious actor, and he wasn't interested in having a Hollywood-star image and didn't do a lot of interviews, and it took him quite by surprise, whereas I had already kind of thrown myself into that whole world. And therefore we deal with it differently."

Unfortunately, Penn's way has often been belligerent: He has perhaps become more famous for fighting than for acting—which has led him to legal difficulties, as well as a troubled public image. Madonna herself has been present for some of the fisticuffs.

"It was very traumatic," she says. "I mean, I don't like violence. I never condone hitting anyone, and I never thought that any violence should have taken place. But on the other hand, I understood Sean's anger, and believe me, I've wanted to hit them many times. I never *would*, you know, because I realize that it would just make things worse. Besides, I have chances to vent my anger in other ways than confrontation. I like to fight people and kind of manipulate them into feeling like they're not being fought, do you know what I mean? I'd rather do it that way.

"But yes, those were very traumatic experiences for me, and I think . . ." She pauses thoughtfully. "I don't think they'll be happening anymore. I think that Sean really believes that it's a waste of energy. It antagonizes the press more and generates even more publicity, and I think he realizes that. But once they realized he was a target for that, they really went out of their way to pick on him, to the point where they would walk down the street and kind of poke at him and say, 'C'mon, c'mon, hit me, hit me.' It's not fair. And they insult me, and they try to get him to react that way, so, God, you just have to have the strength to rise above it all."

Madonna looks suddenly tired. In just a few hours, she will be landing in Los Angeles, then shortly winging off to Miami, Florida, where the American tour begins. One has to wonder: With all this work, all this scrutiny of her private life, does she ever question whether the fame is worth all the trouble?

"Sure," she says quietly. "There have been times when I've thought, 'If I'd known it was going to be like this, I wouldn't have tried so hard.' But I feel that what I do affects people in a very positive way. That's the most important thing, and that's what I always set out to do. And you can't affect people in a large, grand way without being scrutinized and judged and put under a microscope, and I accept that. If it ever gets too much, or I feel like I'm being overscrutinized, or I'm not enjoying it anymore, then I won't do it."

Isn't it possible, though, that things are just heating up? That by the end of this year, she might be an even bigger star? Maybe even, if only for a while, the biggest star?

Something in Madonna's face closes off at the question. "I don't like to think about it," she says. "It's . . . distracting."

But is the prospect . . .

"Is it scary? Sure, it's both scary *and* exciting. Because who knows what will come of it and what responsibilities I'll have and what things will be taken away and what I'll lose and what I'll gain? I mean, you don't know until you get there."

MADONNA'S LIFE stays interesting after her return to America. On the day she arrives in Los Angeles, the press is abuzz with the latest about Sean Penn, who has just been sentenced to sixty days in jail for punching an extra during the filming of his movie *Colors* and for a reckless-driving charge. Several local commentators seem downright gleeful about what they view as the actor's comeuppance; some, in fact, urge his jailers to lock him up with dangerous criminals— an attitude that seems no less odious than Penn's violence.

Matters grow even worse a few weeks later, when—after having won a reprieve of his jail term so that he can finish work on a new film in West Germany—Penn apparently violates his agreement with the court by turning up in New York to see his wife's AIDS benefit concert at Madison Square Garden. Back in Los Angeles, the city attorneys grow furious and obtain a warrant for the actor's arrest, then quash the warrant when Penn belatedly heads for Europe to make his movie. Madonna, meantime, prefers to stay mum on the issue. "I don't know all the details," she says, "and I don't want to."

Still, the whole affair manages to kick up several rumors—namely, that Penn's sentencing has either saved or helped finish what has reputedly been an often tempestuous marriage. "All this talk," says Madonna, "is heightened dramatics. We are a 'Hollywood couple,' so people are going to pay a lot of attention to our marriage and whether it's going to work or not. . . . If we have our fights, I think that's pretty normal for young people in their first few years of marriage. It's normal for anybody who's married, but when you put all the pressures that we've had on top of that, I think the fact that we're still together is pretty amazing. You know, we're working it out, and that's all I can say. . . . It's easy to give up, but it's not easy for me to give up."

Amid all the hoopla about Penn, Madonna's AIDS benefit is relatively overlooked. Shaken by the death of a good friend, artist Michael Burgoyne, and mindful that much of her initial support came from the gay, black and Latin communities—the same groups that have been hardest hit by AIDS—Madonna decided to lend her name to the cause of raising money for medical research against the deadly disease and, in the process, became the first major American pop star to stage such a large-scale fund-raiser. Not surprisingly, many of the concert's songs, such as "Open Your Heart" and "Holiday," take on a new resonance in the context of the event, though none is more affecting than "Live to Tell," dedicated on this evening to Burgoyne. Indeed, the moment when Madonna pushes herself up off the stage floor and back to her feet comes across as both an act of hope and a gesture of solace in the face of terrible, fearful impossibilities. Two days later, the *New York Times* calls the show "shallow, kitschy pop entertainment." Madonna says, "There are still those people who, no matter what I do, will always think of me as a little disco tart."

As the tour progresses, "Live to Tell" seems to take on more and more of the focus in the show. By the time she hits Los Angeles, Madonna has taken to halting in the middle of the song and gazing thoughtfully up at the large photo of herself that looms above her head. What is she thinking about while looking at her own larger-than-life image? "I see it and I say, 'Oh, God, what have I done? What have I created? Is *that* me, or is *this* me, this small person standing down here on the stage?' That's why I call the tour Who's That Girl: because I play a lot of characters, and every time I do a video or a song, people go, 'Oh, *that's* what she's like.' And I'm not like any of them. I'm all of them. I'm none of them. You know what I mean?"

## JEAN ROSENBLUTH

# *WHO'S THAT GIRL* BOMBS

THE QUESTION POSED by the film's title was "Who's that girl?" The answer provided by the box-office receipts was, alas, "The same one who appeared in *Shanghai Surprise.*"

In its first weekend of release, August 7th–9th, the screwball comedy—which reportedly cost between $17 million and $20 million to make—grossed just $2.55 million, compared with $5.17 million for *Stakeout* and $4.88 million for *Masters of the Universe.* By the following weekend, *Who's That Girl* was grossing just $1.1 million, a drop of 57 percent. In its first nine days of release, total receipts were a disastrous $5.1 million.

Warner Bros. hasn't been able to count on critical acclaim to widen the film's audience. The most charitable review from a major newspaper was that of the *New York Times,* which described the movie as nearly achieving "its fairly modest goals." Other reviews were at best mediocre, ranging from "a retread of better films old and new" *(USA Today)* to "a rattling failure" (the *Los Angeles Times*).

Madonna, as Nikki Finn—a woman who spent four years in prison for a crime she didn't commit—leads [Griffin] Dunne, playing straight-as-an-arrow Loudon Trott, through a series of escapades that combines the most improbable elements of *Something Wild* and *Bringing Up Baby.* Along the way—yawn—they fall in love, despite Trott's impending marriage to his rich boss's beautiful daughter.

Warner Bros. might have had some inkling of the problems to come; it opened the movie without any press screenings. A company spokesman denies this was an evasive tactic: "No advance showings were held because reviews either way wouldn't affect the film's success. Madonna is such a draw, you don't need anything else." Then what about the box-office stillbirth of *Shanghai Surprise,* Madonna's last film? "Well, that's a whole different story."

Indeed, *Shanghai Surprise* was not the beneficiary of a hit sound-track. And even though she doesn't sing in *Who's That Girl,* Madonna's appeal as a vocalist may ultimately prove the financial saving grace of the film. The title-track single had risen to Number Two on *Billboard*'s Hot 100 chart by the time of the film's release, while the LP was lodged at Number Forty-six on the album chart in only its second week of release. However, several retailers say the *Who's That Girl* soundtrack, which contains four Madonna tunes as well as tracks by Club Nouveau, Scritti Politti and others, hasn't received enough promotion. "A lot of consumers came in asking for the latest Madonna single off her [*True Blue*] album," says Dave Roy, head buyer for the more than 200 record stores owned by Trans World Music of Albany, New York. "They didn't know there was a movie coming out and a soundtrack already available."

## VINCE ALETTI

# WHO'S THAT GIRL
# ALBUM REVIEW
# (VARIOUS ARTISTS)

THOUGH SOUNDTRACK ALBUMS have an increasingly tenuous connection to the films they accompany into the marketplace—padded as they are with music that never even wafted through the background of the actual movie—one link remains strong: A box-office hit may not guarantee boffo record sales, but an immensely successful soundtrack is virtually impossible without an immensely successful movie. Unless, of course, that movie is Madonna's *Who's That Girl*, whose immediate flop has not kept its soundtrack from bounding into *Billboard*'s Top Ten in its fourth week on the charts.

At least half the songs on the *Who's That Girl* album are buried in or absent from the film, but on celluloid or vinyl, even the best of them are likely to be perceived as filler. Forget Scritti Politti's charming "Best Thing Ever," Club Nouveau's crunchy "Step by Step," Coati Mundi's rambunctious "El Coco Loco" and Duncan Faure's uncannily Beatlesque "24 Hours"—for most buyers, this is the new Madonna album. Her four cuts can't save the film, but they certainly make the LP.

Madonna's songs here, produced in collaboration with old standbys Patrick Leonard and Stephen Bray, are instantly familiar, almost predictable. These are trademark Madonna groove records—no revelations, no departures, no quirks—pure pop in its most potent form. But if the singer is taking no risks on these cuts, there's no sense that she's lying back and sinking into formula.

A good deal of Madonna's appeal on record lies in her ability to invest the flimsiest material with feeling. Her sincerity is beside the point; it's the combination of enthusiasm and empathy she projects into the lyrics (the way an actress projects herself into a role) that clinches her songs. Madonna has an instinctive understanding of pop spirit, that timeless blend of the trashy and the sublime, and an unerring feel for the snagging hook.

So the title tune, at first so unpromising, bobbing up in the wake of "La Isla Bonita," grabs hold with its bright bilingual chant, its vaguely mournful undertow. "Causing a Commotion" and, to a lesser extent, "Can't Stop" match Stephen Bray's irrepressible rhythmic drive with Madonna's alluring, unsettling mix of warm maturity and chirpy adolescence.

But *Who's That Girl* cuts deepest with "The Look of Love," Pat Leonard's song of regret that obviously reprises his "Live to Tell" but clicks just as surely. The song's hypnotically liquid quality and Madonna's soft, aching vocals combine for the soundtrack's one poignant moment, an emotional anchor in otherwise cheery, choppy seas. If Madonna's pop savvy won't sell her movie, it's more than enough to sell her songs.

## February
### CYNDI LAUPER'S TOUR SHOWS OFF HER TRUE COLORS

"When people say to me, 'Aren't you Cyndi Lauper?' I say, 'No, I'm Madonna, and watch out, 'cause Sean Penn is gonna come at ya any second and beat the shit outta ya.' " La Lauper winds up her U.S. tour and is off to Paris to film a concert special for HBO.

## May
### SEAN: INTO THE PEN

While Madonna gets into shape for her tour, Sean Penn once again makes it into the headlines, this time for reckless driving—his second probation violation. He is sentenced to sixty days in the county jail.

## June
### NOTABLE NEWS

Heart launches its U.S. tour June 26th in Portland, Oregon; Madonna begins hers the next day in Miami.

## July
### MADONNA CAUSES A COMMOTION FOR A GOOD CAUSE

Madonna reveals a new, sleek figure and a more powerful voice during her well-choreographed Who's That Girl Tour. Her July 13th appearance at New York's Madison Square Garden is a benefit show that raises $400,000 for AIDS research.

## August
### THE GIRL CAN'T HELP IT

Nothing—not even Madonna's star power—can save the disastrous *Who's That Girl* from box-office oblivion.

## September
### NOTABLE NEWS

*Forbes* magazine declares Bruce Springsteen rock's biggest moneymaker for the last two years, with an estimated income of $56 million. Other major-league bread-winners cited by the magazine are Madonna ($47 million) and Michael Jackson ($43 million).

**December**

## ROCKERS COME TOGETHER FOR 'A VERY SPECIAL CHRISTMAS'

"Why don't we sing 'Jingle Bells'?" says Sting during the photo session for the holiday album *A Very Special Christmas.* Proceeds will benefit the Special Olympics, an organization that offers sports programs for the mentally retarded. Produced by Jimmy Iovine, the album features Christmas songs from Sting, Bruce Springsteen, Eurythmics, Run-D.M.C., John Cougar Mellencamp, Bob Seger, Madonna, Bon Jovi, Stevie Nicks, the Pointer Sisters, Whitney Houston, Bryan Adams, Alison Moyet and the Pretenders. A highlight is U2's cover of "Christmas (Baby Please Come Home)."

"U2 would like to write a Christmas song of our own sometime," says Adam Clayton. Maybe next year.

### ■ RANDOM NOTES (January 14, 1988)

In the wake of Madonna's split with Sean Penn (her divorce papers cited "irreconcilable differences"), the singer's fans are wondering what her next move will be—besides a new hair color. Judging from her recent visit to Prince's Paisley Park Studios, she may be focusing attention back on her music career, though she and Prince have no immediate plans to collaborate.

Next month, Penn stars in *Judgment in Berlin* (see top photo), based on the true story of a hijacking by three East Germans seeking political asylum in the West. Penn plays one of the would-be defectors.

### ■ NOTABLE NEWS (January 28, 1988)

Two weeks after filing for divorce from Sean Penn, Madonna withdrew the papers.

**■ RANDOM NOTES** (March 24, 1988)

"Everyone's dressing rooms were separated by shower curtains," says director Howard Brookner of working conditions on the low-budget *Bloodhounds of Broadway*. "There was Madonna, Matt Dillon, Randy Quaid, Jennifer Grey and Rutger Hauer, all separated by shower curtains with their names scrawled on in Magic Marker." (Brookner's previous credits include a documentary he made on William Burroughs featuring Patti Smith.) Madonna plays chorus girl Hortense Hathaway in the 1920s gangster comedy, which is based on four Damon Runyon stories.

"She's got an eye for the diamonds, you know?" says Grey of Madonna's character. "She's a gold digger." Grey plays a fellow chorine named Lovey Lou.

Quaid says that even though this is another comic role for Madonna, her acting has improved since *Who's That Girl*. "She's more herself in this," he says. "She doesn't use any funny voice."

Madonna is now rehearsing *Speed-the-Plow*, a play by David Mamet, with Joe Mantegna and Ron Silver. It begins a limited run off-Broadway this month.

**■ RANDOM NOTES** (May 19, 1988)

"It's not Judy Holliday time," says director Gregory Mosher of Madonna's acting in David Mamet's *Speed-the-Plow*, now playing on Broadway. "She doesn't snap gum and talk in a funny secretary voice. It's a big change for her. And she works her ass off." Two years ago, Mosher presented Madonna and husband Sean Penn onstage in *Goose and TomTom*. In *Speed-the-Plow*, Madonna does indeed play a temporary secretary to two Hollywood producers (Joe Mantegna and Ron Silver). "Joey is the one onstage every second of this play," says Mosher. "We're trying not to make people think it's the Madonna show."

## JIM FARBER

# LIVE IF YOU WANT IT
# *CIAO ITALIA* VIDEO REVIEW

THIS VERSION of Madonna's Who's That Girl Tour returns the star to the medium where she belongs: television. The tour itself, a glitz-packed stadium spectacle, was supposed to provide the ultimate proof of Madonna's versatility and endurance. In fact, its bloated scale simply overwhelmed her.

Back on the small screen, however, the pleasures of her campy pop presence can be seen in proper context once again. The contrived Las Vegas kitschiness of the event (complete with goofy choreography and throwaway costume changes) seems more at home on video, and the star no longer appears to be straining to push herself beyond her flat pop image.

Of course, the show (captured here in Turin, Italy) still has its baffling moments, including her grade-school imitation of Cyndi Lauper in the "Dress You Up/Material Girl" medley. In addition, the camera work isn't always up to snuff: When the director chooses long shots to capture the full spectacle of the staging, all we see is a blur.

Then there's Madonna's voice. It's a thin enough yap in its strongest range (the high notes), but when she dips down low, she is forever veering off key. Luckily, most of her material is so irresistible it more than carries her. In a ballad like "Live to Tell," she doesn't need to sing with great emotion; there's feeling enough in the words and melody. And the same goes for upbeat tracks like "Holiday" or "Into the Groove."

Then again, the effervescence of Madonna's material and production has never been the issue. Her succession of contrived media images has. That's what made her live show such an alienating experience. On videocassette, however, Madonna makes manipulation seem like an exciting message indeed.

**■ RANDOM NOTES** (September 22, 1988)

"I will be running," says Dave Stewart. "I don't know which country I'll be in. I might be in Britain; I might be in America. I'm not sure yet." Stewart, Sting and Madonna are just a few of the celebrities who've registered to take part in the Race Against Time, an International charity run sponsored by CARE/Sport Aid '88. The race, which will take place on six continents, will raise money for the world's needy children. Other prospective runners include King Sunny Adé, Donny Osmond, Bill Wyman and Peter Gabriel.

Stewart is currently producing an album for Russian rock singer Boris Grebenshikov for CBS Records. (Annie Lennox and Chrissie Hynde sing on the record, due next year.) Stewart says he's also been recording with Harry Dean Stanton. The actor? "He sings great," Stewart says.

Madonna, who's been writing with frequent collaborator Patrick Leonard, plans to go into the studio now that her run in *Speed-the-Plow* is over.

**■ NOTABLE NEWS** (December 1, 1988)

That's Madonna singing under the nom de croon Lulu Smith on Peter Cetera's latest LP, *One More Story*.

**■ RANDOM NOTES** (January 12, 1989)

"Sean Penn is into some pretty scary stuff: guns, fire, mud, mad dogs," says singer-songwriter Joe Henry, who got a firsthand look at the actor's peculiar obsessions when Penn directed the video for Henry's single "Here and Gone," from his impressive forthcoming album, *Murder of Crows*.

"We filmed in the Mohave desert, and he came out there very heavily armed," says Henry, who's married to Madonna's sister Melanie. "He's a very strange man, and I mean that in the nicest way." The video marks Penn's directorial debut.

**■ NOTABLE NEWS** (January 26, 1989)

Despite a string of box-office failures, including *Who's That Girl* and *Shanghai Surprise*, Madonna has managed to swing her own production deal with Columbia Pictures. Five movies are planned under her new Siren Films banner during the next two years. Madonna is not obligated to appear in all of the productions.

**■ NOTABLE NEWS** (February 9, 1989)

Madonna will play Breathless Mahoney in Warren Beatty's movie version of the cartoon classic *Dick Tracy*. Beatty is starring in, producing, and directing the film.

**■ NOTABLE NEWS** (February 23, 1989)

Amid sordid tales of her husband's violent, abusive behavior, Madonna petitioned for divorce from Sean Penn in January. The singer also filed assault charges against Penn with the Malibu sheriff's office, but they were later dropped. A spokesman for Penn has called the divorce "amicable"; Madonna's people say they have no comment. Perhaps Madonna's forthcoming album, *Like a Prayer,* will shed some light on her personal strife. Penn, meanwhile, is off to Canada to film a remake of *We're No Angels* with Robert De Niro.

## BILL ZEHME

# MADONNA

## The ROLLING STONE Interview

"**D**O YOU SEE a black jaguar?"

The voice, small and insistent, issues from the passenger seat, where the world's most famous woman burrows deep into the upholstery. She slumps and scrunches, lying decidedly low. Her rump is poised perilously above the floor mat. Her boots are propped against the dashboard. Her tresses are piled beneath a leather cap, and tiny dark specs pinch at her nose. Occasionally, her head bobs up, and she peers through the windshield in order to give navigational tips. Then, just as quickly, she ducks back into hiding. Madonna is on the lam. She is incognito. She is in my car. I am driving her home. It was her idea.

"The paparazzi won't recognize your car," she says, hatching her intrepid scheme after our first interview session. For her part, Madonna recognizes her most dogged pursuers. She knows what they drive. Every TV in her house is wired to the security system and transmits a continuous picture of the front gate and the street beyond. She sees those who park and lurk and obsess. She watches and remembers their movements. All of which might explain why she is cowering in my rented Chevy Corsica, fretting about a particular black Jaguar that is nowhere to be seen. "At this point," she says, sighing wearily, "I know them all."

Madonna has a new home—a sanctuary, really—nestled high in the Hollywood Hills. As it happens, an aerial photograph of the spread, snapped from a helicopter, was published in this morning's paper. The accompanying text: "The soon-to-be-divorced Mrs. Sean Penn took title to the house Jan. 18. She paid $2,950,000." She had not yet seen the item when I showed it to her a few hours earlier. "They say how much I paid for it?" she asked, sounding surprised and violated. " 'The house has seven bedrooms and six bathrooms'? *They are so misin-formed!"* (Indeed, the next morning the same column reads, "A friend of Madonna's called to say we were incorrect to report . . . seven bed-rooms. 'It has three bedrooms plus a maid's room,' said the caller.")

The point being, she is beset. Her woes dangle like shredded pulp from the jaws of gossip carnivores. Among supermarket-literature queens, she is the ultimate checkout girl. Her reign currently rages, due to the noisy unraveling of her three-and-a-half-year marriage to actor-pugilist Sean Penn. Divorce papers were filed by her attorneys on Jan-uary 5th—thirteen months since the last time it happened (when she just as hastily rescinded the action). Like before, "irreconcilable dif-ferences" were cited. But this recent connubial rupture was reportedly prompted by a mysterious post-holiday altercation about which noth-ing is known for sure. Speculation abounds, however, and gallons of tabloid ink have been expended to document it. Why conserve now?

Rumors surrounding Madonna's "night of terror" (December 28th, 1988): A drunken Sean explodes at Madonna in their Malibu es-tate because *(a)* having a baby in the near future does not jibe with her plans; *(b)* he is annoyed at her friendships with Warren Beatty and/or Sandra Bernhard. Sean demonstrates his displeasure by *(a)* roughing her up; *(b)* threatening to thrust her head into an oven; *(c)* hogtying her with leather straps (and/or twine) to a chair and leaving her "trussed up like a turkey" (tabloid description) for nine hours. She per-suades him to release her and/or escapes to the Malibu sheriff's office, where she swears out an assault complaint against her husband. (The complaint, which was actually filed, is withdrawn by her days later.) She then seeks refuge in the home of *(a)* photographer friend Herb Ritts; *(b)* her manager, Freddy DeMann.

Meanwhile, Malibu police descend upon the Penn house and order Sean to come outside with his hands up. He does so but later denies abusing Madonna, claiming she trumped up the charges because she is jealous that he has been dating a stripper.

The veracity of any of the above is questionable. Maybe even su-perfluous. Throughout the ordeal, Madonna remained mum; by drop-ping charges, she implied that her marriage has been more than ade-quately scrutinized, that an ensuing trial would be a macabre circus. What is curious, however, is that she has chosen instead to bare her soul musically on the matter. On her forthcoming album, *Like a Prayer,* there is a jarringly urgent song titled "Till Death Do Us Part" that chronicles a violent and harrowing marriage: "He takes a drink, she goes inside/He starts to scream, the vases fly. . . . I wish that it would change, but it won't if you don't," she sings, her voice soulful and plaintive. The performance is arguably her finest artistic moment, and that in itself is a sadly ironic notion.

Similarly, *Like a Prayer* as a whole represents the maturation of Madonna Louise Veronica Ciccone. The record largely scoots away from her previous gum-snapping *oeuvre*—although some pleasant, chirpy confection is left over—and she emerges as a thoughtful introspective songwriter. Also, she sings with more womanly import: On "Love Song," a sultry duet with Prince, she transcends girlish flirting and musters palpable eroticism. On "Promise to Try" and "Oh Father," individual odes for her parents, her voice shimmers with beseeching emotion.

The ethereal title song itself, which opens with Madonna quietly reciting the Rosary, seems to portend a personal spiritual purge. It is the debut of the philosophical Madonna, who, at thirty, seems to be making a public-policy changeover: Getting It On has been stoically supplanted by Getting On with It.

Lately, she is consoling herself with capitalism. On the day I meet with her to begin the first of two wide-ranging discussions, Pepsi announces that it has enlisted the singer to blitz the cola-war zone. (She will reportedly earn $5 million for one year's allegiance, which would include commercials and tour sponsorship.) In addition, she has been busily overseeing the editing of the "Like a Prayer" video and preparing for her role as a cheeky vixen in Warren Beatty's film *Dick Tracy*.

Nevertheless, she arrives at the designated Hamburger Hamlet, alone and serene, and at once disposes herself with playful confidence. Scruffily dressed in tattered chic, she slides into a back booth and pertly flags down a waitress. ("Yoo hoo! Could we get some coffee?"). She is discovered only once, by an archetypal young Hollywood hustler who presses into her hand a film script he hopes to direct. She endures his protracted schmoozy pitch with bemused graces. "Being rude doesn't get you anywhere," she tells me after the interloper says, "*Ciao,*" and disappears. "You end it quicker by being nice."

For the second session, I am summoned to the new hilltop hacienda—a white, stark, airy affair, replete with marble floors and important art. Among her collected *objets* is a painting by her idol Frida Kahlo, whose own marriage to Mexican muralist Diego Rivera was notoriously stormy. Also on display are a few framed photographs of Rivera's mistresses. Accordingly, when Madonna steps out of her bedroom, she has traded guises. Hair down, heels spiked, she radiates retro-glamour—a gossamer goddess in billowy black lounge wear with matching brassiere showing through the gauzy décolleté. Even her bearing this time seems a tad regal as she flounces onto an overstuffed ocher-satin divan and accepts inquiries. "Please," she wryly instructs a few chattering associates in the next room, "don't anyone bother me. I am being interviewed!" Throughout both conversations, however, she good-naturedly plumbs her feelings and, even in the matter of Sean, manages to comport herself with jaunty charm. Still, as an icebreaker, I brandish an early copy of the *Playboy* issue containing La Toya Jackson's nude pictures, thinking Madonna might enjoy the momentary reprieve of basking in another woman's scandal. And, of course, she does.

*Have you seen La Toya? Perhaps you could share any spontaneous observations.*

[*She lunges for the magazine*] Give me that! No shit! [*She pores over the pages, amused.*] She had a tit job, for sure! This isn't bad. They're funny. But you see only tits? Major tit job! Well, La Toya, *this* is a *shocker.* Oooh! The Jackson family must be outraged. This is desperation. Well, maybe she'll get a job out of it.

*Jumping from one kind of exposure to another, I suppose there's no tactful way to ask you about the dissolution of your marriage.*

[*She smiles coyly*] Inquiring minds want to know? Now you're gonna get all nosy, huh? Well, this is something incredibly close to me right now, and very painful. I have a difficult time talking about it. You can ask, but I can refuse to answer you.

*Fair enough. You've said in the past, "I'd rather walk through a fire than walk away from one." Are you attracted to flame?*

Am I attracted to pain? Is that what you're trying to say? I'm attracted to obstacles I need to overcome. I'm interested in facing challenges, things that are going to be harder rather than easier.

*The song on your album "Till Death Do Us Part" portrays a tormented, volatile and dangerous marriage. The implication is autobiographical. How honest are the lyrics?*

Like most of the songs on my album, it's very much drawn from my life, factually speaking, but it's fictionalized, too. "Till Death Do Us Part" is about a destructive relationship that is powerful and painful. In this song, however, it's a cycle that you can't get out of until you die. It's futile. I wanted the song to be very shocking, and I think it was.

It's about a dysfunctional relationship, a sadomasochistic relationship that can't end. Now that's where the truth stops, because I would never want to continue a terrible relationship forever and ever and ever until I die.

*Has Sean heard the song?*

Yes. And he loves it, strangely enough [*laughs*]. But Sean is very, very keen on being brutally frank in his work. He's attracted to writers and artists who don't mince words.

*Do you ever think you married too young?*

No.

*Do you think the odds were stacked against this marriage from the start? It seemed people defied it to succeed.*

Oh, yes. I felt that no one wanted us to be together. They celebrated our union, and then they wanted us to be apart. There were rumors about us getting a divorce a week after the wedding. We fought that. And, yes, that is difficult. I don't know if anyone can do it [under those circumstances]. You have to be really, really strong and immune. Very sure of yourself.

*In terms of your chemistry, you are two strong-willed individuals, volatile in your own ways.*

Both passionate people. Way over the top [*laughs*].

*Did your marriage thrive on friction?*

Yes. I have an incredible fascination and attraction to it. Like I said about walking into the fire. Well, he's fire, that's for sure.

*Do you regret you ever got married?*

No. Ultimately, I have twinges of regret, but I feel more sadness than anything. Feeling regret is really destructive. I have learned a great deal from my marriage, so much. About everything—mostly about myself. Please don't ask me what. I just couldn't say.

*You almost seemed an old-fashioned girl in your enthusiasm for marriage.*

I'm a *very* old-fashioned girl. Marriage is a great thing when it's right. And I did celebrate it and embrace it, and I wanted the whole world to know that this is the man I loved more than anything. But there's a price to pay for that, which is something I now realize. Ever since I was in high school, when I was madly in love with someone, I was so proud of this person, I wanted the world to know that I loved him. But once you reveal it to the world—and you're in the public eye—you give it up, and it's not your own anymore. I began to realize how important it is to hold on to privacy and keeping things to yourself as much as possible. It's like a runaway train afterward. So if you ask, Did I complicate things by being very public about [my feelings]? Yes, I did.

*And he is as famous for his shyness as you are for your forth-rightness.*

Yes, he is shy. But I have my shyness, and he also has his moments of exhibitionism. But I really don't want to analyze Sean in this interview. The point I was trying to make before was just about saving something for yourself. The romantic side of me wanting to announce my love, given my position in life, would ultimately work against me in the future. It's an incredible strain on the relationship. Because if you want everyone to know about the great things, then you're saying too that you want them to know about the bad things. So you never get left alone.

*Are you a woman who loves too much?*

No. I don't think you can ever love enough.

*Your public persona is characterized by flirtatiousness, and Sean appeared to be a traditional guy, jealous of his woman's sharing herself so openly.*

But I'm not immune to jealousy? We're both jealous.

*Do you think you're the right woman for him?*

I don't know. Life is long. Who knows? I couldn't say for sure. *Was* I the right woman, or *am* I the right woman? I was the right woman at the time. I mean, there are no accidents. What happened happened. I'm sure we learned a great deal from each other.

*Are you a challenge to live with?*

Definitely! Do you think it could be any other way? Yes, I'm pretty headstrong. And stubbornness comes with that, a certain amount of inflexibility. In going after what I wanted, other things tend to fall by the wayside, things you should maybe pay more attention to. Most passionate people are headstrong. [We were] two fires rubbing up against each other. It's exciting and difficult.

*How accurate are the tabloid tales of your night of terror—the nine hours in bondage?*

Extremely inaccurate, as they usually are. They made it all up. But I expect it. They're always making shit up. I've completely reconciled myself to that fact.

*So there wasn't one single breaking point?*

It's been a slow breaking point all the way. I can't say there's anything specific that happened.

*But you did file and later drop charges with the Malibu police, right?*

[*Pauses*] I understand your position. People want to hear the dirt. But this is not really anything I want to talk about here. It's totally unfair to Sean, too. I have great respect for him. It's like most relationships that fail. It's not one thing, it's many things that go on over a period of time.

*You've spoken before of your fascination with the painter Frida Kahlo, whose marriage to the muralist Diego Rivera was famously tempestuous. Are you drawn to the parallels in your lives?*

I see some parallels. I mean, she was crippled physically and emotionally in ways that I'm not. But she was also married to a very powerful and passionate man and was tormented by him. Although he loved her and was supportive of her as an artist, there was a lot of competition between them. There weren't that many female artists at the time, and the Latin community is a very macho environment. It was very hard for her to survive that and have her own identity. And I can identify to a certain extent with having that awareness of the male point of view of what a woman's role is in a relationship. It's tough to fight it. She was very courageous, and I admire and can relate to that.

*You've maintained in your music that dreams come true. What are your dreams like?*

Most of my dreams are really violent. But then, obviously, my life is pretty crazy. I'm always in the public eye. People are always sort of chasing after me and imposing on my privacy, my area, my space. So I have those kinds of dreams, where people are chasing me or I'm naked—you know, exposed. Also, I dream of children a lot. Specifically, I see different people in my life as children. That may be because, in a way, I feel I take care of a lot of people. But, yes, dreams are an important part of my life.

*You're an insomniac on top of it, right? What's your secret to falling asleep? Do you count sheep?*

No. You know what I do? I remember the past when I can't go to sleep. I think of a very specific moment in my life, like when I was nine years old and I was the fourth-grade hall monitor, and everyone in class was all lined up to go to the bathroom. I remember every detail—what people were wearing, what I felt like, what I was wearing, the smell of the school. It works my mind and tires me out. Then I find myself drifting into sleep. Although I spend many a night not going to sleep at all.

*How have you been sleeping lately?*

I'm sleeping all right now, actually. When I'm really upset, I do actually sleep. The times I don't sleep are when my mind just won't shut off, and I'm either working on something or worried about something, or I've had too many cups of coffee.

*Let's discuss your new album. How do you think it reflects your musical development?*

I don't really know. I just do what I do. It's not calculated. Although, in the past, my records tended to be a reflection of current influences. This album is more about past musical influences. The songs "Keep It Together" and "Express Yourself," for instance, are sort of my tributes to Sly and the Family Stone. "Oh Father" is my tribute to Simon and Garfunkel, whom I loved. Also, the overall emotional context of the album is drawn from what I was going through when I was growing up—and I'm still growing up.

*Does the preponderance of Madonna clones blaring from the radio bother you? Who comes closest to the real thing?*

When it first started happening, I kind of got pissed off. You know, if you create a sound, then you want to have dibs on it. But then I felt flattered. But it *is* confusing sometimes, because I'll hear a song on the radio and for a second I'll think it's me. It's uncanny sometimes. There's one girl in particular, a girl named Alisha, who's had a couple of songs that ripped off the chord progressions of some of my songs. And her *voice* sounds so much like mine when I sing in a higher register. I was shocked! She's definitely one who stunned me. I think a lot of the imitators are black.

*Do you ever feel black?*

Oh, yes, all the time. That's a silly thing to say though, isn't it? When I was a little girl, I wished I was black. All my girlfriends were black. I was living in Pontiac, Michigan, and I was definitely the minority in the neighborhood. White people were scarce there. All of my friends were black, and all the music I listened to was black. I was incredibly jealous of all my black girlfriends because they could have braids in their hair that stuck up everywhere. So I would go through this incredible ordeal of putting wire in my hair and braiding it so that I could make *my* hair stick up. I used to make cornrows and everything. But if being black is synonymous with having soul, then, yes, I feel that I am.

*Whose voices blow you away?*

Ella Fitzgerald has an incredible voice. She's the greatest. Joni Mitchell. Patsy Cline. Chaka Khan—I *love* her voice! I love all the old soul singers—Marvin Gaye, Frankie Lymon, Sam Cooke. I like really smooth voices like Belafonte and Mathis. My father had all their records. Then there are the gravelly voices—Joe Cocker. Tom Waits. And Prince—Prince has an incredible voice.

*You wrote and performed "Love Song" with Prince on your album. How did the collaboration come about?*

Well, we've been friends for years and admirers of each other's work. So we'd always talked about getting together to write. And, in fact, there was a moment last year when we were possibly going to write a musical together. I went to his studio in Minnesota and worked on some stuff, just to get the feel of what it would be like to collaborate. Because it's a very intimate thing to write a song together. I can't write with everybody. I've tried with a lot of people, and it doesn't always work.

Prince and I didn't really finish anything, though. We started a bunch of stuff, then we would go on to the next thing. We just tried to start as many things as we could. We worked for a few days; then I had to leave to do some other things. I decided that I didn't want to do a musical with him at that time.

Meanwhile, I went and did *Speed-the-Plow* on Broadway. He came to see the play and brought me a rough mix of one of the songs we'd worked on. I thought it was just fabulous. I'd sort of forgotten about it. So I called him up and said I loved it and that, after I was finished with the play, I wanted to get together with him and work on it for my album. As it turned out, we did it in a very funny way. We sent tapes to each other back and forth between L.A. and Minnesota. Then we would talk on the phone, and he would play stuff for me over the line. I loved working that way.

*What surprises you about him? For instance, what does he smell like?*

He does smell good! I'm really aware of people's smells. I love fragrances and perfumes. Ever since I've known Prince, I've attached a smell to him, which is lavender, and I don't know why. He reeks of it. And I'm sure he would probably disagree with me. He's very private, you know, and very shy. He's great when you get to know him. Charming and funny, in his own way. More than anything, he really comes alive when he's working.

*Since he is the preeminent pop spiritualist, did the two of you have any discussions about religion?*

We never talk about religion or politics. But "Love Song" does have a spirituality about it, the kind that exists between two people. It's really about that push and pull of a relationship. The back and forth: I love you, I hate you. I want you, get away from me. You build me up and tear me down. That constant rubbing.

*You dedicated the album to your mother, who taught you to pray. When do you pray?*

Constantly. I pray when I'm in trouble or when I'm happy. When I feel any sort of extreme. I pray when I feel so great that I'll think I need to check in with myself and recognize how good life is. I know that sounds silly. But when it seems there's so much bullshit around, it's important to just remind myself of the things I have to be grateful for. On the other hand, when I'm feeling really bad or sad, I pray to try to reassure myself. It's all kind of a rationalization. I can't describe the way I pray. It has nothing to do with religion.

*You've forsaken your Catholicism?*

Once you're a Catholic, you're always a Catholic—in terms of your feelings of guilt and remorse and whether you've sinned or not. Sometimes I'm wracked with guilt when I needn't be, and that, to me, is left over from my Catholic upbringing. Because in Catholicism you are born a sinner and you are a sinner all of your life. No matter how you try to get away from it, the sin is within you all the time.

*Would you raise a child a Catholic?*

No, I don't think so. That's a tough question. I don't know what sort of information I would pass on to them in terms of God. Catholicism is not a soothing religion. It's a painful religion. We're all gluttons for punishment.

*You're using the song "Like a Prayer" in your Pepsi commercial. You're not going to call it "Like a Pepsi," are you?*

Well, I wouldn't put Pepsi in any of my songs. Pepsi is Pepsi, and I'm me.

*But why do the commercial? You don't need the dough, do you?*

No, but I do consider it a challenge to make a commercial that has some sort of artistic value. I like the challenge of merging art and commerce. As far as I'm concerned, making a video is also a commercial. The Pepsi spot is a great and different way to expose the record. Record companies just don't have the money to finance that kind of publicity. As it is, the music will be playing in the background, and the can of Pepsi is positioned very subliminally. The camera pans by it, so it's not a hard-sell commercial.

*Do you ever think you missed your era in this town? I can imag-*

*ine you running Hollywood as the Bombshell Queen of the Forties and Fifties.*

How do you know I'm not running it right now [*laughs richly*]? But, yes, I do in a way feel it would have been great in those days. Hollywood was so different then. The studio system really nurtured and cared for you in a way it doesn't now. On the other hand, your life was not your own. Now you have more individual freedom, but you don't have anyone looking out for your career the way they did then.

*The studios used to arrange dates between its stars. Who would you have wanted on your arm?*

Oh, Jimmy Stewart! I love him so much. I would die to meet him! I can think of two incredibly favorite moments in his films that just melt me. In *It's a Wonderful Life,* there's that scene where he's standing with Donna Reed, who's talking on the phone, and he's telling her that he doesn't love her as he's kissing her, and he's crying. Clearly, he loves her so much. [*She swoons.*] *Ohhh!* And then the other moment is in *Rear Window* when he gives Grace Kelly this look. She's spending the night with him, and he turns and rests his chin on the back of a chair and looks at her so lovingly. I can't describe it, but that is the way I want someone to look at me when he loves me. It's the most pure look of love and adoration. Like surrender. It's devastating.

*How do you think old-line Hollywood sees you?*

I don't really think they understand me well enough to think of me in any way. A lot of them see me as a singer.

*Do you consider yourself a movie star?*

Yes, if I could be so immodest to say so.

*Do you want to become a mogul someday?*

[*Laughs*] I would rather own an art gallery than a movie studio. Or a museum. I would rather be Peggy Guggenheim than Harry Cohn.

*But you do have a production company set up to find movies for yourself.*

Yes, Siren Films. You know what a siren is, don't you? A woman who draws men to their death.

*Is that how you see yourself?*

Oh, I suppose I've had my moments of sirendom [*laughs*].

*You're about to play your first movie villain, Breathless Mahoney, in Warren Beatty's "Dick Tracy." Are you researching the role by doing evil things?*

Oh, I don't have to research *that*. [*She laughs coquettishly.*] She's a siren, definitely. She's a nightclub singer. Stephen Sondheim is writing the music I perform. And she falls in love with Dick Tracy in spite of herself. I don't think she's inherently evil, but she's quite accomplished in her villainy. She's basically a good person. She's not bad, she's just drawn that way. [*She flutters her eyelashes.*]

*Last year you took nine months to do the David Mamet play "Speed-the-Plow" on Broadway. Yet, if we're to believe your crack on the David Letterman show last July, you hated the experience.*

Oh, but I loved it, too. I hated to love it, and I loved to hate it. It was just grueling, having to do the same thing every night, playing a character who is so unlike me. I didn't have a glamorous or flamboyant part; I was the scapegoat. That's one of the things that attracted me to it. Still, night after night, that character failed in the context of the play. [Madonna essayed the role of a manipulative, possibly altruistic and ultimately beaten Hollywood secretary on the make.] To continue to fail each night and to walk off that stage crying, with my heart wrenched . . . It just got to me after a while. I was becoming as miserable as the character I played. So when I did the David Letterman show, it was very much toward the end of the run, and I really was marking off days on the calendar!

*Your character withstood epic verbal abuse from the Ron Silver and Joe Mantegna characters. Had you been playing yourself, wouldn't you have just punched their lights out?*

Absolutely, I would have. So many times I wanted to smack Ron Silver. I wouldn't have taken their shit after two minutes in the office. I wouldn't have had a job, if it was me up there.

*What kind of material do you find yourself drawn to? Weren't you interested in acquiring film rights to a novel called "Velocity"?*

Oh, yeah! It's a great story. The girl who wrote the book, Kristin McCloy, told me that when she wrote it, the two pictures she had on the wall by her desk were of the Dalai Lama and of me. She wrote it with me in mind. I couldn't put the book down. It really moved me. The story is about a woman whose mother dies, and she goes back home to try to develop a relationship with her father that she'd never had. It's very strained—and I can relate to that. And in the midst of this, she falls in love with someone who is all wrong for her—and I can relate to *that*. She doesn't get the guy in the end. But she becomes very close with her father. It's very touching.

*How're you getting along with your father these days? Do you understand each other?*

Yes, we get along very well right now. I mean, it's been up and down. You know, my father is not an incredibly verbal man, and that's been my frustration. He doesn't really express himself. And more than anything, I want my father's approval, whether I want to admit it or not. But he's always been very affectionate with me. I have a million different feelings about my father, but mostly I love him to death. What's difficult for my father is the idea that I don't need him. But I do need him.

*Has he been able to comfort you lately?*

Yes, absolutely. I can confide in my father. It wasn't that I couldn't before, but I didn't want to. For years, I resented him. You see, when my mother died I attached myself to my father. He was my only parent. So I felt in many ways that my stepmother stole him from me. I felt deserted. All my life I harbored that resentment. For five years after I left home, in fact, I barely spoke to him. But we've made our way back into each other's lives. Whenever I need him, he's there for me.

*Do you think about death much?*

Yes, but in spurts. Sometimes I just assume I'm going to live forever. I don't want to die. It's the ultimate unknown. I don't want to go to the dark beyond. I want to stay where I know where everything is.

*Had she not died, what kind of role do you think your mother would have in your life right now?*

If she were alive, I would be someone else. I would be a completely different person. I have to be careful sometimes. When someone dies and the years go by, you tend to make them into something they're not.

The song "Promise to Try" on the new album is about letting go of that. It's about a yearning to have her in my life but also about trying to accept the fact she's not. As in the lyric "Don't let memory play games with your mind/She's a faded smile frozen in time." Yes, I wish, but it's not going to be. I do talk to her often. I mean, I always have. I don't know if she can hear me or not, but I tell her things that a girl can only say to her mother. Private things.

*What kind of mother do you think you'll be?*

Very affectionate, but probably domineering—maybe too domineering. And I'll have to acquire patience, but I think when you go through the nine months of pregnancy, you learn to be patient. I would love to have a child. But you've got to have a family first. . . . Can't do it by yourself. But it's definitely up high on the list of things to do.

*Maybe you noticed this already, but a number of songs on the new album have sort of antimale themes.*

[*Surprised*] Well, gee, I never thought of that. This album definitely does have a very strong feminine point of view. Hmmm. I've had some painful experiences with men in my life, just as I've have some incredible experiences. Maybe I'm representing more of the former than the latter. I certainly don't hate men. No, no, no! Couldn't live without them!

*Are you a good women's friend?*

Yes. I used to think I had more men friends than women friends, but over the last few years—especially since I got married—I've nurtured a lot more female relationships. My mother's death was the catalyst in this, because I didn't have any strong female role models as I was growing up. I was the oldest girl and kind of took care of everyone. So I thought I really didn't need women. I didn't really look for it and had no women that I confided in. I saw the world as a man's world for a long time. I discovered that it isn't, though.

*Your Letterman appearance with your friend Sandra Bernhard was history-making television. I understand it was your idea that you two dress identically that night.*

To dress alike? Definitely. Whenever we would meet up for dinner or whatever, we were constantly showing up in the same or very similar clothes. So then, when we decided that I'd go on the show with her, I just thought we should follow through with that. In retrospect, it was all a little mysterious to me why that was so interesting to everyone. We were just having fun, which is what I always do with Sandra. She's a gas. I felt totally comfortable out there.

*You stirred some controversy that night by suggesting you two hung out at a New York lesbian club called the Cubby Hole.*

Well, yes, we threw that out there to confuse people. It was definitely an inside joke for people in New York. I mean, I've never been to the Cubby Hole. I just think it's hysterical.

*At the moment, you're a brunette. How different does brown feel from blond?*

I can't dwell on it too long because I have to dye my hair blond again for *Dick Tracy*. Being blond is definitely a different state of mind. I can't really put my finger on it, but the artifice of being blond has some incredible sort of sexual connotation. Men really respond to it. I love blond hair, but it really does something different to you. I feel more grounded when I have dark hair, and I feel more ethereal when I have light hair. It's unexplainable. I also feel more Italian when my hair is dark.

*Speaking of your look, you were recently named to Mr. Blackwell's annual worst-dressed list. Is there any list on which you'd like to name him?*

I'd put him on the list of men I'm least affected by. [*She grins mischievously.*] I think I always make the worst-dressed list. It's just silly. But it is kind of nice having something you can count on.

*If you could change anything about the way you look, what would it be?*

I always wanted to be taller. I have the little-person complex. People who are smaller are always trying to be bigger, I guess.

*You seem mighty big.*

Well, that's good, because I've been working on being big for so long [*laughs*].

*What of life can you see from behind tinted glass?*

It looks even more inviting. If I'm in a hotel and I know there are paparazzi downstairs, I find myself looking out the window wistfully. Last summer, during the play, I would look out my window in the theater and see tons of people outside waiting for me every night. And I would find myself enviously watching some anonymous woman just carrying a shopping bag, walking down the street, just slowly window-shopping and taking her time, with nobody bothering her. I envied her.

*What becomes a legend most?*

[*Puzzled*] You mean like the fur you're wearing? Is that a question? I don't know. I think that's one of the great mysteries.

*Do you make your own bed?*

Yes, I do. The maid comes three days a week, so on the days she doesn't come, I make my bed. I've even been known to wash my own clothes.

*Well, that ought to be worthy of legendary behavior. Confess your worst fault.*

Impatience. I just can't stand waiting. I always want everything right away. Nothing came as fast as I wanted it.

*Over the years, you've jokingly called yourself a bitch. Do you think you're a bitch?*

Oh, I can be. Deep down inside, I'm a really nice girl. But, certainly, I can be a bitch. I'm a perfectionist, and I'm under lots of pressure. Sometimes you have to be a bitch to get things done.

*You mean in light of the Bush administration, you haven't become a kinder and gentler Madonna?*

No! [*She laughs devilishly.*] The world isn't ready for that!

China may be against Western materialism, but the country apparently has nothing against the Material Girl. According to the China Youth News, Chinese promoters have talked to Madonna's representatives in hopes of arranging a tour for the singer there this spring. She would be the first major American pop star to perform in the People's Republic.

## J.D. CONSIDINE

# MADONNA'S TRUE CONFESSIONS
# *LIKE A PRAYER* ALBUM REVIEW

★ ★ ★1/2

EVER SINCE MADONNA'S bellybutton first undulated its way into mass consciousness, her fame has been more a matter of image than artistry. Never mind whether there was any depth or resonance behind it; for many of her fans, the image alone—Madonna as wily, wanton boy toy, gleefully manipulating the material world—was resonant enough. For others, it was just an act, a coolly calculated pop ploy designed to sell records.

With *Like a Prayer,* Madonna doesn't just ask to be taken seriously, she insists on it. Daring in its lyrics, ambitious in its sonics, this is far and away the most self-consciously serious album she's made. There are no punches pulled, anywhere; Madonna is brutally frank about the dissolution of her marriage ("Till Death Do Us Part"), her ambivalence toward her father ("Oh Father") and even her feelings of loss about her mother ("Promise to Try"). Yet as intensely personal as these songs are, the underlying themes are universal enough to move almost any listener. Likewise, the music, though clearly a step beyond the pop confections that earned the singer her place on the charts, remains as accessible as ever.

Don't expect to be won over instantly, though, for *Like a Prayer* is more interested in exorcising demons than entertaining fans. The album is in large part about growing up and dealing with such ghosts from the past as parents, religion and the promises of love. At times, the album can be heartbreaking in its honesty—read through the lyrics to "Till Death Do Us Part," and you'll feel guilty for ever having glanced at a tabloid with a MADONNA & SEAN WEDDING SHOCKER headline.

This is serious stuff, and nowhere is that more apparent than on the title tune. Opening with a sudden blast of stun-gun guitar, "Like a Prayer" seems at first like a struggle between the sacred and the profane as Madonna's voice is alternately driven by a jangling, bass-heavy funk riff and framed by an angelic aura of backing voices. Madonna stokes the spiritual fires with a potent, high-gloss groove that eventually surrenders to gospel abandon.

The tracks that Madonna coproduced with Patrick Leonard—which include "Like a Prayer"—are stunning in their breadth and achievement. "Cherish," which manages a nod to the Association song of the same title, makes savvy retro-rock references, and "Dear Jessie" boasts kaleidoscopic *Sgt. Pepper*-isms. When Stephen Bray replaces Leonard as coproducer, even an unabashed groove tune like "Express Yourself" seems smart and sassy, right down to Madonna's soul-style testimony on the intro: "Come on, girls, do you believe in love?"

Believing in love doesn't seem as easy for Madonna as it once did, though. "Till Death Do Us Part" takes its wedding-vow title almost mockingly, as the singer contemplates all the ways her marriage seems to be killing her. "The bruises, they will fade away/You hit so hard with the things you say," goes one verse, and it's hard not to be shocked. But the saddest thing about the song isn't the abuse endured by Madonna (for this hardly seems a fictional "I"); it's her helplessness in the face of her husband's self-loathing: "You're not in love with someone else/You don't even love yourself/Still I wish you'd ask me not to go."

But difficult love seems a familiar refrain in this collection of songs. "Oh Father" mirrors many of the horrors hinted at by "Till Death Do Us Part" (which provides plenty of material for armchair psychiatrists), and despite the song's lush string arrangement, there's still a disturbing amount of ache in lines like "You can't hurt me now/I got away from you, I never thought I would." Not that it's all bad love and childhood trauma. "Promise to Try," for instance, is about gathering a certain strength from feelings of loss and abandonment, as Madonna tries to live up to the memories she holds so dear.

The worst that can be said of the album's obviously confessional numbers is that they engender such powerful emotions that an admirable pop song like "Keep It Together" seems almost trivial by comparison (when in fact it's a rather impressive invocation of the importance of family). Fortunately, Madonna maintains an impressive sense of balance throughout the album, leavening the pain of "Till Death Do Us Part" with the lighthearted love of "Cherish," contrasting the trauma of "Oh Father" with the libidinal power games of "Love Song" (a coy, musically adventurous duel-duet with Prince) and juxtaposing the ecstatic fervor of "Like a Prayer" with the Catholic in-joking of "Act of Contrition."

As for her image, well, you may see her navel on the inner sleeve, but what you hear once you get inside the package is as close to art as pop music gets. *Like a Prayer* is proof not only that Madonna should be taken seriously as an artist but that hers is one of the most compelling voices of the Eighties. And if you have trouble accepting that, maybe it's time for a little image adjustment of your own.

# MADONNA'S "LIKE A PRAYER" CLIP CAUSES A CONTROVERSY

MADONNA'S CONTROVERSIAL video for "Like a Prayer" has provided the singer with a miraculous bounty of publicity: Religious groups both here and abroad have condemned the clip as blasphemous, while Pepsi-Cola—with whom Madonna has a reported $5 million sponsorship deal—has canceled some ads featuring the pop diva.

The video—which shows a scantily clad Madonna singing in front of burning crosses, suffering wounds on her hands like Jesus and kissing a saintly statue that turns into a man—was immediately denounced by the fire-and-brimstone crowd after its debut March 3rd.

Pepsi's two-minute TV commercial, which aired worldwide the night before, uses a similar church-choir scene but has a different story line and was shot by another director.

The Reverend Donald Wildmon has called for a nationwide boycott of Pepsi. Wildmon, a Methodist minister who heads the American Family Association in Tupelo, Mississippi, led a boycott against the film *The Last Temptation of Christ* last year.

The video also caused controversy in Italy, where a Roman Catholic organization protested TV broadcast of the clip. Madonna's record company agreed to delay those showings.

A news wire quoted Pepsi spokeswoman Becky Madeira as saying the soft-drink company expressed its concern to Madonna's management and asked that the video be pulled.

The video apparently also upset gospel singer Andrae Crouch, who sang on "Like a Prayer" and was expected to appear in the clip. He bowed out after learning about the theme.

**■ RANDOM NOTES** (April 20, 1989)

I'm really here for two reasons," Madonna told the crowd that had packed L.A.'s Shrine Auditorium for an AIDS benefit dancethon. "Number one is that I really believe in AIDS Project L.A. . . . And the second reason is that I love to dance." The singer, who's gone back to the bleach for her upcoming role as Breathless Mahoney in *Dick Tracy*, made good on that claim when she and her posse—including pal Sandra Bernhard—took to the floor to bump and grind for nearly an hour. Bernhard, who is making a film version of her outrageous stage show *Without You I'm Nothing*, says she and Madonna hang out together a lot. "Our favorite thing to do," says Bernard, "is to go to 7-Eleven and buy junk candy late at night."

## JEFFREY RESSNER

# PEPSI GOES FLAT ON MADONNA

THE PEPSI-COLA COMPANY, which touts its products as "a generation ahead," has apparently knuckled under to some old-fashioned intimidation. Facing pressure from religious groups and consumers, Pepsi dropped its multimillion-dollar commercial featuring Madonna, claiming too many people confused the ad with the singer's controversial video for "Like a Prayer."

Pepsi had reportedly agreed to pay Madonna $5 million for a year-long contract that would include a series of commercials and sponsorship of her upcoming tour. But after the TV spot was yanked in early March, company spokesmen refused to comment on whether Pepsi would continue to have any ties with the singer.

Michael Patti, a vice-president at the advertising agency BBDO, which helped create the Madonna commercial, says everything, including plans for a follow-up commercial, has been put "on hold."

Madonna herself declined to comment on Pepsi's sponsorship challenge. But when asked what would happen if Pepsi fizzled out on its commitments, a source familiar with Madonna's plans replied, "See you in court."

The original two-minute Pepsi ad premièred worldwide on March 2nd. Since then, it has run in shortened form overseas but has never been shown again in the United States. Nor will it ever be, according to the soft-drink company.

Although the commercial and the video use the same song and a similar church scene, the story lines are completely different. In the Pepsi pitch, Madonna relives a childhood birthday party; in the video, she rescues a black man in a scenario with religious imagery.

Despite the thematic differences, both the commercial and the video were blasted by the American Family Association, whose leader, the Reverend Donald Wildmon, threatened to call for a boycott of Pepsi products if the company didn't pull its support of the singer. When Pepsi agreed to stop the ad, Wildmon also dropped his boycott plans. A Pepsi spokesman said the company arrived at its decision "independently" of Wildmon's threats.

Nevertheless, Pepsi's move has angered a group of former fundamentalists. The organization, Fundamentalists Anonymous, recently launched a crusade to force Pepsi to put Madonna's ads back on the air. "When we're through with this campaign," says group cofounder Richard Yao, "we'll have taught college kids that it's uncool to drink Pepsi."

■ **NOTABLE NEWS** (June 1, 1989)
**Madonna** handpicked about fifty male actors and models to appear with her in the video for her next single, "Express Yourself." The clip, directed by David Fincher, cost nearly a million dollars. Offscreen: According to recent press reports, Madonna's name can now be added to Warren Beatty's list.

■ **RANDOM NOTES** (October 5, 1989)
If it had been any slicker tonight, it would have been Las Vegas," said Roger Daltrey after the Who's benefit performance of the rock opera *Tommy* at L.A.'s Universal Amphitheater. The show—featuring special guests Billy Idol, Elton John, Phil Collins, Patti LaBelle and Steve Winwood—raised $2 million for children's charities and the Rock and Roll Hall of Fame. The audience included Madonna, Sylvester Stallone and Timothy Leary.

■ **RANDOM NOTES** (October 19, 1989)
Madonna's opening performance of "Express Yourself"—complete with voguing and a crotch grab—set the tone and the energy level for this year's MTV Video Music Awards at L.A.'s Universal Amphitheater. Though she gave her all onstage, offstage she wouldn't give anyone the time of day.

■ **NOTABLE NEWS** (October 19, 1989)
Fresh from her portrayal of Breathless Mahoney, the vamp in *Dick Tracy*, Madonna may take a part in the upcoming sequel *The Godfather, Part III*. Meanwhile, Madonna's own production company is developing a project based on the life of her favorite artist, Mexican painter Frida Kahlo.

"Elvis is alive—and she's beautiful," said Madonna after meeting Canadian country singer k.d. lang following lang's show at the Wiltern Theater in Los Angeles. The admiration is obviously mutual. Lang said of the encounter, "I've been baptized." It was baptism by lipstick. Madonna and an entourage including Warren Beatty, Sandra Bernhard and Jennifer Grey traipsed backstage after the show. When a photographer showed up, Madonna whipped out her makeup to share with the singer.

Madonna is now working on the *Dick Tracy* soundtrack, which will also feature lang.

# THE 100 BEST ALBUMS
# OF THE EIGHTIES

A T DECADE'S END, ROLLING STONE editors chose the top albums of the Eighties. Madonna's debut came in at Number Fifty.

# #50 Madonna

Five years after arriving in New York City from her hometown of Pontiac, Michigan, Madonna Louise Ciccone had little to show for a lot of work. By 1982, she had managed to get only a few gigs singing with drummer Stephen Bray's band, the Breakfast Club, at clubs like CBGB and Max's Kansas City, and the future looked far from bright.

"I had just gotten kicked out of my apartment," Madonna says, "so the band let me live in their rehearsal space at the Music Building, on Eighth Avenue. Stephen had keys to all the rehearsal rooms, so when I decided to make my own demos, we'd go into other people's studios at night and use their four-track machines."

Armed with a tape, Madonna began making the rounds of New York's dance clubs. "I had heard that a lot of A&R people hung out at the clubs," she says, "and I thought trying to go see them at their offices would be a waste of time." It proved a good strategy: Through Mark Kamins, the DJ at Danceteria, the tape found its way to Sire Records, and Madonna was signed by label president Seymour Stein. "Seymour was in the hospital at the time," she says. "I got signed while he was lying in bed in his boxer shorts."

The contract with Sire guaranteed just one single, but it had options for recording albums as well. With Kamins producing, Madonna cut the moody disco track "Everybody" as her debut single. But when Sire picked up its option to record an album, she decided to try a different producer. "I wanted someone who'd worked with a lot of female singers," she says.

Reggie Lucas, the Grammy-winning songwriter who had produced Stephanie Mills and Roberta Flack, was selected. After recording the album's second single, the Lucas-penned "Physical Attraction," he and Madonna cut the rest of the album, with the exception of "Holiday," which was produced by Jellybean Benitez.

"Things were very informal and casual," Lucas says of the sessions. "It was my first pop project, and she was just a new artist. I had no idea it would be the biggest thing since sliced bread."

Indeed, initial response to *Madonna* gave no indication of the mania to follow. It took a year and a half for the album to go gold. But its assured style and sound, as well as Madonna's savvy approach to videos, helped the singer make the leap from dance diva to pop phenom, and it pointed the direction for a host of female vocalists from Janet Jackson to Debbie Gibson.

"It influenced a lot of people," says Madonna, who cites Chrissie Hynde and Debbie Harry as her own musical heroes. "I think it stands up well. It just took a long time for people to pay attention to me—and I thank God they did!"

## DAVID FRICKE

# *LIKE A PRAYER* YEAR-END ALBUM REVIEW

WITH ITS ADROIT MIX of point-blank confession and chart confection, *Like a Prayer* is Madonna's attempt to finally get some artistic respect—and continued multiplatinum sales, of course. Even the most hardened skeptic cannot help but admire her stylish reconciliation of bitter trauma and sweet dance-floor release in "Till Death Do Us Part." The whole tenor of the album is neatly summarized in her examination of hardball bedroom politics in "Love Song," with co-writer and duet partner Prince. To some degree, Madonna remains a prisoner of her own commercial expertise; the real attraction of the title hit is the juxtaposition of heavy funk and high gospel fire, not her struggle with the sacred and profane. Yet, the cover art notwithstanding, it is a treat to find Madonna baring something other than her navel for a change.

■ **NOTABLE NEWS** (January 25, 1990)
Madonna, Tracy Chapman, Jack Nicholson, Elton John and Sylvester Stallone were among the guests who showed up at L.A.'s Fahey/Klein Gallery for a party and exhibition celebrating photographer Herb Ritts' new book, *Men/Women*. Last year Ritts shot his first video, for Madonna's "Cherish."

In honor of her role as Breathless Mahoney in *Dick Tracy*, Madonna has titled her next album *I'm Breathless: Music From and Inspired by the Film Dick Tracy*. *Breathless*, one of the movie's two soundtrack LPs, features the single "Vogue," songs by Stephen Sondheim and duets with Mandy Patinkin and Warren Beatty. For those who don't have a penchant for Patinkin, the *other Dick Tracy* soundtrack, produced by Andy Paley, features songs from k.d. lang, Ice-T, Jerry Lee Lewis, Darlene Love, Tommy Page, La Verne Baker and Paley.

**KEITH CAHOON**

# MADONNA LEAVES JAPAN *BREATHLESS*

The singer kicks off her Blond Ambition Tour near
Tokyo with a show full of sexual shenanigans

G ENKI DESU KA?" Madonna shouted from the scaffolding on the stage of the Marine Stadium, in Chiba, Japan. "How ya doin'?" she added by way of loose translation. "I feel nice."
Kicking into "Express Yourself," the singer initiated a double baptism: the launch of her worldwide Blond Ambition Tour and the official opening of Chiba's new outdoor venue. The seductive and glitzy show—more on the order of a Broadway production than a standard rock & roll stadium date—was given a decidedly surreal touch by the locale. Chiba, a densely populated suburb, is the home of Tokyo's Disneyland and the setting for science-fiction author William Gibson's *Neuromancer,* a futuristic novel of nerve splicing and techno-crime.

The huge, modern facility does indeed have a certain sci-fi look to it, an impression that was only enhanced by the muted light shining through the clouds at sunset as 35,000 people found their seats. As if on cue, rain began to fall just as the concert's opening notes sounded. But the weather wasn't the only thing contributing to the surreal atmosphere at Marine Stadium: A team of male dancers embellished the opening number by reconstructing the industrial macho-slave feel of the "Express Yourself" video.

The Blond Ambition Tour is a nifty summation of the spectacle that is Madonna, combining convincing moments of musical performance, over-the-top stage production, and choreography with a healthy dose of old-fashioned promotion. The tour, which was slated to begin a leg in the United States in Houston on May 4th, coincides with the release of the singer's new album, *I'm Breathless,* itself a wittily titled plug for Madonna's role as gun moll Breathless Mahoney in Warren Beatty's movie *Dick Tracy.*

Indeed, three tunes from *I'm Breathless*—"Sooner or Later," "Now

I'm Following You" and the sizzling big-band number "Hanky Panky"—were spotlighted in the eighteen-song, two-hour-plus show. And although *Dick Tracy* will not be released in Japan until December, the audience was shown previews on huge screens near the stadium exits. The clips included Madonna reciting such clever gems as "Dick—my body hurts just thinking about it" and "Dick—that's an interesting name."

Onstage, the singer proved equally suggestive. Although the show was fast paced and tightly choreographed, Madonna kept a loose attitude and threw in casual S&M quips. "When I hurt people, I feel better—you know what I mean?" she joked, and she later followed her rendition of "Hanky Panky" by adding, "You all know the pleasures of a good spanky."

Nor was the licentious attitude limited to stage banter. Madonna's costumes consisted largely of lingerie, and a team of dancers and backup vocalists helped the singer work her way through suggestive performances of most of her hits.

For the song "Like a Virgin," Madonna posed on a bright red bed while being attended to by two men caressing huge pointed "breasts" strapped to their naked chests. To cap off the song, the singer rubbed her body and frantically humped the furniture. Lust temporarily sated, Madonna turned to her Catholic-girl sex-and-salvation obsession, performing "Like a Prayer," "Live to Tell," "Oh Father" and "Papa Don't Preach."

Although the Japanese press focused on the show's more overt sexual shenanigans, the performances ranged over a broad terrain of styles, from the psychosexual "Like a Virgin" to the Hollywood flash of "Open Your Heart" and the cartoonish comedy of "Cherish."

If Madonna has an obstacle left to overcome in Japan, it is the weather. Three years ago, strong winds affected one show on her Who's That Girl Tour. And on this year's opening night, despite constant toweling of the stage, one dancer slipped and fell, which led to the shortening of several dance numbers during another rainstorm on the third night. The Material Girl did manage to turn the adverse conditions to her advantage though, as raincoats proved the best-selling items at the extensively stocked souvenir counters.

Whatever money Madonna earns on merchandise is a drop in the bucket compared with her gross from ticket sales: Although scalpers offered tickets at below their face value of 7000 yen (about $45) just before the opening show, the singer could sell nearly $14 million worth of tickets for her nine Japanese shows.

Madonna's most recent Japanese hit, "Keep It Together," served as the finale and featured a spirited dance routine based on *A Clockwork Orange*. The band, which includes guitarist David Williams, percussionist Luis Conte, bassist Darryl Jones and musical director/keyboardist Jai Winding, prefaced the song with a brief reading of the tune that inspired it, Sly and the Family Stone's "Family Affair."

As the Blond Ambition show in Chiba reaffirmed, Madonna's primary inspiration comes from her ability to alternate soul-searching songs with narcissistic self-obsession. And once again, the creative results—which mix state-of-the-art production values with a street-savvy sensibility—provided an entertaining and provocative show.

## MARK COLEMAN

# NEW MATERIAL
# FOR THE MATERIAL GIRL

*I'm Breathless: Music From and Inspired
by the Film "Dick Tracy"* Album Review

★ ★ ★1/2

A N ALTERNATIVE SUBTITLE could be *Madonna Goes Broadway in a Major Way.* She pulls it off with brass and panache, but then everybody knows Madonna doesn't mess around. Compared with Prince's mechanical-sounding *Batman* LP, at any rate, *I'm Breathless* stands as a unified whole—a fully realized concept album. Whether that's a *compliment* depends on what you think of the concept itself. This recording may seem like a conceit to listeners who are unenchanted by—or have barely heard of—the musical stage tradition. (The vast majority of Americans, in other words.) Madonna's new album will automatically introduce Stephen Sondheim—who wrote three new songs for Madonna to sing in *Dick Tracy*—to a whole new audience, but exactly what kind of impression Sondheim will make, well, *that* remains uncertain.

The *Dick Tracy* juggernaut just might trigger a sudden mass craving for this stuff: campy, acutely stylized musical period pieces that recall the late Forties. After *Batman,* anything is possible. Among a more select audience, Sondheim is already regarded as the most imaginative composer working in his field. His musicals, like *Sweeney Todd* and *Sunday in the Park With George,* are light-years beyond *Cats* or *Phantom of the Opera.*

More than you'd expect, Madonna measures up to the challenging new material, holding her own against Sondheim's heavy credentials *and* his penchant for studied, solemn melodies. Her breathy emotionality fits "Sooner or Later" like a glove: Madonna doesn't coo, "I always get my man"; she spits it out like fire, bringing fresh conviction to a somewhat generic line. Even during this album's most melodramatic or self-conscious moments—and there are several—Madonna never sounds like she's "just acting."

At times, though, the wit and sophistication of Sondheim's lyrics work against Madonna's more forthright charms. There's a certain distance inherent in these songs; the music consciously draws on the pre-rock past, while the lyrics savor tricky wordplay and dispense witty observations about love and life. It's satisfying to hear Madonna's voice amid a genteel acoustic piano and reeds arrangement, for a change, on "Sooner or Later," but the other two Sondheim contributions included here sound a bit forced.

"What Can You Lose" unfolds slowly; it's a courtly his-and-hers torch song, with the veteran Broadway performer Mandy Patinkin supplying the male voice. At first, his voice is a warm contrast to Madonna's, but then he leaps up an octave or three, assuming a grating, obviously affected tone—pure Felix Unger to anyone with rock & roll ears.

"More," meanwhile, is something of a kick. A swaggering, jivey uptempo number, this gold digger's anthem would seem custom-made for Madonna. She recites the ditzy, materialistic mantra with aplomb and a winking sense of irony, but something vital is missing from "More." The tip-off comes near the end of the song: Once you "have it all" with Mr. Right, Madonna allows, this all-consuming quest for "More" becomes redundant. That comes with the territory—most musicals offer a happy ending *and* a tradition-affirming moral. But the "Material Girl" would never have indulged in such tidy sentimentality. The brazen sexiness and vulnerability that have always supported Madonna's image of toughness and resolve are deeply buried on most of *I'm Breathless* under new layers of artifice and theatricality.

The album's other songs don't appear in the film, but they could have. Working with longtime collaborator Patrick Leonard, as well as Andy Paley, among others, Madonna has come up with several more-legitimate sounding and confidently sung show tunes without a trace of disco. "Cry Baby," "I'm Going Bananas" and "Hanky Panky"—the titles alone are enough to conjure up visions of the elaborate production numbers on Madonna's summer tour. That's good news for ticket-buying fans, but on the record the long-term appeal of these shenanigans is sharply limited.

*I'm Breathless* does have its commercial ace in the hole—maybe a pair of them. The album's opening track, "He's a Man," chugs with the churning inevitability of a power ballad, and Madonna's haunting vocal hangs in the air long after the music has faded. "Back in Business" flirts with the kind of catchy slow-verse-fast-chorus construction that begins as a novel hook and ends as a nagging headache. Remember, you've been warned.

Madonna has still got a redeeming sense of humor. Just at the point *I'm Breathless* starts to sound terminally indulgent—when warblin' Warren Beatty comes a-callin' on the hokeypokey "Now I'm Following You (Part I)"—Madonna gives herself a giant poke in the ribs and brings the whole affair back down to earth. "Now I'm Following You (Part II)" is nothing more or less than a scratch mix of part I. By laying some much-needed beats atop this nostalgic riff, Madonna turns the whole album upside down and indicates that she still knows what time it is.

"Vogue" preceded *I'm Breathless* as a single, and at first it sounded a bit lackluster, but when heard as the last song on an ambitious, inconsistent album, this simple dance-craze celebration gains a startling resonance. Voguing is disco dancing at its most narcissistic: a true escapist fantasy. A series of improvised model moves struck to the deafening sound of house music, this inner-city trend may already be passé. But if any singer can claim to understand and embody the transcendent appeal of posing, it's Madonna.

She's been voguing since the beginning of her career, acting like a superstar and waiting for the rest of the world to catch up. For all her shrewdness, savvy and image-mongering, the magic in Madonna's music has always come from the overwhelming, incredible sense of empathy in her singing. On "Vogue," Madonna communicates exactly how vital and important a silly dancefloor ritual can be to its practitioners—more primitive, and also much more real, than any Broadway musical.

No other pop star today could—or probably would—make an album like this, but the throbbing beat and emotional wallop of "Vogue" make the rest of *I'm Breathless* seem academic, a brisk exercise as opposed to a sweaty, cathartic workout. More than any pop singer since her Motown forebear Diana Ross, Madonna seems obsessed with making it big in the more-traditional showbiz world of musicals and movies. And like the ruling Supreme, she may yet become a prisoner of her own aspirations toward Hollywood. That's entertainment. In the meantime, whatever the fate of *Dick Tracy* and *I'm Breathless,* "Vogue" proves Madonna can still deliver that indefinable something extra. For now, that's enough.

**■ RANDOM NOTES** (June 28, 1990)

Madonna has been named in a $500,000 lawsuit filed by a thirteen-year-old New York boy who claims he has suffered from nightmares and bed-wetting problems stemming from an incident that occurred in May 1988 outside the singer's Central Park West apartment. In his complaint, Keith Sorrentino charges that Madonna grabbed his camera, hurled him to the ground and choked him after he asked permission to take her photo. In turn, Madonna has filed a third-party countersuit against the boy's older sister, Darlene Sorrentino. The countersuit, which paints the older Sorrentino as an obsessive fan who has subjected Madonna to a torrent of "threatening, abusive, vexatious and obscene statements" over the years, alleges that the woman impersonated Madonna's business manager to obtain Madonna's whereabouts and that Sorrentino, on a "star-watching expedition," orchestrated the 1988 confrontation, using her brother as a tool for harassment. Darlene Sorrentino was unavailable for comment. A state Supreme Court judge has ordered Madonna to appear in the offices of Sorrentino's lawyer before October 22nd to provide a deposition.

**■ NOTABLE NEWS** (June 28, 1990)

Warren Beatty came twice during Madonna's week-long run of shows at the L.A. Sports Arena. Prince showed up the same night as his ex, Kim Basinger, and security guards went to great lengths to make sure that they didn't bump into each other. (Prince is now seeing singer Elisa Fiorillo.) The L.A. audience also included Richard Gere, Billy Idol, Dennis Quaid and Meg Ryan.

**■ RANDOM NOTES** (July 12–26, 1990)

"She said, 'Freddy, I ain't changing my fuckin' act,' " says Madonna's manager Freddy DeMann about the brouhaha that developed in Toronto after police showed up—minutes before her show at SkyDome—saying that they wanted to talk to the singer about altering her performance. The police told DeMann that some of the choreography was "lewd and obscene" and that he had two choices: Madonna could tone it down or be cited, and then she'd have to return to Toronto to face charges. DeMann presented them with a third choice. "I said, 'We can cancel the show, and you'll have to tell 30,000 people why,' " he says. After considering that option, the police backed off. "As we all know," says DeMann, "Madonna tries to titillate, not offend."

## PETER TRAVERS

# A DICK WITH NO KICK: THERE'S MUCH TO ADMIRE BUT LITTLE TO ENJOY IN WARREN BEATTY'S *DICK TRACY*

*Dick Tracy* Film Review

AFTER ALL THE HYPE, the movie of *Dick Tracy* turns out to be a great big beautiful bore. Many viewers (myself excluded) felt the same thing about *Batman,* last year's box-office biggie, with which *Tracy* shares more than an origin in the funny papers. *Batman* also has a loner hero, a grotesque villain, a blond bombshell, a marketable pop soundtrack and a no-mercy merchandising campaign. But *Batman* possesses something else: a psychological depth that gives the audience a stake in the characters. *Tracy* sticks to its eye-poppingly brilliant surface. Though the film is a visual knockout, it's emotionally impoverished.

It's not that producer-director Warren Beatty hasn't thought things through. Beatty's been talking about filming Chester Gould's classic comic strip for five years. And casting himself in the title role isn't the problem. At fifty-three, Beatty still has the looks and bearing to play the square-jawed crime fighter whose only fears are a desk job and marriage.

What Beatty can't do is make Tracy compelling. Gould couldn't either. That's why the cartoonist surrounded his duty-bound cop with a jazzy wardrobe (a yellow raincoat and fedora), gimmicks (a two-way-radio wristwatch) and misshapen villains (Flattop, Pruneface, Itchy, et cetera). Violence was unheard of in newspaper comic strips in 1931, when *Tracy* debuted, so the strip was a shocker and an immediate success. Today, five years since Gould's death, the strip still appears in hundreds of newspapers, written by Max Allan Collins and illustrated by Dick Locher; it's an intriguing curio.

But the strip is more than that to Beatty—he sees Gould's creation as an evocation of prewar America on the brink of losing its innocence. Gould's drawings, influenced by postexpressionist art, which showed a bright world growing dark and twisted, became the film's blueprint. Production designer Richard Sylbert *(Reds)* employed only the seven basic colors used by Gould—a color scheme Milena Canonero followed in her costumes. Makeup experts John Caglione Jr. and Doug Drexler *(Cotton Club)* created faces for the villains that exaggerate the baser human instincts. To preserve the strip's vignette structure, cinematographer Vittorio Storaro *(The Last Emperor)* took care not to move the camera too much within the shot. Editor Richard Marks *(Broadcast News)* then cut the film sharply from frame to frame to mimic the abrupt transitions of the comics. Under Beatty's exacting direction, these artists did incomparable work.

The trouble is that all this technique hardly gives the actors room to breathe. Glenne Headly *(Dirty Rotten Scoundrels)* as Tess Trueheart, Tracy's loyal love, and Charlie Korsmo *(Men Don't Leave)* as the Kid, a tough orphan who tries to get Tracy to adopt him, don't have roles— they have plot functions. Young Korsmo is a feisty wonder, but he's there only to humanize Tracy.

Madonna does substantially more with the role of torch singer Breathless Mahoney, a moll with a yen for Tracy. It's still hard to tell if Madonna is an actress, but she is a definite presence. "That's what I call a dame," says the Kid to Tracy. The Kid's got a point. Madonna suggests the glamour of Marlene Dietrich in everything from *Blonde Venus* to *Witness for the Prosecution.* Dressed in something black, clinging and transparent, Madonna exudes enough come-on carnality to singe the screen. "You don't know whether to hit me or kiss me," she tells Tracy. "I get that a lot." Though the movie heats up considerably when Breathless tries to get Tracy to give in to his dark side, Beatty only hints at the possibilities of this kinky attraction.

More surprisingly, Beatty fails to use the music to arouse thoughts of romance and eroticism. Danny Elfman's score, uncomfortably close to his work on *Batman,* sticks to ominousness. Beatty also wastes the three songs Broadway legend Stephen Sondheim *(A Little Night Music, Sweeney Todd)* has written for Madonna. The melodies are not remotely near the composer's best, but his intricate lyrics suggest there are many kinds of fires burning in Breathless. So why does Beatty go out of his way to bank their flame? He never allows Madonna to complete a song without cutting away to car chases or gunshots. The most tellingly romantic Sondheim number is "What Can You Lose"—a duet for Madonna and the gifted Mandy Patinkin, who plays Breathless's lovesick accompanist, 88 Keys. But the song is mostly played over shots of Tracy and the Kid at a diner.

The villains are another missed opportunity. William Forsythe's Flattop, Lawrence Steven Meyers' Little Face and Paul Sorvino's Lips Manlis are artfully outlandish creations given too little screen time to properly register on an audience. Dustin Hoffman, in a blond wig and with a twisted mouth, does better as Mumbles; he seems to be controlling the makeup instead of vice versa. But all—even the Blank (the faceless villain who gives the picture its surprise ending)—fall before the evil Big Boy Caprice of Al Pacino. Fitted with a hunchback, padded hips and a Hitler mustache, Pacino offers a grandly conceived comic creation. Big Boy threatens Tracy, mauls Breathless and fulminates in a manner that makes Jack Nicholson's Joker in *Batman* look timid. But even this performance grows repetitive and wearisome. Pacino is defeated by the same culprit that ultimately brings down the movie: a lousy script.

Credited to Jim Cash and Jack Epps Jr.—a pair whose movies *(Top Gun, Legal Eagles, Turner and Hooch)* make money but no sense—the screenplay is exasperatingly witless. Beatty is so concerned with how things look that he's forgotten the importance of verbal style and friskiness. By confusing artifice with art, Beatty has deliberately made a movie with no depth. For all its superficial pleasures, *Dick Tracy* ultimately flounders because it provides an audience with nothing to take home and dream about.

■ **NOTABLE NEWS** (September 20, 1990)
Madonna closed her world tour in Nice, France, thanking her musicians and crew for putting up with her. "I should pat you all on the back for surviving me," she said. " 'Cause God knows I'm a bitch."

■ **RANDOM NOTES** (October 18, 1990)

Steven Tyler called it. While accepting Aerosmith's MTV award for Best Hard Rock video, he thanked Tipper Gore and Jesse Helms "for making sure that as long as there are a few four-letter words on the album, it'll sell an extra million copies!" This year's Video Music Awards—held at L.A.'s Universal Amphitheater—were a three-hour slap in the face to the censors.

Best New Artist Michael Penn did his bit, proclaiming, "Holy shit!" on air. And Penn's former sister-in-law, Madonna, showed a flair for comedy in her baroque-cum-camp performance of "Vogue."

The next night, Madonna reprised her risqué role at a benefit for AIDS Project Los Angeles at the Wiltern Theater. She was honored—along with David Hockney and Ian McKellen—for her work in the fight against AIDS. The lineup featured something for everyone: Burt Bacharach and Herb Alpert did "This Guy's in Love With You," Rod Stewart wiggled through "Hot Legs," McKellen recited Shakespeare, and a street dance troupe called the Brat Pack was fittingly introduced by Rob Lowe.

## PAUL EVANS

# MADONNA: IMAGE OF THE EIGHTIES

*I*N THE LAST ISSUE *of a special series celebrating the four decades of rock & roll, Madonna was crowned the Image of the Eighties. The following essay appeared with a collage of photos of her various "images."*

YEARS SINCE SHE CAME across as anything even remotely like a virgin—a spunky Michigan girl arriving in New York and wishing on her "Lucky Star"—the Madonna of today confronts us with consummate power. Material Girl for a thousand pinups, she now seems sprung full-blown from the head of Fantasy. Absolutely artful, a dream sent earthward from the soft-focus heaven of movie stills and fanzine spreads, she is flesh and blood become pop archetype: Vamp, Tramp, Star, Madonna. She is a conglomerate of images, a one-woman bonfire of the vanities, arguably the most famous female in the world. True to form for the work-mad Eighties, she has dripped big sweat for her celebrity, her Greek-marble thighs the product of militant aerobics, her multimillionaire's wages won with entrepreneurial cunning.

In 1983, starting out, Madonna Ciccone was punky and populist— the boy toy next door, if your neighborhood happened to be a cross between *West Side Story* and *Mean Streets*. Enticing the nice girls of America into the trash-and-flash gear of lingerie and thrift-shop castoffs, she spawned an eager army of wanna-be's. By the time her look had conquered the mall, however, she was already upwardly mobile. Having begun, like any credible rocker, by crossing the borderline of Good Taste, she revolted next into High Style. Tailor-made for MTV, she recycled moves from classic cinema: A chorus line of tuxes adoring her, she was Marilyn come again, demanding that gentlemen prefer blondes.

Wed briefly and stormily to mini-Brando Sean Penn, she progressed from videos to the real Big Screen, scoring a hit with the 1985 film *Desperately Seeking Susan*. Hanky-panky with the likes of Warren Beatty seemed fated; with one of the last of the legendary lovers embracing her, it was as though she'd been awarded the showbiz imprimatur, sealed with a kiss.

If *postmodern* more or less means the art of the deft rip-off, the canny revamping of styles, Madonna is our Postmodern Goddess—her every gesture is a shadow of some past vogue: the platinum blaze of Jean Harlow's hair; the hot boyishness of Louise Brooks; the dark, smoldering earth angels of Italian films. Partly, this posing can be read as *hommage*; mainly, though, it seems like conquest. Armoring herself with every wink and prop of the all-pro *femme fatale,* Madonna manufactures an elusive artwork self, a Sex Machine as hard, magnetic and irresistible as any cool-hearted gigolo.

AIDS activist, crusader for freedom of expression, rebel gender-bender, postfeminist, mascaraed amazon, Madonna is more than her baby-breathless voice, trademark navel, stallion's nostrils. Nonetheless, her look is a crucial medium of her message. And what is that message, echoed endlessly in the sighs of her global fan club? Express Yourself.

## JIM FARBER

# SWEET TRANSVESTITE: *THE IMMACULATE COLLECTION* MUSIC VIDEO REVIEW

T HIS TAPE COLLECTS twelve of Madonna's greatest videos and her performance of "Vogue" from the 1990 MTV Video Music Awards show. You can see her grow from a street kid who touches herself (1984's "Lucky Star") to a high-fashion model who touches everybody (1990's "Vogue"). In between, she fondles fish ("Cherish") and screws a black saint while solving a rape case ("Like a Prayer"). It's the best—and most sacrilegious—stocking stuffer for Christmas.

■ **RANDOM NOTES** (November 29, 1990)
Madonna's patriotism knows no bounds, as she demonstrates, wearing only a G-string and draped in a flag, in her current public-service spot promoting freedom of expression and voter registration. On the self-promotional front, she has just released *Immaculate Collection*, a greatest-hits package that features two new tracks.

## DAVID FRICKE

# I'M BREATHLESS: MUSIC FROM AND INSPIRED BY THE FILM "DICK TRACY" YEAR-END ALBUM REVIEW

THREE SOUNDTRACK ALBUMS? If you count Danny Elfman's orchestral score (which was just Bernard Herrmann-meets-the-Sunday-funnies) and the actual *Dick Tracy* soundtrack album (featuring such strange bedfellows as Erasure, Jerry Lee Lewis and Ice-T), enough music was written and recorded for Warren Beatty's comic-book noir salute to ol' Chisel Face to fill a Tracy screen trilogy. Okay, Madonna cheated; the three saloon-siren numbers by Broadway composer Stephen Sondheim constitute the only real *Tracy* music on *I'm Breathless*. As for the "inspired" stuff, "Cry Baby" and "I'm Going Bananas" are just period boop-boopee-doo fluff, and the notorious spanking song, "Hanky Panky" . . . c'mon, that's just not Tracy's style.

Even the Sondheim collaborations are less than breathtaking. It may be a rare treat to hear Madonna fire her vocal engines over some light acoustic swing in "Sooner or Later," but she puts more irony than attitude in the gold-digging "More," and "What Can You Lose" is a routine Great White Way torch song. Not surprisingly, "Vogue" remains the album's enduring highlight, a lavish, propulsive house-music salute to the art of posing. The song has zero to do with *Dick Tracy*, but the narcissistic energy and wicked glee in her voice (missing from so much of the record) confirm that, most of her recent movies aside, Madonna still knows a hell of a lot about acting.

## ■ RANDOM NOTES (January 10, 1991)

Madonna's provocative "Justify My Love" video may be the marketing coup of the season. MTV's ban of the clip has set off a hypefest that's nothing short of an ad campaign for the first *ever* "video single." During her appearance on *Nightline,* Madonna was quick to point out the ease with which MTV airs videos depicting violence and degradation of women. But the former "boy toy" lost a few people while making the case that such things never creep into her own work, because she's in constant control: *"I've* chained myself. . . . *I've* crawled under my *own* table." Judging from the clip at which her latest clip is selling—at $9.98 a pop—she's definitely got the upper hand this time out.

## ■ NOTABLE NEWS (January 24, 1991)

Sire Records has a 900 hotline (900-990-SIRE) that features a "breathless" safe-sex message from Madonna.

## ■ RANDOM NOTES (January 24, 1991)

As if the hype surrounding the video for Madonna's "Justify My Love" weren't enough, a round of bickering has begun over who wrote the song's lyrics. The tune is credited to Lenny Kravitz, with additional lyrics attributed to Madonna, but in December, Prince's *Graffiti Bridge* sidekick Ingrid Chavez told a Minneapolis newspaper that *she* penned the words. After Chavez spilled the beans, Kravitz promptly released a statement admitting that Chavez had written "some" of the lyrics to the song and that the two had signed an agreement entitling Chavez to 25 percent of the songwriter royalties. According to Kravitz, he and Chavez agreed "for personal reasons" that Kravitz would receive sole credit for the song. In a subsequent statement of her own, Chavez made no mention of a written agreement waiving her right to a songwriting credit. "I did not go seeking public recognition for my contribution," she said, "but when a local paper got wind of the story and called to confirm it, I did not deny it. 'Justify My Love' is my expression . . . and I am proud to take credit for it."

# 1990 MUSIC AWARDS

MARCH 7, 1991

## READERS PICKS

### ARTIST OF THE YEAR
Sinéad O'Connor
**Madonna**
M. C. Hammer
Stevie Ray Vaughan
Janet Jackson

### BEST SINGLE
"Vogue," **Madonna**
"Nothing Compares 2U,"
   Sinéad O'Connor
"Epic," Faith No More
"U Can't Touch This," M.C.
   Hammer
"Something to Believe In,"
   Poison

### BEST FEMALE SINGER
Sinéad O'Connor
**Madonna**
Mariah Carey
Janet Jackson
Bonnie Raitt

### WORST FEMALE SINGER
Sinéad O'Connor
**Madonna**
Paula Abdul
Janet Jackson
Tiffany

### BEST VIDEO
"Vogue," **Madonna**
"Epic," Faith No More
"Cradle of Love," Billy Idol
"Nothing Compares 2U,"
   Sinéad O'Connor
"Janie's Got a Gun," Aerosmith

### WORST VIDEO
"Cherry Pie," Warrant
"Step by Step," New Kids on
   the Block
"Nothing Compares 2U,"
   Sinéad O'Connor
"Vogue," **Madonna**
"Black Cat," Janet Jackson

### BEST TOUR
**Madonna**'s Blond Ambition
   Tour
Paul McCartney
Aerosmith
Janet Jackson
Billy Joel

### WORST TOUR
New Kids on the Block
**Madonna**
M.C. Hammer
The 2 Live Crew
Sinéad O'Connor

### BEST-DRESSED FEMALE ARTIST
**Madonna**
Janet Jackson
Paula Abdul
Sinéad O'Connor
Mariah Carey

### SEXIEST FEMALE ARTIST
**Madonna**
Paula Abdul
Janet Jackson
Mariah Carey
Lita Ford

## CRITICS PICKS:

### BEST VIDEO
"Justify My Love," **Madonna**

### BEST TOUR
**Madonna**'s Blond Ambition Tour

# HYPE OF THE YEAR

**MADONNA'S "JUSTIFY MY LOVE" VIDEO CONTROVERSY**

# ARTISTS PICKS

**CARNIE WILSON of Wilson Phillips**

(Sort of a particular order.)

1. Tears for Fears, "Woman in Chains": My favorite song of the year. The first time I heard it was on headphones, and I couldn't believe it. I almost died.
2. **Madonna,** "Vogue": The music is unreal and has the best beat of the year. Her lyrics are neat, and the video kills me. I don't vogue myself. I wish. Sometimes I play around with it, but only at home.
3. Don Henley, "The End of the Innocence": It's beyond. I love Bruce Hornsby and Don Henley, so the combination of them playing together was incredible.
4. Sinéad O'Connor, "Nothing Compares 2 U": When I heard this, I was in my apartment and my boyfriend brought home the tape. I was depressed for three days. I had to listen to that song only. And when I heard Prince wrote it, I said, "Oh, no wonder."
5. The B-52's, "Roam": The B-52's are my favorite group. I love their harmonies. All of their songs have great off-the-wall lyrics.
6. Deee-Lite, "Groove Is in the Heart": This record cracks me up. The music is classic. She's beyond funny, and the amazing lyrics are almost weirder than the B-52's, like "Horton Hears a Who."
7. Jon Bon Jovi, "Miracles": He's really talented and sings with soul.
8. Billy Joel, "I Go to Extremes": I love his piano playing. He wails on this song, and the lyrics are like poetry. This song represents what goes on in people's lives—we go nuts and we don't know why.
9. Phil Collins, "Another Day in Paradise": Phil Collins is a genius, in my opinion. It's a great song, and I had to pick it because of the message.
10. Aerosmith, "What It Takes": My favorite vocal of the year. Steven Tyler is so awesome, he's perfect.

## PETER WILKINSON

# MADONNA'S FAVORITE FILMMAKER IS ONE SMART ALEK

T HE MOVIE WAS STILL a few minutes too long, the sound a bit out of sync, the trailer too raunchy for a G rating, but already Alek Keshishian was hot. An East Coast boy is our Alek, an Ivy Leaguer, so he's dealing with it today, a few weeks before the première. Besides all the postproducing, Alek has been hanging out with the star, which might explain why he arrives late at Paddington's, an English tea parlor on La Cienega Boulevard, a suitably low-profile establishment with that rathskeller feel. Only a few years out of Harvard, Alek still takes the acoustic, coffeehouse vibe where he can find it amid the electric circus that is West Hollywood.

"People tell me my whole life's going to change in May," Alek says, rubbing sleep from a pair of well-rubbed eyes. "Is it? All I know is, I've got these thirty scripts to read." Why think of the future now? The film is still being edited, for Christ's sakes, and, as he says, "black and white is the fucking most difficult stock to work with." There have been budget problems, crew problems, union problems; the film labs in New York are like delis—"Take a numba!"—and there are unseen demons, powerful specters lurking on the fringe even now who, given the chance, would cast a spell so dark on Alek's movie that it might never reach an American screen.

Better prerelease publicity than this you cannot buy.

*Truth or Dare: On the Road, Behind the Scenes, and in Bed With Madonna* is the most arresting antidote to self-serving tour films you will see this year. The documentary follows our preeminent cultural icon through her four-month Blond Ambition Tour, from Tokyo and Paris to her hometown of Detroit, where Madonna's dad, a man not unlike most dads, comes to the show. Madonna, the film shows you, is not unlike most people. To prove this, she has given Alek nearly complete access: backstage, hotel rooms and bedrooms; Alek was rolling tape even when Madonna went to the bathroom.

*Truth* is a picture full of firsts. Madonna's nipples. Madonna and Warren bickering. Madonna fellating a water bottle and recalling a finger fucking by a high-school girlfriend, men frenching men and Queer Nation on parade. The overlong concert sequences are boring in comparison, because *Truth or Dare,* like Madonna herself, is about something more than music. It is about what it takes and what it means to be a star.

If *Truth or Dare* doesn't give us the Real Madonna, it comes as close as any movie can to capturing her essence. Or does it? Peel away one of Madonna's masks, and you'll usually find another. More than anything else, it's a fan's movie, made by a fan, and Alek Keshishian, at the wise old age of twenty-six, is a world-class fan.

Keshishian found his conceit for the film early: Madonna as mother to a fragile group of dancers and other needful retainers. Unlike other touring superstars, Madonna doesn't want to be alone. She and the kids—some of whom were leaving home for the first time—huddle like a basketball team before every concert, so Mama may lead them in prayer. There is joy in the family, the shared triumph of entertaining millions of people. There are also tears, because the children go through all manner of trauma—sexual harassment, reunions with estranged parents, even a rape. As Alek says, "They were all emotional cripples on some level." Capturing their tribulations and Madonna's soothing reaction pays double dividends: It adds poignant subplots and shows a side of Madonna few have seen, though Madonna herself, of course, knew full well it had existed all along. "I *thought* I had an amazing capacity to deal with humanity," she says, "and it was good to see it."

Projects like these usually come with histories that seem, in retrospect, as perfectly scripted as the art produced. *Truth or Dare* is no exception. The story of Alek and Madonna is as irresistible a fable as the movie. Alek Keshishian, four years in Hollywood, had never directed a feature film. His résumé included a handful of videos, including Bobby Brown's hit "My Prerogative," Elton John's "Sacrifice" and "He's Got the Look," by Vanessa Williams. They were MTV slick but broke little new ground, with screens full of writhing women clad in scraps of black fabric. It was difficult to detect a signature directorial style.

Alek was helped by two old standbys—luck and connections. Just weeks before the Blond Ambition Tour opened in Tokyo, David

Fincher, the man originally chosen to document the tour for the ages, dropped out. Madonna still wanted some footage, probably for a television special. Who might be available on such short notice? She remembered the self-assured kid brought to her attention by some Creative Artists Agency (CAA) agents—Harvard alums—who were also acquaintances of Alek's.

And so last March, as Alek was pitching video ideas to a budding diva named Mariah Carey, the phone jumped out of the cradle at his sparsely furnished apartment near Vine Street.

"Hi-Alek-this-is-Madonna-how-are-you?" It was the voice of his mistress, rapid and bratty as always. Could he come watch a Blond Ambition rehearsal? Could he actually come right away? Flipped out as he was, Alek maintained Harvard-man composure. "It was like a bad *Brady Bunch* episode," he says, "where what you were thinking was different from what your mouth was saying." Sure, Alek finally managed, he probably could make it to that rehearsal. Three days later he joined Madonna in Tokyo, and Mariah Carey ended up with somebody else.

At this juncture in his recitation of the tale, tea arrives, and Alek detours briefly into Sanford Meisner's reality-based theory of acting. Whenever his long, black hair gets out of whack, which it often does, Alek employs whichever open palm is available to fold it back. His eyes do not wander while he speaks; they are the kind of eyes that are best seen, and see best, through loops of cigarette smoke. Alek lights Camel Light after Camel Light, talking easily, knowing when to listen, like someone who has grown up among cultivated conversationalists. As a friend of Alek's put it: "He's the most single-minded person alive who isn't boring. He has an amazing capacity to jolt dead space."

He also has no trouble speaking up, as Madonna and her staff learned. "Can you put on something less offensive than Styx?" Alek asks the waitress, a bubbly sort with a Glaswegian accent, who is startled at the request. "A place like this should have on some Kate Bush, low level."

It was Kate Bush, in a sense, who helped Alek get his chance with Madonna, but Kate Bush had not been his first diva. Cher had been Alek's first, at Harvard. It happened in 1985, when the Hasty Pudding Club voted her Woman of the Year. Alek, producer of the award show, drew baby-sitter duty. Cher's first words to him off the plane were *"Parev, inch-bess-yes"*—"hello, how are you," in Armenian. They got along famously.

With Kate Bush, Alek says he made Harvard history. As a senior, he spent $2000 producing *Wuthering Heights* as a pop opera, with music by Bush, Billy Idol and Madonna—the first time a theater piece had ever been approved as a senior thesis in those hallowed groves. "He liked dance music, and Madonna was the queen of the dance divas and had a killer personality," a school friend says. "But she was part of his art at that point, one of the characters in this grand design of his." While the show was in performance at the American Repertory Theater, a reviewer called it "Robert Wilson meets MTV." Alek says, "You couldn't buy a Kate Bush album anywhere in greater Boston after that."

Alek had always seemed destined for Cambridge, Massachusetts. Born in Beirut, where many Armenians had settled after oppression at home, he grew up in Boston and Manchester, New Hampshire, the son of a radiologist and a mother active in charity work. After prep school at St. Paul's, he took a year at the Sorbonne. A student who could play the violin, act, sing and dance, as well as direct, Alek had "totally blind commitment and a clean, tight visual mind," a friend says. "He could idealize and control any environment he created, and that's a big thing with Alek. He's a little Richard Attenborough and a little Bob Fosse." Visiting friends' houses, Alek would move lamps around to improve the lighting.

Whoever his influences, Alek knew how to handle a beat. Madonna recognized this when she saw a videotape of Alek's *Wuthering Heights* back in 1989. "He had a simplicity about his directing," Madonna says. "He let whoever was in front of the camera shine through, didn't always impose directorial ideas or impose funny shots." But Madonna had never called. Until last March, with that invitation to Tokyo.

"Those were the most insane five days of my life," Alek says as tea turns into lunch, which for Alek is a meatless sandwich. It became clear Tokyo was a sort of trial run. Few people, except Madonna's brother Christopher Ciccone, the tour's art director, seemed willing to help. Madonna was indifferent. "She was completely testing me, being almost abusive," Alek says. "I felt like I was in junior high school on the bus in the same row as the class bully. But I could keep up a banter with Madonna better than anybody in her company. It was like an old Howard Hawks movie. Very fast." As the story goes—Madonna legend 1,000,001 in the making—when Alek and Madonna saw the Tokyo dailies, they knew right away they had more than typical backstage footage. They had a *movie* on their hands.

"I was really taking off with videos," Alek says. "So I said, 'I don't want to spend four months just filming sound checks. I don't want it to turn into *Rattle & Hum.* Let's work with the rules of a documentary.' " They argued. Alek stayed firm. "I'll film you without makeup," he told her. "I'll film you when you're being a complete bitch. I'll film you in your room after the show when you don't want anybody around. I'll film you in the morning before your sleeping pill's worn off."

Madonna, of course, wasn't used to being talked to this way and loved it. "There was a mutual attraction, but it wasn't necessarily sexual," Alek says, though not everybody agreed. "By the second day I was telling her exactly what I thought about things."

So Alek joined the Madonna family, but on his own terms. "I was an older brother," he says. "I wasn't one of Madonna's kids." Her preshow candlelight massage was the only thing off-limits to him. But could Brother stay with Sis after she sent the kids and boyfriend Warren away? That question fueled their own little side drama.

With its use of sixteen-millimeter black and white for everything except song segments, the film may be dismissed by cynics as scripted intimacy of the first order, but Christopher Ciccone says: "It is extremely realistic. It is Madonna as I know her."

Others may see it as a New Grit style they would like to mimic, forcing upon us unexpurgated M.C. Hammer or Vanilla Ice. "Whether it's truth or it's acting is a moot point," Alek says. "It's a bit of both." The debate, of course, signals that Madonna has made yet another sly career move, this time using an undiscovered directing talent to recast herself as herself and make another fortune. *Truth or Dare,* which cost $4 million, may be one of the most-successful concert documentaries ever made, *the* biggest if the Sunbelt preachers try to keep it out of theaters. "But," says Alek, a picture of the seasoned Hollywood hand, "I don't have a single point on the back end."

As the movie developed, as you might imagine, so did Alek and Madonna's friendship. During those months on the road, they traded books, creating their own little history. After *The Sheltering Sky,* he was Port and she was Kit Moresby. At 7:00 A.M., she'd bull her way past the do-not-disturb order on his hotel phone and ask: "Port, are you up yet? What are we going to do today?" Alek may have been flying by the seat of his pants, sleeping five hours a night, but for his leading lady the movie was a reassuring constant, part of the tour ritual. They thought of calling the movie *The Adventures of Louise,* after Madonna's middle name.

When the camera annoyed her, Madonna slammed her suite door

and locked it. She'd scream, he'd scream back. More therapy. As savvy as Alek was, he also turned to Christopher Ciccone for Madonna-handling advice. "He talked to me a lot and asked me what he should do," Ciccone says. "I was a very good source."

Gradually, over the objections of Madonna's longtime manager, Freddy DeMann ("He thought I was the antichrist who'd descended into their lives," Alek says), the entourage became accustomed to Alek and his black-garbed crews. "Freddy and I went through some very hard times, some very hard times," Alek says. "They're still nervous. Somebody in her group told her she should buy the movie back and put it in her closet. But at some point she started to appreciate the challenge I had, and she started to help me." Madonna tipped him that her father was coming to the Detroit show—a top *Truth or Dare* emotional moment—and about the Toronto cop's threatening to stop the music because of its simulated onstage diddling. A great scene, Alek says, "but it would have been incredibly cool if she had been arrested."

Madonna, being Madonna, didn't tell Alek everything, though he was learning something about diva psychology. On one occasion, she walked into a room to get her hair bleached and found Alek ready to shoot. She immediately nudged her chair out of the best light.

"Madonna, can you please move your chair back six inches?" said Alek, in his even, respectful way.

"I *can't* move my seat six inches, *Alek!*"

"Okay, it'll look more tragic this way," Alek said, which became a running line. Wherever they were, when the lighting wasn't going to be right, and Madonna wasn't going to look 100-percent glam, the scene would just look more tragic.

"Even now, when we're doing the looping," Alek says, "I'll ask her to say something again, and she'll say, 'No, I won't do it, I won't. It's fine.' And I'll wait. I'll be silent and not give her anything. Then she'll say, 'Okay.' Her impetuousness last about fifteen seconds."

Besides Madonna's early reluctance, *Truth or Dare* had other cards stacked against it from the start. Remember *Who's That Girl* and *Shanghai Surprise*? It was clear Madonna couldn't deviate too far from Madonna, couldn't *act* all that much, which wouldn't be as simple as it sounded, because, as Alek said, "playing yourself is by far the hardest role to play."

There was also the Warren Problem. "Come over here, Warren, you pussy man!" Madonna cries early in the movie, summoning Dick Tracy to her dressing table. Things didn't improve.

Beatty hated the twenty-four-hour-a-day camera intrusion; his girl-friend's willful exhibitionism drove him crazy. When Madonna's throat doctor wants to examine her without Alek and his camera around, Warren, from behind sunglasses, taunts: "Turn the camera *off?* She doesn't want to *live* off camera, much less talk." In the end, Madonna won the day because, as Alek says, "it became painfully evident I wasn't going anywhere, the film wasn't going anywhere, and Warren was the only person going anywhere."

They were like two suitors. "Warren was never rude to me, never confrontational, but he was incredibly weirded out that I was doing this thing," Alek says, "and I'd hear what he was saying later from other people. She's his antithesis. She says whatever is on her mind. And he wouldn't accept the fact we weren't involved. We took some extra days in the south of France, after the shoot. And Warren was going, 'If you're not sleeping with Alek, who are you sleeping with?' "

"**C**AN YOU PLEASE close the door," Alek says, when another couple thirsty for tea brings a rush of cold air into Paddington's. The tea drinkers seem to have gone mad. They have raised their voices to an alarming pitch, and Alek's nemesis, the waitress, has turned up the volume again on her radio. Alek's nerves are about gone. For the second time, he suggests relocating. He rolls his eyes and rubs them again. "This is unbelievable," he says. "This place is never like this." The waitress summons Alek to the phone. It's his office with a message: Be at Madonna's house by 5:30.

Warren's suspicion, by the way, was unfounded. Alek and Madonna were no Cathy and Heathcliff. "I knew if I met Madonna, we could be friends," Alek says, and people who see the movie may feel the same way, because Madonna sure seems like she needs some friends. ("Who would you like to meet?" Sandra Bernhard asks her in a Paris hotel room. Madonna mulls it over and says, "I think I've met everybody.")

Now Alek's firmly in her circle. "You're another me, Alek," Madonna tells him. She calls almost every day, several times. They get together often, whether it's dinner with George Michael or a glittery party at the home of Al Pacino's girlfriend, Lyndall Hobbs. They attended a *Truth or Dare* screening and cocktail party at CAA with David Geffen, Barry Diller and Jeff Katzenberg (everybody loved it, *loved* it) and dropped in at Miramax's pre-Oscar do at the Beverly Hills Hotel. Alone together they drink margaritas and "gossip about everybody," says Madonna, who is getting Alek to exercise, because as hard as he works, "he is one of the world's laziest people."

She has bought him a stereo and an outfit for their visit to Cannes in May: a Matsuda vest and a Gaultier jacket. "We both have to look fabulous," she says. They write poems for each other and have even exchanged rings—an antique beauty with a huge gem from her for him, a cobra with ruby eyes and diamonds along the back for her from him. It has gone no further. "If we'd had a romance," says Madonna, "we wouldn't be friends right now."

The movie gave her more than a new friend. "Seeing it was better than five years of psychoanalysis," Madonna says. "It was over-whelming to see how much did happen, how much responsibility I did have. I was exhausted more than anything. I was drained. I also liked myself a lot more than I had in the past. I didn't think I was so awful. I learned to love myself. Everybody should make documentaries about themselves."

Ah, Madonna, Madonna who couldn't find success in other people's movies, made her own movie about her own success that will be hugely successful as a movie, proving once again that Madonna knows what she is doing, whether she can act or not. And it was an educational experience too! *Truth or Dare* also leaves its audience with a bittersweet truth: Family or no family, mother goddess or not, Madonna will probably throw off her kids as soon as their last dance is over. Mothers mother, but Madonnas need control.

While Alek waits for his life to change, for the premières in New York and Los Angeles, the reviews and the box-office numbers, he's living the single life, searching for a project in those thirty scripts and considering his options. "I don't feel like I've gone far enough at twenty-six," Alek says, sounding like his star did at that age. "I feel miserably underachieved. How old was Orson Welles when he made *Citizen Kane*? Twenty-five or twenty-six?"

Irving Azoff wants to develop his *Wuthering Heights*. Madonna is seeking his advice on choosing her next leading man. In the meantime, Alek says he wants to get laid: "Getting this movie meant I couldn't sleep with anyone."

Probably for the best, that decision, because you never know how sister Madonna might have felt about somebody else's mixing life with art.

## PETER TRAVERS

# MADONNA CAUSES A COMMOTION
# *TRUTH OR DARE*
# FILM REVIEW

WHATEVER YOU THINK of this hot-to-shock documentary, which tracks Madonna on and off the stage during her 1990 Blond Ambition World Tour, don't call it "neat." That's the word Kevin Costner uses when complimenting Madonna backstage in L.A. Hearing such a candy-assed adjective for the two-hour assault of en-ergy and high-tech flash that is her act sends the diva into jerk alert. In a pure Madonna moment, she sticks two fingers down her throat and pretends to barf. Costner slinks out of her dressing room, exposed as an abject dweeb in the ruthless glare of her pop-icon hipness. The *Dances With Wolves* Oscar winner would have been better off chatting up the star in Lakota.

We already knew Madonna had attitude. What gives freshness and snap to *Truth or Dare* is what the film uncovers about the origin of that attitude and the gargantuan ambition that fuels it. Shrewdly directed by Alek Keshishian, a Harvard alumnus noted for his video work with Bobby Brown, Edie Brickell and Elton John, the film alternates glitzy concert footage shot in color with grittier personal material shot in black and white. The symbolism may be heavy-handed but the movie is not. It's the most revealing and outrageously funny piece of pop demythologizing since D.A. Pennebaker blew the hype off Bob Dylan's 1965 English concert tour in *Don't Look Back*.

Madonna gave Keshishian near-total access to her inner sanctum during the four months of the tour. The movie begins in Tokyo with Madonna entertaining a stadium audience in a downpour. The stage footage is striking but can't match the raw charge of a live performance. And by now, familiarity has blunted the edge of Madonna's crotch-grabbing bit. What does come through is the star's unnerving stamina. Holding hands with her staff before each concert, Madonna prays for the strength to bring off her behemoth of a show. You may not leave *Truth or Dare* loving Madonna, but you'll respect her as a force of nature.

During a sound check that's going badly, Madonna barks for an engineer. "I'm waiting," she says, like Salome demanding the head of John the Baptist. After one show she harangues her manager for letting those "so distracting and depressing" industry types sit with their arms folded in the front rows. For fun she plays the game of truth or dare with her entourage, at one point going down on a bottle to show how she gives a blow job.

Madonna's need to shock often causes her problems. Warren Beatty, Madonna's privacy-driven *Dick Tracy* costar—and lover at the time—berates her for the "insanity" of making her life a public spectacle. A woman friend from her high-school days—who doesn't share Madonna's memory of their "finger fucking"—shows up for a reunion only to get a polite brushoff. "You little shit," says the woman, as the star blithely exits.

But much is also made of the tyrant's soft side. She plays mother confessor to her seven male dancers, most of whom are new to the road and celebrity, by arranging family reunions and soothing fragile egos. She also gets confused, frightened and stressed out. Alone in her hotel room, juggling phones in a bathrobe and no makeup, Madonna looks exhausted. But she's not complaining. This is her fantasy, and she's living it to the hilt.

There are times when the movie snags on mawkishness, as when Madonna visits the grave of her mother or phones her conservative Catholic father to coax him to her hometown concert in Detroit, despite his dread of her stage antics with crucifixes. Madonna's lost-lamb routine doesn't play as well as the scenes that show her running her career the way Iacocca runs Chrysler. She's not going to change her act for her father any more than she did for the censors in Toronto and Rome. What they see as obscene or sacrilegious she views as "artistic expression." Madonna's talent is less God-given than Madonna-made. She's exercised her body into pinup shape, toughened her vocal cords and brought precision to her dancing. And she's proud of her handiwork. Immodesty becomes her.

So does self-mockery. For the first time on film, the bitch goddess descends from her pedestal to laugh at her narcissism. She bares her nipples and her soul. She wants to be liked. Is this vulnerable Madonna the real thing or a ploy to ingratiate herself with film audiences who've found her chilly and strident? You be the judge. But there's no denying that *Truth or Dare* is at its raunchy best when Madonna is kicking ass instead of kissing it.

## ADRIAN DEEVOY

# "IF YOU'RE GOING TO REVEAL YOURSELF, REVEAL YOURSELF!"

Madonna Talks Tough About Life and *Truth or Dare*

"THIS IS MADONNA."

The introduction seems a trifle unnecessary. She is probably the most famous woman on the planet and you are, after all, standing in the middle of her living room.

Up above you, as you shake hands, is a beautiful Langlois ceiling painting of the naked Hermes flanked by similarly unclad women. All around the walls are works of art from Mexico, England and France, and original black-and-white photos—mostly female nudes—by Edward Weston, Man Ray, André Kertész and Herb Ritts. To your right in this low, white, ten-room home, perched atop Hollywood Hills, is a spacious office area, complete with chattering fax machine and sleek filing cabinets. Across the lounge, which is dominated by the somber presence of a huge grand piano, you can just see into the bedroom, where a sleeveless black dress is hanging on a wardrobe door. Off the bedroom is a small bathroom, which, judging from the minimasterpieces on display, could qualify for the world's most compact art gallery. In keeping with the arty ambience, there is a copy of *The Andy Warhol Diaries* beside the lavatory.

Madonna's Los Angeles home has the strange atmosphere of a lived-in modern-art museum: stark and sophisticated, but somehow comfortable, even homey. But look out through the full-length windows, past the pool, and there lies the reason why this residence is just so desirable: a genuinely breathtaking view that seems to take in all of Los Angeles.

"Isn't it beautiful?" asks a rough-edged and slightly nasal voice from behind you. Madonna is standing close enough for you to smell (the pleasingly uncomplicated aroma of warm, clean skin) and to notice the flesh-toned cover-up on two small pimples on her left cheek. It immediately makes her seem human.

She is a small woman, maybe five feet four, with large hands and a lean, almost sinewy body. Today she is wearing a loose-woven thigh-length green cardigan (beneath which, it is plain to even the untrained eye, she is sporting a black bra), loose-fitting black trousers cropped above the ankle and threadbare green espadrilles. Her bleached hair is tied back in a bun, exposing her dark roots, and she is fully made up. Her legendary beauty spot is reassuringly present.

"Uncommonly beautiful" is the phrase that springs to mind as she walks with an almost regal grace across the room and composes herself on an eighteenth-century European chair. She has agreed to this rare interview to promote her new movie, *Truth or Dare*. The controversial film has prompted the *New York Post* to declare "What a Tramp!" and has raised the highbrow eyebrows of critics and censors the world over.

As you are probably aware by now, *Truth or Dare* chronicles the behind-the-scenes fireworks during the superstar's 1990 Blond Ambition Tour and focuses unflinchingly on her relationships, professional and otherwise, with her colorful entourage, which includes a fleet of catty dancers, a long-suffering road crew and Warren Beatty. It is Madonna's attempt to give us mortals a glimpse into her complex life. It is a touching, vulgar, erotic and revealing documentary that—like most things given the Madonna touch—will be the subject of much heated moral debate for some time to come.

*Do you think "Truth or Dare" will change people's perceptions of you?*

[*A quaver in her voice betrays a slight nervousness.*] First of all, everyone overreacts to *everything* I do. They overreact to really simple, mundane things I do. So I can just imagine the overreactions to this. People are *primed* to overreact to everything I do, and this isn't a three-minute video dealing with some touchy issues. This is a two-hour movie and it's real life. But I don't think it's my real life, as such. I think it's life in general.

*It's a very emotional film.*

Well, I'm a very emotional person. Then, being on the road is a really emotional thing anyway. The insanity of the life I lead is very emotional also. So, to me, it was a very emotion-packed time.

*Presumably your life outside of your work isn't as emotionally hectic as that?*

I'm afraid to say, it is! [*laughs*]. Yes, it is. It truly is. Because I'm very maternal with people. Like with the dancers in the movie: I mother them all during the movie and I still do. Still! I'm still very close to them and completely embroiled in their lives and trying to help them. In addition to that, I have my own, very large family, who are all emotional cripples in one way or another. So I'm the matriarch of all these little families. I can't keep my hand out of the fire. I just keep getting pulled into everyone's lives and try to help them out of their messes. Meanwhile, I'm neglecting all of my own. So . . . my life remains completely insane. Don't let this calm facade fool you.

*The impression one takes away from "Truth or Dare" is of someone who wants desperately to be in charge but also wants to be looked after.*

Is that the only impression you came away with? I think the impression of me will be twofold. I think people will think, Oh, she isn't just a cold, dominating person. I think that's the world's perception of me, that I'm power-hungry and manipulating. I think a great deal of the movie shows a gentler side of me.

*Could you explain the film's ending, where you inexplicably appear in bed with a bunch of naked men?*

That's there because it's me bidding farewell to everyone. You'll notice throughout the montage, I'm saying, "I love you. I hate you. I love you." It's my need to be loved and my need to dominate. So, to me, it's like a witty presentation of the whole thing. In two minutes it underlines what you've just seen in two hours. It's my need to be loved but also my need to be in charge.

*Parts of the film could almost be described as too revealing.*

Yes. But if you're going to reveal yourself, *reveal* yourself. I mean, what do I do, say I'm only going to reveal myself up to a point?

*Most people would.*

I'm not "most people." And if I'm going to make a documentary and tell the director that I want to reveal truths, then I'm not going to say, "But this is where I draw the line." If you take all those parts out, what would you have? Life is about the highs and the lows, and if you just present the mids, then what's the point? I chose to show that part of myself because I know that other people feel the same way. The only difference between this and other movies is that I don't have the safety net of saying, "This is fictional." These issues are dealt with in drama all the time, but I think the hard thing for people to take will be that there isn't someone playing the part of my life in a movie fifty years from now when I'm dead. I'm doing it myself. No one has ever done this before.

*Can we discuss some specific incidents in the film? You appear very nervous when your father turns up in the dressing room after your show.*

Oh God, yeah [*laughs*]. I always do these supposedly immoral things, and then after I've finished, I go, My God, what if my father sees this? I still think like that. Like the *Vanity Fair* issue that just came out, I was laying in bed last night and I just heard that my father was in town and I was thinking, My God, what if he gets on the airplane and, God, someone hands him the magazine and, oh my God, he'll see me without a shirt on and, Oh God! What I keep trying to impress upon my father is that he mustn't take what I do *personally.*

*You worry about this and, yet, later in the film, you fellate a bottle.*

Yeah [*shrugs*]. But my father wasn't in the room.

*But he'll see the film. Won't he find that shocking? Is that shocking?*

Is *what* shocking? My giving head to a bottle? Why? You see people doing it in movies all the time. It's a joke. What's shocking? Why don't you know if it's shocking or not? Don't you know your own feelings? It's a *joke!* The idea of Truth or Dare is a joke. It's like all those childhood games: "I dare you to do this." It's all a game. If everybody put on film what they did in those games when they were children, or what they did in their fraternity games, I mean, my God, they'd all be *arrested.*

*Why did you start playing Truth or Dare?*

The dancers used to play it all the time in the beginning. I was never really part of it. The point of it is to relieve boredom, fucking with people. It's great for relieving tensions and animosities. Or if someone has a crush on somebody and the other person wants to find out. In the guise of the game, you can find these things out. Sometimes it would turn into these heavy sessions where it was all truths and no dares. Did you really do this? Were you sleeping with so-and-so? Everyone gets their feelings out and then, after you've played the game, everyone is closer. That's the theory. It's like group therapy.

*Isn't it dangerous?*

It is, yeah. But every time we played it and went all the way and got into it, it was really intense. Like, "I think you are behaving really stupidly." Or, "You did heroin the other night and we all know." Everybody looks at each other differently the next day because the truth brings people closer together.

*The game seems to start with a lot of sexual stuff. You dare a dancer to expose his penis.*

That's right [*chuckles*]. The sexuality is always at the beginning and everyone goes through these primal curiosities about . . . *things.* The exhibitionistic tendencies come out: "You show me this, I'll show you this." Then you get down to the nitty-gritty. This has happened with me when I've been playing the game with friends since my tour's been over with, and the same thing always happens. Everyone gets past the sex things, then you get into the real shit about people."

*You seem to have a strange relationship with your brother Martin. In the movie, you expose him as an alcoholic.*

Martin is a very hard person to get along with. He's an elusive, enigmatic character. He's very charming, but, yes, he is an alcoholic. He's very tortured, and I speak to him, but it's hard for me because I find myself being very judgmental. What I always do is start saying, 'You've got to stop doing that, you must do this.' The mother thing again. In Alcoholics Anonymous it's called a codependent. You get into this thing of dealing with their drinking by harping on it. I've had to get him out of the habit of calling me whenever he needed something from me. I have to feel that he loves me for just me and not for my money. We have a strained relationship. I know he loves me and I love him, but it's difficult.

*Families are funny things. You don't choose them . . .*

You certainly *don't!* All of my brothers and sisters are individually . . . unique. I have completely different relationships with all of them. Emotionally we're all pretty needy in some way, because of my mother. I became an overachiever to get approval from the world. It's unconscious, but it's always there.

*The most moving part of the film is where you visit your mother's grave.*

I still cry when I watch that [*apparently on the verge of tears*]. It was the single most . . . the greatest event in my life, my mother dying. What happened when I was five years old changed forever how I am. I can't describe in words the effect it had. That's when the die was cast. I know if I'd had a mother I would be very different. It gave me a lot of what are traditionally looked upon as masculine traits in terms of my ambitiousness and my aggressiveness. Mothers, I think, teach you manners and gentleness and a certain kind of, what's the word? I don't want to say subservience, but a patience, which I've never had. Then, when my mother died, all of a sudden I was going to become the best student, get the best grades. I was going to become the best singer, the best dancer, the most famous person in the world, everybody was going to love me. I've been to analysis and I understand that about myself. My brother, on the other hand, decided he was going to set fire to everything.

*There are cynics who might perceive the visit to your mother's grave as contrived or choreographed.*

It wasn't choreographed *in the least*. I hadn't been to the grave in many years. Actually, it took us forty-five minutes to find it. It was very sad in a way; we just could not find the gravestone. Then . . . we found it.

*When, in the film, you visit a throat specialist and he asks you whether you want the consultation filmed, Warren Beatty says, "She doesn't want to live off-camera, much less talk!" Is there a grain of truth in that?*

I think what Warren was *trying* to say is that he is very shy and private and he doesn't understand my lack of inhibition because he's the opposite of me. What's so intimate about my throat? I mean, my God, everyone knows when I'm having an abortion, when I'm getting married, when I'm getting divorced, who I'm breaking up with. My throat is now intimate? Anyway, the cameras didn't follow me around twenty-four hours a day. They weren't in the room when I was *fucking*.

*That's an almost surprising omission.*

But the point of that scene is that it serves to show how different Warren and I are. He lives a very isolated life. I maintain that as much as I've revealed about myself, I haven't given up my complete deck of cards and been totally emotionally raped.

*Were you upset that the Vatican objected to your stage show?*

The Italians, typically, overreacted. They said all the religious imagery and symbolism was really sacrilegious, that there were men in bras and I was masturbating onstage. So they put all this propaganda in the Italian newspapers to try and put kids off coming. It really hurt me because I'm Italian, you know? It was like a slap in the face. I felt incredibly unwelcome. And misunderstood.

*Did it make you reappraise your Catholic beliefs?*

No. I've always known that Catholicism is a completely sexist, repressed, sin and punishment-based religion. I've already fallen out of love with Catholicism.

*When was the last time you went to mass?*

I go to church once in a while. I love the rituals, particularly of Catholicism, and the architecture of grand, beautiful churches, and the mysteriousness of it all, especially if they say the mass in Latin, and the incense and the classical organ music. It's a beautiful ritual, but often the messages are not so beautiful.

*Did you think your stage show was shocking? How would you feel if you went to see George Michael and he pretended to masturbate on-stage? Would that upset you?*

It would depend on the context. It's hard to say, isn't it? I don't do any of those things without humor. It's a bit difficult for me to see someone like Michael Jackson grabbing his crotch and humping the ground simply because I feel he's a very androgynous person. I don't believe him. So it would depend how it's used.

*The song in your show that attracted the most controversy was "Like a Virgin." You've always claimed it was about a newness, a freshness, but obviously you were aware of the song's ambiguity.*

*Weeeell,* there's many meanings to it. That's what I like about everything. I like innuendo. I like irony. I like the way things can be taken on different levels. But, yes, "Like a Virgin" was always absolutely ambiguous.

*At one point during your live performance of "Like a Virgin"— where you romp on a harem-style bed—the simulated masturbation suddenly changed into something that didn't seem quite so simulated.*

*Did* it? Yeah, I guess it did. The idea was to make it funny and serious. Passion and sexuality and religion all bleed into each other for me. I think that you can be a very sexual person and also a very religious and spiritual person. I think I'm religious in the broadest sense of the word, and I am very sexual in that I'm very aware of my sexuality and other people's, and am very interested in it. Not in the sense that I want to go out and fuck everything that moves. So I'm a very sexual, very spiritual person. What's the problem? People's sexuality and the way they relate to the world is very important.

*It transcends just the trousers.*

Exactly! It's beyond trousers! It's so much more than just fornication. Your sexual identity is so important. The more you pay attention to it, the more you realize that just about everything in the world is centered around sexual attraction and sexual power. You also become aware of people who are not in touch with their own, or have the wrong idea about it or abuse it.

*Do people often misunderstand the humor in your work?*

Yes. That's the death of anybody. I find all artists who take themselves seriously boring. I hate it when singers go, "I don't want to be a pop star, I want to be taken seriously," blah, blah, blah. Or when actors talk about their "method" and all that stuff. It's such a fucking bore. If I took my show seriously, I would hate it, do you know what I mean? But you only have to have half a brain in your head to see that I'm quite often making fun of myself. I mean, how obvious can I be?

*Your sense of humor can be quite coarse.*

That's your opinion. *Coarse?* It's aggressive, if that's what you mean.

*You resort to vulgarity very quickly.*

Uh-huh, I s'pose. Maybe that's from not having a mother.

*You can't attribute everything to that.*

Like I said, I have a lot of boyish traits about me. That's probably one of them.

*Are you aware that you aren't treated like other people?*

Yes, I am. Very. I'm always aware of that. I've developed mechanisms, I guess. It's funny, like the way my father seems to be unaware of my fame and fortune and place in the world, I sometimes am too. I have to keep telling myself I'm not like everyone else. I have to go around looking for the ulterior motive all the time.

*Does it make it difficult to find new friends?*

Oh [*pauses*]. I guess. I haven't really thought about that much. I tend to go to social occasions and hang around people who are celebrities as well. Celebrities kind of flock together. It's like, I'm okay, what can they get from me?

*Do you discuss being famous?*

*No!* We don't. God, what a *boring* thing to talk about!

*Do you feel guilty about being rich?*

Yes I do. It's because of my upbringing. I was raised by a working-class father and we never had money. I continue to feel guilty about it, like I don't deserve to have it, or something, even though I work really hard. I can't help it. No one in my family has had any money and they continue to not have any money and I feel guilty about it. That's just my upbringing. I feel sometimes that someone will come and take it all away from me. That makes me work really hard, all the time.

*Do you think men are afraid of you on a one-to-one basis?*

There's two different fears. There's the superficial fear that they would have just because they'd read all these things about me. And if they've had the bad fortune to believe everything, then they would have a lot of preconceptions about me and probably be afraid and be very guarded. Then there is the fear that they would have once they'd gotten to know me, which is that I am very much in charge of my life and a dominating and demanding person and a very independent person. A lot of men aren't ready to deal with that.

*Are they not daunted by this image of the Olympian sexual athlete? They might imagine that it would be terrifying to sleep with you.*

I think that's something a lot of men feel about me. They're shocked when they find out I'm not. Everybody has their image that precedes them. My sexual image is looming out there in front of me. Everyone probably thinks that I'm a raving nymphomaniac, that I have an *insatiable* sexual appetite, when the truth is I'd rather read a book.

*Do you lecture boyfriends about condoms?*

I will if they refuse to wear them.

*Would you prefer an alternative contraceptive to condoms?*

If there was one, *hell* yeah! They're a *drag*. Such a drag. They interrupt *everything*. It's like, "Wait a second, wait a second. Do you have a rubber? I think I've left them in my coat! Aaargh!" Then, the worst thing, they say no! And it's, "Oh God! Well, well now what!" And then it's, "Well, sorry." You know the best people of them all are the ones who just have them, that are thinking and aware enough to have them. They're not great but they make sense. They've saved my life.

*What are you like when you're in love?*

What am I like? Well, I'm . . . *happy.*

*Do you find it difficult to fall in love with people who aren't famous or powerful?*

Well, power is attracted to power and power threatens power. And certainly people in a similar position to me understand better what I have to do. So I think that's probably a benefit. And anyway, I *have,* I've fallen in love with people who aren't famous. The question is, can you maintain it?

*What is the attraction of power?*

Well, power is a great aphrodisiac . . . and I'm a very powerful person!

*Do you ever suffocate people?*

No [*laughs*]. I've never been accused of that. If anything, it's the opposite. I give people a lot of room. Sometimes I give people far too much room and they're just begging me to come into the room.

*You seem to have pinballed through quite a few relationships since your marriage.*

Not any more than most people I know.

*Are you difficult to have a love relationship with?*

Yeah, I'm difficult on a lot of levels. Just my situation alone is pretty daunting and probably keeps a fair share of men away from me. You have to be prepared for your private life to be spilled to the world, because the minute you start going out with me, that's what happens. So they have to find that out and understand that their past is now public domain. I try to warn them, but you can never warn people completely. Some people take it very well, and others are destroyed by it. It does affect my relationships.

*In "Truth or Dare," you answer a question someone asks you by saying, "Sean." What was the question?*

Who is the love of your life?

*You must miss him?*

I do [*whispers*]. I still love Sean and I understand very clearly, now that time has passed, why things didn't work out between us. I miss certain things about our relationship because I really do consider Sean to be my equal—that's why I married him. I don't suppose I've found that yet with anybody else.

*There seemed to be something good between the two of you. You were more like buddies than husband and wife.*

Really? We did make a really good couple, didn't we? But we had our problems. I hate to keep talking about it. It's all over. But . . . there's something to be said about people being the love of your life. Even if it doesn't work, there's always that person that you love. I did have a real connection with Sean and I still do. I feel close to him even though we're not physically close. Going through what we went through made us very close. There was a lot of pressure. I mean, it really is amazing we didn't kill each other. But I don't feel like it was a waste of time. I still love him.

*Are you a happy person?*

I'm a very tormented person. I have a lot of demons I'm wrestling with. But I want to be happy. I have moments of happiness. I can't say I'm never happy. I'm working toward knowing myself and I'm assuming that will bring me happiness. I'm slowly getting rid of the demons. You see, I don't think you can truly be loved until you know and love yourself. Then, you can be truly loved and that's what I want.

## ANITA SARKO

# CHILDREN OF A LESSER GODDESS

B Y THE END OF THE TOUR, they called her simply "Ma." It might have meant "Mother." Then again, maybe it was just short for "Madonna."

Madonna as mother. It makes sense, in a perverse sort of way, and as *Truth or Dare* keeps reminding us, here is yet another role that Her Blondeness revels in. With her seven male dancers, Madonna had to be Mother to these frivolous and, at times, downright disobedient children. But were they kids or simply Madonna's posse?

In her advertisement for the dancers' audition, Madonna expressly asked for "fierce male dancers . . . wimps and wannabes need not apply!" Attitude she wanted and attitude she got. "Once you walked into the audition," dancer Luis Camacho, 21, recalls of his first meeting with the superstar, "you knew who was the boss. She just radiates power."

When one of the dancers' homophobia threatened some of the others, Madonna showed who was boss. "The tour has just started," the dancers recall her telling them. "I can have you all replaced." Oliver Sidney Crumes, 21, a heterosexual, felt taunted by some of the gay dancers, especially Camacho, whom Madonna described as being "someone born to play a male courtesan."

"He was Mr. Macho Man," Camacho says of Crumes. According to another dancer, Salim "Slam" Gauwloos, 22, "Oliver was a toy for Madonna. He was dumped and he gagged, and we laughed because we knew it would happen. They started up at the end of rehearsal." What they actually "started up" is something *Truth or Dare* leaves open to speculation. But all hell broke loose in Madonna's posse when a tabloid reported that Crumes had replaced Warren Beatty as the man in her bed.

"I was carrying on an Oedipal relationship, a mother and son,"

Madonna waxes on about Crumes. "It wasn't fully realized. He played 'Little Boy' to my 'Mother.' I took him under my wing and wanted to educate him. I'd give him books. He got attached."

On tour, the affections between mother and children ran every which way and loose. Kevin Stea, 21, another Blond Ambition dancer, claims that at the last performance, Madonna revealed a secret. "Madonna told me she had a crush on me when we first started," he says. "And I thought she hated me because she treated me in a very businesslike manner." Madonna remembers it differently.

"Dream on!" she lashes back. "He can say anything he wants. I kept my distance because he didn't bathe!"

And how do the other boys feel about Madonna today? Let's just say they make her sound like the only serious challenge to sainthood for Mother Teresa. And why not? For the duration of the four-month world tour, they were paid top dollar and stayed in deluxe hotels, each getting his own room when they played Los Angeles. Any 21-year-old could get addicted to that kind of a lifestyle, and some did. "I did a Linda Blair," Camacho says of his withdrawal from life on tour. "Getting off the plane, I didn't get into a Mercedes limo, I got into my father's Ford Reliance. When I got up [in the morning], I reached over and gagged because there was no phone for room service."

And of course, there was no Madonna. "She was a very maternal figure," says Stea. "She was always worried about us. There were always condoms in our per diem."

## ANTHONY DeCURTIS

# FLESH AND FANTASY

T HE SECOND PHOTO ESSAY on Madonna to appear in ROLLING STONE featured her collaboration with photographer Steven Meisel, with whom she would soon collaborate again for her book *Sex*.

"F OR ME, it was a great chance to re-create an era that I feel I would have really flourished in, that nothing I would have done would have been censored." That's how Madonna describes her collaborative effort with photographer Steven Meisel to conjure the demimonde of Paris in the Twenties and Thirties. The inspiration for the images was the work of Brassaï, the photographer who, with the curiosity of an anthropologist and the vision of an artist, haunted the brothels, alleyways, cabarets, backstages, opium dens and gay and lesbian nightclubs of the nocturnal world he called "the secret Paris." Brassaï's frank, nonjudgmental depictions of life in the sexual underworld were not published until the mid-Seventies, decades after he had attained international recognition for his other work. "Rightly or wrongly, I felt at the time that this underground world represented Paris at its least cosmopolitan, at its most alive, its most authentic," Brassaï wrote about his forbidden photographs.

In her poses for Meisel, Madonna characteristically erases distinctions between artifice and reality in pursuit of ever-shifting, always elusive emotional truths. If you are a woman who loves other women, or a man who longs to be a woman, which is more true: the daylight world in which you assume your conventional identity and pretend such feelings do not flow inside you, or the concealed, ideal world in which you dress and act as you see yourself in your mind, as you believe you truly are?

In the erotic theater of the imagination evoked by Madonna and Meisel, roles are taken on and cast off—the obedient bordello performer straining to sip from a glass held tightly between her feet; the butch mistress surrounded by transvestite supplicants; the kinky pinup girl, resplendent in heels, seamed stockings, a garter belt and the American flag—their meaning an impulse of the moment.

Describing his approach to his typically camera-shy subjects, Brassaï wrote, "What I wanted was for the suggestion to take photographs not to seem to come from me, but from them." "I think if you know anything about Brassaï and you know anything about me, you can see my attraction to his work and what he's trying to say," Madonna says. It's photography and performance as the seducer's promise, images that whisper: "You think you know Paris, you think you know Madonna, you think you know yourself. I can show you more."

## CARRIE FISHER

# TRUE CONFESSIONS:

The ROLLING STONE Interview with Madonna,

Part One

**M**ADONNA AND I had met many times over the years, but we had never actually had a conversation. It took this interview to bring us together—she as icon, I as inquisitor of icon (after all, I have already distinguished myself as friend of icon, relative of icon and ex-wife of icon). I had never done an interview before, and I don't know that I will again. For me, this has all the makings of a Waterloo.

The first of the two sessions for this interview took place in the restaurant of the Four Seasons Hotel in Los Angeles. Madonna wore gold lamé; I probably wore black. The last session took place in the offices of her manager, Freddy DeMann. Madonna wore a negligee; I probably wore black.

I was late for that first meeting because a friend who had AIDS and who was staying with me had suddenly developed a fever. I called Madonna to say I was on my way. "You're late," she informed me. I explained about my friend. "Well, okay, that's a good excuse," she said. By the time of our final meeting the following week, my friend had died. He had been extremely courageous, fighting an unbelievable battle. I relate this because it factored somehow into our meetings, making them even more bizarre and certainly changing the tone of our conversation from time to time.

Madonna has no equal at getting attention. She often seems to behave like someone who has been under severe restraint and can now say and do whatever she likes without fear of reprisal. She delights in being challenged, in telling more than she had planned, in going further than she had intended. And judging from her new film *Truth or*

*Dare,* there is no "too far" for Madonna. She has a quality that I've always enjoyed in some people, mainly public ones: She will answer any question because she is genuinely interested in her own reply. A conversation or an interview, then, can become an opportunity for self-discovery, or just discovery. It's a hearty mix of self-consciousness and self-confidence. It's a type of courage, a free fall into the perplexing public now.

I had heard a rumor that Norman Mailer was the first choice to do this interview but that it didn't work out. I'm sure he would have cost more than I. No doubt that Norman on Madonna would have been a historic piece. But this time around, history was not in the budget. Unfortunately or not, I was. So a lot of money was saved, and history was not made. Or made, at least, of cruder material. Discount history, at those low, low, no-Mailer prices.

*We have a lot of things in common. We go to the same shrink.*

Yeah, everything I do is measured by what I think her reaction will be.

*The choice is to be either her worst patient or her best patient, but to be distinct somehow.*

I'm so worried about impressing her—not impressing her, but being good—that when I know I'm fucking up—

*She becomes the superego mommy conscience.*

Absolutely. And so far she's disapproved of everything I've done since I've started seeing her. That's why I haven't gone lately.

*We've also been married and divorced.*

How many years were you and Paul [Simon] married?

*We did a six-year stint on "not married," and then suddenly it was "Let's fix this relationship," or "We might as well be married." Then we were married for two years, and it was very on again, off again, as it was for the whole relationship over thirteen years.*

So nothing changed after you and Paul got married?

*It got worse because it was supposed to get better. Now I was supposed to be a better wife.*

But you weren't.

*No.*

We also both got married on August 16th.

*The day Elvis died.*

Is that why you got married on the sixteenth?

*No. I don't remember why. Why did you? Because Elvis died? No,
I know it was because that's also your birthday, and his [Sean Penn's]
is the next day. Do you still speak to him?*

I have been speaking to him recently. You know how it is. First it's
like anything bad you can say comes out.

*I never heard you slam him.*

No, I never slammed him publicly. But I went through a hostile period. My heart was really broken. You can be a bitch until your heart's
broken, and when your heart's broken, you're a superbitch about
everything except that. You guard that closely. So, no, I never really
slandered him. And then we went through a period where I never
would have known I was even married to the guy. It was like that part
of my life did not exist. Four years. The first year was good—sort of.

*But you weren't together that long before you got married.*

Seven months. It was really a romantic thing. We were madly in
love with each other, and we decided quite soon after we started seeing each other that we were going to get married—and then we got
married. He didn't get a tattoo on his arm.

*You weren't like Cher and Josh [Donen]?*

Or Winona and Johnny? Actually, Sean did get a tattoo but not
until after we were married. It's my nickname on his toe. So none of
his girlfriends can see it unless they're really inspecting him.

*Which I should think they would.*

Yes, at this point. It's DAISY.

*Your nickname is Daisy?*

It was when I was with him. No one calls me Daisy now. Now it's
Dita, from Dita Parlo, an actress from the Thirties. She did a lot of silent
movies.

*And who gave you this one?*

Actually, I gave it to myself, but everyone thought it was very fit-
ting, so it just stuck. You know how you have to pick names when you
stay in hotels. After Daisy there was Lulu.

*Why were you named Daisy? For Daisy Buchanan, Daisy Miller?*

Daisy Miller. There are a lot of good Daisys.

*Mostly high-strung.*

Yeah. And then there was Lulu because I was worshiping Louise
Brooks. My name was Lulu Smith.

*Why did you worship Louise Brooks?*

Because she was hyperactive, she didn't mince words, and she was
a rebel—at least from what I've read. I thought she was a fab girl.

*Who else do you like who doesn't mince words?*

Bette Davis. Oh, everybody I like is dead. The next name, while I was on tour for six months, was Kit Moresby from [the book] *The Sheltering Sky*. She's fairly high-strung but not exactly my personality.

*She was a lesbian and insane. Kit was based on the writer Jane Bowles.*

So they say. Anyway, I loved the book, but after I saw the movie, I didn't want to be Kit Moresby anymore, because it was so disappointing. I didn't want people to think that I was Debra Winger.

*So we're staying with Dita until further notice.*

Until I find somebody else to be enamored of.

*Someone from the past who's dead. Dorothy Parker?*

She's good, but I don't like the name Dorothy.

*Dotty. She wore those little puffy dresses and was apparently a really mean drunk.*

Well, you know what we have to say about mean drunks.

*What? Oh, that's your ex.*

Shhhh.

*Yeah, it's a really big secret. Nobody knows.*

Okay, back to things we have in common. Let me ask you something: Did you fuck Warren?

*No.*

You didn't?

*I'm one of the few. I could have.*

Okay, but we both made a movie with him, so we both could have fucked him.

*At the time, I was seventeen and making "Shampoo." He offered to relieve me of the huge burden of my virginity. Four times. That was the big offer. I decided against it. I decided for reality over anecdote.*

Next, we're both fag hags.

*I prefer "fag moll."*

Next, we both have a hostility toward men, which rears its ugly head often in our work.

*I guess so.*

I'm not saying it's bad. I think it's good to work it out. Which leads me to the next common thing—our work tends to be confessional and semi-autobiographical.

*But yours hasn't been so autobiographical until lately. "Truth or Dare" is wildly so.*

I finally decided that it was okay. That's the most interesting thing to talk about. I couldn't go on pretending that everything was peachy keen.

*They always say, "Write about the truest thing you know."*

Exactly. And another thing in common, last but not least—mother complex.

*And probably father complex.*

For different reasons.

*Well, you didn't have a mother. How old were you when she died?*

Five.

*And did you have a stepmother?*

Yeah, my father remarried three years later. So that's a lot we have in common. And—we both have the same shrink.

*And also a lot of your humor is not dissimilar to something that I do. It is shock over wit. I've read interviews in which you say things like "Look how big his dick is!"*

It's a kind of vulgarity.

*It's funny to me that you do it, because sometimes it seems like you have the attention of the world and sometimes you behave as though you don't. It's like you haven't caught up with the reality. It would be a very abstract reality to get behind.*

It's not something I sit around and think about. It's rather unconscious. I just sort of naturally say things to shock, not necessarily to offend. It's like pulling the tablecloth off the table to disarm everybody.

*You enjoy being controversial. That used to mean talking about things that were never talked about. Now, it seems controversy is just a diluted form of pornography or obscenity. I'm not suggesting that you do pornography, but you do obscenity.*

You want to be more specific about that?

*You express yourself in crass language. Like the woman in your documentary that you say finger fucked you when you were schoolmates.*

But that's what really happened!

*Well, she denied it in the film. But I wanted to ask about that. Who is that girl?*

She was a girl that I grew up with when I was little. She lives in North Carolina now; she moved there with her family. She recently had a baby and named it after me. I have spoken to her and written to her since then. To me, a lot of obscene things happen to people in their lives. I just didn't happen to cut it out of my movie.

*I don't think it's obscene, actually, it's personal. The language you use to talk about it can be obscene.*

Yeah, but I ended up making a personal movie. To me it was like

"Where do I draw the line?" Should I cut this out? If I cut out that, then why aren't I cutting out this?

*And you have total say over what you can cut and what you can't?*

In the end, Alek [Keshishian], the director, has final cut, but we never disagree on anything.

*And he was there for how long?*

He was there through the whole rehearsal period, which was a couple of months. He didn't start filming until we got on the road. In total, he was with us for about seven months.

*So you were constantly being observed?*

Absolutely.

*But you are constantly being observed anyway, so the experience was probably just heightened.*

Yeah. I didn't really know Alek that well. I was a bit wary of him in the beginning, and I didn't set out to make such a personal movie. I wanted to document the show because I thought it was really theatrical and I wanted it to be a film. But before we even got on the road, I started developing a relationship with my dancers. I was so fascinated with them that I thought: "No, I don't want to make a movie about the show. Fuck the show. I want to make a movie about *us*, about our life." I thought they were so amusing and inspiring.

*Why inspiring? Because they worked hard?*

They were hard workers, extremely talented, and I didn't think they were jaded. They hadn't been on tour with other people and hadn't traveled. They hadn't been associated with—I hate to say the word—"celebrity." Everything was completely new to them.

*You could trade on their innocence a little bit.*

Absolutely. And I could show them things and be a mother to them. Take care of them. Assuage my guilt for having so much money by taking them shopping at Chanel and buying them everything their hearts desired.

*That handles your guilt?*

It makes me feel better for a while.

*I've always felt that the nice thing about having a lot of work is that you feel required and essential to the process. Does your work use you up well enough?*

Yeah, I think it does. It has to, because I ultimately end up making my own work. I don't sit around waiting for other people to give it to me. I've had to do this to ensure myself constant employment. I honestly don't think I could just announce to Hollywood, "Okay, now

I want to be an actress," and then wait for people to give me movies. I also couldn't be just a recording artist who puts out a record once a year. I have to keep finding things for myself to do.

*Like producing films? What do you do? Do you option books, or have writers come in and pitch ideas?*

It's almost never ideas people pitch. One film I want to do is the Frida Kahlo story, which I got interested in because I love her paintings. I started collecting her artwork, and all of a sudden everybody loved Frida.

*She's one of the dead people you admire.*

Absolutely. I'd never call myself Frida, though. Now I hear that there are a million people who are all doing Frida projects, but I don't give a shit.

*Wasn't she supposed to be an unattractive woman?*

I don't think so.

*Actually, I have a pin of her that looks like you.*

In self-portrait she kind of over-exaggerated her facial hair. Her eyebrows didn't actually meet together, but she painted them to meet together. And she had dark hair on her upper lip because she was Latin American. And she overemphasized that in her paintings, which made her masculine and hard looking. In later years she had health problems. She started taking some kind of medication like steroids and her facial hair got really thick. She had almost a beard; she had to shave practically.

*How do you shave practically?*

You know what I mean. And I'm just starting to develop Martha Graham's life story.

*So you're doing a lot of women.*

I couldn't do any men.

*As a producer you could.*

That's true, but I'm not interested in doing things that I'm not in. Although by the time one of these things comes along, maybe I'll be too old for it, and then I'll just direct it.

*You want to direct?*

Definitely. After I made this documentary and having gone through the step-by-step process of making movies, definitely.

*I'd like to do it eventually too. At my height, I'd like to boss a group of men around. How tall are you?*

Five four and a half.

*I'm five one and a half, and it's incredibly important to me. Except that I stoop, which is attractive. I have one of those dowager's*

*humps; it's from reading when I was a kid. For some reason I don't
bring the book up, I bring my head down, like it's a feed bag. So I read
like a horse.*

Short people try harder.

*I'm compensating for it. What are you compensating for? Didn't
you think you were attractive?*

When I was little, absolutely not.

*So when did you?*

When did I think I was attractive? When I started hearing it from
my ballet teacher at about sixteen.

*But by then you had solidified the impression that you were not
attractive.*

I thought I was a dog from hell.

*You certainly carry yourself as though—*

I'm a dog from hell?

*No, quite the opposite. I remember when we were at Ron Silver's
Seder together and I had the impression that you were in a documentary, waving. You looked like you were moving through warm, thick
liquid. It was very slow and—*

Maybe it's because I was drunk.

*You were drunk? You get drunk in a very, very graceful way, then.*

I was so out of my element there.

*Who wasn't? Excuse me!*

Ron was out of his mind.

*Screaming at his mother.*

I'm not even Jewish. It was all very strange. So if I was moving like
I was going through warm liquid, it's because I felt like I was.

*That was just my impression. I usually watch people and decide
that they're just a lot more comfortable with how they're coming off
than I am.*

Did I look like I was comfortable?

*You always look like you're comfortable. My impression of you
is, arm's length. I've always felt that you were abrupt toward me, not
impolite but close to it. You're not an ingratiating personality.*

With you?

*It's actually gotten better over time, but you've always been like
[blasé] "Hi, Carrie."*

I know. I think you probably intimidated me.

*If so, then it seemed like you were working at intimidating me or
removing me from the scene.*

I do that all the time to people that I'm afraid of.

*In your documentary, you come across more girllike, whereas I've always experienced you as, I don't know, a commando. I never understood why you felt the need to attack when you've certainly won the battle, if not the war, in your mind.*

Well, that's all part of how I'm going to conquer the world: conquer my loneliness.

*But the impression I got from the movie was more girlish.*

Yeah, because those are people who I really trusted and I spent a lot of time with, so it was very easy for me to be that way.

*I saw you with them when I went backstage after I saw your show with Penny Marshall. We stood where the short people stand—sort of in the corner.*

That's the funny thing about you in my life, Carrie. I see you in a lot of places, and you know a lot of people that I know, but for some reason I always feel like whenever I see you, I see you unexpectedly. In other words, no one ever tells me that you're coming or they're bringing you. So I feel like if I knew, then I would be ready.

*I like the idea of preparing for me, like getting cookbooks or something.*

Exactly. But I always see you and go, "Oh!" You seem to always kind of be—

*Around.*

You're on the periphery, but you have a very commanding personality. Maybe I see some of myself in you and I can't deal with that.

*I offend you greatly. My line is that too many village idiots spoil the village. So if you're in the room, it's your village, man, and you be the idiot. I would certainly take a backseat to your drive. You're what I would call a focus puller. You would have been a star in any incarnation.*

You mean whatever I chose to do?

*But you could not have chosen to do anything but what you do, could you? Did you ever want to do anything else?*

No.

*Like John Lennon once told Paul [Simon] that he wanted to be a hairdresser. Yeah, right.*

Well, I wanted to be a nun. I saw nuns as superstars.

*How could you have wanted to be a nun, given your attitude? Sister Mary Blowjob.*

Sister Mary Fellatio. When I was growing up I went to a Catholic school, and the nuns, to me, were these superhuman, beautiful, fantastic people. To me, that was as close as I was going to get to celebrities. I thought they were really elegant. They wore these long gowns, they seemed to glide on the floor, everyone said that they were married to Jesus. I thought they were superhuman and fabulous.

*So you grew up believing in God.*

I still believe in God.

*Do you go to church?*

I don't like to have to visit God in a specific area. I like him to be everywhere.

*Here with us now.*

Part of my air.

*Well, I like the idea. My doubt is heavier.*

You probably weren't raised with a devoutly religious parent. It sort of rubs off on you.

*So your father is devoutly religious?*

Absolutely.

*Does he go to church still?*

Every Sunday.

*So your big thing is probably rebelling against the church. I'm going to figure you out yet.*

Rebelling against the church and rebelling against the laws decreed by my father, which were dictated through the church, I suppose.

*Do you believe in the afterlife?*

Oh, I believe in everything. That's what Catholicism teaches you.

*So you go to confession? I'd love to be there.*

I don't now, but I did.

*You don't even go to your shrink.*

But mind you, when I did go to confession, I never told the priest what I thought I'd really done wrong. I'd make up other, smaller crimes. I thought, look, if I think I've done something wrong, I have a private line to God, and I'll just tell him in my bedroom.

*Do you still think that you have a private line to God? "Hello, God, it's Madonna." No, not even Madonna, just say, "God, it's me."*

He knows my voice by now. I suppose I still pray.

*Well, you do before your shows, as we see in your film. I was so impressed. My brother is a born-again Christian, and though we fought over it, I always sort of envied his ability to suspend doubt.*

It's not that my doubt has been suspended, it's just that if something's really horrible and I say enough prayers, it will get better.

*I believe in God in strong air turbulence.*

God seems to be there whenever things are really horrible. I do try to remind myself—I know this sounds corny—to be thankful for things when they're good, to be conscious of God.

*Even during your masturbation reenactments onstage?*

Well, I don't practice Catholicism now. The Catholic Church completely frowns on sex.

*Sex is okay for procreation.*

But *only* for procreation and not for enjoyment.

*Men have to have an orgasm in order to procreate, while we certainly don't.*

Right, that's another thing—Catholicism is extremely sexist.

*Thank God.*

For what?

*That we don't have to have an orgasm in order to procreate.*

Yeah, it sort of takes the pressure off of us.

*Who told you about sex, your father?*

Who did tell me? My stepmother told me, and I remember I was horrified. I was ten and had just started my period. It was like "Okay, we better tell her." I remember my stepmother was in the kitchen, and I was washing dishes. Every time she said the word *penis,* I'd turn the water on really hard so it would drown out what she said. I thought what she was telling me was horrifying, absolutely horrifying. And I hated the word. I just hated the whole thing.

*You certainly had a lot of brothers, so you must have seen theirs.*

I did, and I thought they were disgusting.

*I saw my stepfather's—which was alarming—from the back.*

I never saw my father naked, and I really thought about that.

*So, what did your stepmother tell you?*

I don't remember the exact words, but just that a man has a penis and a woman has a vagina.

*You didn't mind the word "vagina" as much?*

No, because I have one, so I can relate to it. I can barely relate to a dick now; I couldn't at all then.

*Would you like to have one, every now and again?*

Yeah, I'd like to know what it feels like to go in and out of somebody.

*Enter laughing.*

It's enough having my breasts as an appendage. When you jump up and down, or dance, or run, or whatever, they're there. I can't imagine having a third thing hanging off my body. How dreadful!

*I think I'd like to wake up with an erection, even if it was just to not like it.*

Yeah, I'd like to know what those things are like. I'd really like to pee standing up.

*The way to do that is to go to Africa. When you really have to go, you go in the bush. All you think is that a snake is going to come and bite something—hopefully your ass.*

That's what makes women vulnerable, that extra hole.

*But men are vulnerable because their genitals are hanging outside and could be lopped off. Ours have been lopped off.*

Yeah, but we have a big orifice that insects can crawl inside of.

*Have you had that experience?*

No, thank God. But I think I probably had that fear when I was little. Whenever I was out in the woods, I'd sit on my hands to make sure that no bugs could permeate my underpants and go up inside my crotch.

*They'd have to be pretty small bugs, I guess, depending on what kind of underwear you wore. If you were Catholic, you probably weren't wearing lace at that point. You didn't get into really elaborate underwear until recently, I imagine.*

Not until I had money, really.

*How long have you had money? Eight years? I can figure it out because you were becoming famous when I was in the drug clinic. The videos used to be on. The drug addicts only wanted to watch "Star Trek," MTV or "The Twilight Zone." You were part of my recovery, dancing and writhing around on the floor.*

In my lace underwear.

*Speaking of that, how is your personal life now? You're not with that guy anymore.*

I'm in a state of limbo. I find myself singing "Mister Sandman" every night before I go to bed.

*So, do you want me to set you up with some people?*

Excellent.

*Is there something particular that you're looking for at this juncture?*

Intelligence would be good.

*As you get older, the pickings get slimmer, but the people sure don't.*

I'll take a slightly overweight guy if he's smart.

*You can work him out.*

Yeah, I'll put him through a training regime. But what can you do to somebody's brain? The die is cast.

*You don't want to put him through Boyfriend University?*

Oh, God, I'm so tired of that. I'm waiting for the perfect man.

*That's going to be tough. I always thought that I wanted to form an alliance rather than have a relationship—find someone who you fancy as your counterpart. But a counterpart you go to war with, a counterpart you live with. So this is my new theory.*

I've found counterparts, and I've worked with them.

*That almost killed me.*

I have not found a complement.

*I would have thought your last boyfriend [model Tony Ward] was a complement.*

He was a complement, but I insist that whoever complements me has his own identity. Meanwhile, let's skip right to the thing men really enjoy.

*Let's get to the real servicing thing. The quickest way to a man's heart is not through his stomach, it's through blow jobs.*

I don't like blow jobs.

*What do you like?*

Getting head.

*For how long?*

A day and a half [*laughs*].

*So why don't you go out with women? I have the answer from my end.*

Because after they give me head I want them to stick it inside of me.

*My answer is, because there's no payoff.*

Although, I guess a woman could strap on a dildo.

*Not really. There's no way to look at somebody who has strapped on a dildo and still think that they're a human. Their dignity levels are frighteningly low.*

I've never had one inside of me, but for a joke I asked a friend of mine to put one on. I just couldn't stop laughing, so I don't see how anyone could look at them with a straight face.

*That's what you can do at your level of power: Insist that someone strap on a dildo.*

She was happy to do it.

*I bet! Good anecdote, bad reality. Mike Nichols once said that in* relationships there should be a flower and a gardner, and there was the problem with you and Sean: two flowers, no gardener, no nurture. Who's going to mind the relationship?

That's exactly it. Who's taking care of things? "We both need a wife" is what Sean was always saying. We're supposed to be the good wife.

Breadwinner and breadmaker. When you win as much bread as you do, your bread-baking skills are going to go down and it's going to be harder to have a relationship. You have to figure out different compromises. Most men don't want to compromise.

I have to figure out what I can do good for a guy that will take care of the fact that I'm not going to be doing the cooking.

What can you do well? I'm desperate to hear this stuff. You are very attractive.

That's not doing something good.

Well, for guys it is.

I would never be a financial burden to anyone [laughs]. I think I have a terrific sense of humor.

You can joke about the things that they're not getting.

Exactly. I'm a good kisser. I know that.

How do you know?

Because everyone says so. They don't tell me I give good head, believe me, because I don't give it.

Ever?

They just tell me I'm a savage bitch. Who wants to choke? That's the bottom line. I contend that that's part of the whole humiliation thing of men with women. Women cannot choke a guy.

Some would argue.

Yeah, but still, it doesn't go down into their throat and move their epiglottis around.

So you're a good kisser, you have a good sense of humor, and you're not a financial burden. I think we have to find some more stuff.

Okay. I can carry my own suitcases.

Are you supportive or nurturing?

I can be [laughs]. I'm tempted to say it's not my nature, but on the other hand I know that I am nurturing.

Do you remember to ask how their day was?

I do, but only because—

You've been tortured about not doing it.

Exactly. I'm getting better at that. Inevitably, what they did bores me.

*But you know how I've heard boredom described? Unenthusiastic hostility.*

That's good.

*Do you want to have children?*

Yeah.

*When?*

As soon as I find Mr. Right. No, as soon as I just finish one more project!

*But I don't think there is Mr. Right.*

Okay, there isn't Mr. Right.

*I think we have to modify that idea.*

Expectations, absolutely.

*Especially when you're such a piece of work. You'll forgive me, but most men—I was told this by a shrink—will not want to take on a person in your position. He didn't speak specifically of you but of people with large careers.*

I'm sure of that. That's why so many young guys go after me. For me it's either older guys or younger guys. Older guys have already achieved success. They know who they are and generally they have money, one would hope, so they're not about to be that competitive with you. They're in a certain place; they're in the twilight. And then there are the really younger ones, and nothing is expected of them yet.

*And there's also that horrible thing when you go on dates after you're thirty: Everyone's already experienced a bad relationship, so you're living in the blowout of that horror. You have to put up with the ghosts that both of you carry around. A younger guy doesn't have as many ghosts, so you can scribble on their clean slates. You can be their first bad experience.*

And I usually am.

*You can initiate them into the world of dysfunctional relationships.*

I can walk away and say, "Well, that'll really make a man out of him."

*That's right, they've had their Madonna experience. That's what wrecked me for dating guys after I turned twenty. I didn't want to give anyone the opportunity to say they had fucked Princess Leia.*

Laid Princess Leia.

*I think you should put an ad in some very, very high-level newspaper.*

Like what, the *Wall Street Journal?*
*So how are you going to meet guys, go to bars?*
No.
*The bummer about being a celebrity is that guys already know so much about you, which you either have to undo or redo.*
You can always say, "You can't believe *anything* you've read."
*"I'm really very sweet, and I only showed how to give a blow job in that movie because I was stressed out. That's not really how I do it, this is how I do it."*
I guess it is strange. It's kind of hard to date when you're a celebrity, because you can't walk unknown into a place and present yourself to somebody. It's like everybody knows you already. Or here's a good barometer: if you can watch my documentary and not be completely repulsed—not repulsed, but shocked—by me. That weeds them out.
*That's what I think you like to do. You like to test your parameters by exceeding them.*
That's it, absolutely. You got it.
*I was going to ask if you were going to keep topping yourself in each of your videos. Could we expect one of your male dancers to pull a tampon out of you with his teeth? But I don't want to give you any ideas.*
I don't like blood, so you won't see that.
*It could be during the off period, during ovulation.*
I haven't thought of that one. I don't think I would, though, because I don't think any of my dancers want to go anywhere near my pussy.
*They like to go near your breasts, though.*
But that's just a leftover thing with their moms.
*You've been photographed kissing women. Do they kiss the same as men?*
Sometimes better. I've kissed girls that are horrible kissers. I've only *kissed* women, though.
*Well, you've done the finger-fucking thing.*
Okay, okay.
*But that's it.*
Let me put it this way: I've certainly had fantasies of fucking women, but I'm not a lesbian.

## CARRIE FISHER

# TRUE CONFESSIONS

The ROLLING STONE Interview with Madonna,

Part Two

I N THE FIRST part of this interview, Madonna and Carrie Fisher sat around talking about their shrink, the day they both got married and blow jobs. In this second of two parts they delve deeper into the meaning of death, ecstasy and spankings.

*You never took drugs?*

Not really.

*You seem like you're too in control. I like to regain control.*

After you've lost it? No, I never like to relinquish it. I went through a real short period where I very begrudgingly tried a few drugs.

*LSD ever?*

I didn't really enjoy it. I enjoyed ecstasy.

*There's a nickname for ecstasy: St. Joseph baby acid.*

What I like about it was that it took my edge off. I'm a naturally suspicious person, and all of a sudden I didn't see everyone as my enemy. I was really nice to people.

*So next time I want you to be really nice to me, I'll put some ecstasy in your water.*

It was enjoyable a couple of times. But I would feel violently ill after I did it. I'd be bedridden for days, so it wasn't worth it. Good anecdote, bad reality.

*It sounds like it's a good anecdote, bad subsequent reality—which I always used to feel was worth it.*

I never really enjoyed coke because it made me more of a nervous wreck than I am.

*So, if you are a nervous wreck, why wouldn't you have gotten into painkillers?*

They weren't available. I didn't know anybody who did them. I was trying drugs before I had money, and the people I knew were only into ups. Everybody was into coke and crystal meth—stuff that made you chew on the side of your mouth after you took it. If I needed anything, I needed something to calm me down—and nobody seemed to have that.

*Then you're lucky. Also you're not addictive, just compulsive.*

I'm definitely compulsive, but I'm compulsive about being in control.

*I'm addictive-compulsive, and I would have been a drug addict no matter what. The great philosophy of painkillers is that they make you feel better. Well, if you don't feel bad already, that's great; but if you do, that's better still.*

My treatment for feeling bad was not to make myself feel better but to flagellate myself in other ways.

*That's Catholic. What's your mother complex?*

That I don't have one, so I'm always looking for someone to fill up my hole—no pun intended.

*So, then, you're looking for someone to be your mother?*

Yeah. She's gone, so I've turned my need on to the world and said, "Okay, I don't have a mother to love me, I'm going to make the world love me."

*Now that you've gotten the attention and you've gotten a certain amount of respect—*

But it's not enough.

*No. Well, when is enough? David Mamet has a Pulitzer Prize and still doesn't feel like a real writer. I mean, I don't know anybody at any level who goes, "Ahhh!"*

That's good to know. I wonder if there are people walking around who are happy with what they've accomplished? I don't know anyone who's happy.

*Not anybody in this business—*

Which is full of unhappy people—

*And children of alcoholics. You don't have that problem.*

There's alcoholism in my family. My father wasn't an alcoholic, but his parents were. And some of the people in my mother's family are alcoholics.

*You're lucky you're aware of that because it makes it a lot easier to handle.*

Absolutely. I guess some people would say that my father's behavior was alcoholic behavior.

*It would have to be if he's a child of one. Children of alcoholics don't manifest the alcoholism, but they do the behavior. Does your father give you advice?*

No.

*Never? I bet he did. You're rebelling against somebody.*

My father didn't give me advice, he just gave orders.

*Well, that's advice.*

"Do this or else."

*What's the "or else"?*

I was always grounded or had to do chores or was forced to stay at home for the summer.

*No hitting?*

My father never hit me. My stepmother slapped me a lot, and she gave me a bloody nose once. I was thrilled about it because my nose bled all over an outfit that she made me for Easter. I really hated it, and I didn't want to wear it to church.

*How old were you?*

About twelve. We had a very large family and my stepmother was trying to make ends meet, so often she would go to Kmart and buy big bolts of fabric that were on sale. She would sew the exact same Mc-Call's dress pattern for me and my three sisters. I detested that—looking like my sisters. I wanted to be my own person.

*You've succeeded in that.*

I know, I know. Anyway, she made us these horrible lime green dresses.

*It must have looked nice with blood on it.*

What happened was that we got into the car to go to church and I was disgusted that I had to wear this lime green dress with white stripes on it. I had on white ankle socks and white shoes. I thought I looked hideous. I got into the front seat of the station wagon next to my stepmother. The car was completely filled up with all my brothers and sisters. I mumbled something about this horrible ugly dress I was wearing, and my stepmother just went BAM! I always got nosebleeds when I was little and my nose bled very easily. Even though I was in agony, I couldn't have been more thrilled. Not only did I not have to wear the dress, but I didn't have to go to church. My nose wouldn't stop bleeding, so everyone left and I got to stay home.

*So you were supposed to be a good little girl. Were you supposed to be a virgin when you got married?*

Yes. And my stepmother told me I wasn't allowed to wear tampons until I got married. Can you imagine? That's why my friend Moira had to teach me how to wear a tampon. I'm telling you, I put it in sideways and was walking around paralyzed one day. It pinched a nerve or something.

*And you were rebelling by putting it in at all.*

Yes, but I wanted to go swimming. It was during the summer, and who can go swimming with a Kotex on?

*Probably someone.*

Probably Mormons or something. No, you just don't go swimming—just like you don't fuck when you're Catholic if you don't want to get pregnant. There are all these stupid rules.

*My favorite Polish joke is the one where the Polish people have fifty dollars and they go to New York. They're sent out to find something to do. One of them goes out and comes back later with a carton of Tampax. They go, "What is this?" He says: "Look! You can go swimming, you can go horseback riding, you can go sky diving."*

That's cute.

*When did you lose your virginity?*

When I was fourteen.

*So you got into rebelling.*

Right away.

*Did they know?*

Nooo. Oh, no.

*And when did they find out that you had?*

They didn't.

*They'll find out through this article.*

I've never really talked about sex with my father. My parents were virgins when they got married. My mother was very religious, too. I think my father realized I was having sex once I married Sean [Penn]. Before then I don't think he did. I never brought any guys around because my parents lived in Michigan and I lived in New York at the time.

*When did you move away from home?*

When I was seventeen. But I never brought anybody home. Oh, once I brought Jellybean [Benitez] home, but we had to sleep in separate bedrooms.

*Did you sneak?*

No, because my father's bedroom was in between.

*In "Truth or Dare" when your father came to your show, was that the first time he had seen you simulate masturbation and be so explicit about everything?*

I don't know if he's seen all the other things I've done. I'm sure when the nude pictures in *Playboy* and the album *Like a Virgin* came out he went through a period of extreme shock.

*Did he ever say anything?*

No.

*That's nice—I guess.*

I'm not sure. I haven't decided. When I go home, my father absolutely does not acknowledge that I'm famous, or a star, or a celebrity, or that I've made it in any way. He doesn't talk about it so I can fit in and not feel the scorn of my brothers and sisters. I'm not sure that I like that.

*That must be complicated if you go out to dinner.*

I never go out to dinner when I go home.

*So you don't want to make him confront your celebrity.*

No, I would like it if he talked about it, actually, but he never does. Maybe I want him to recognize it so that finally I'll have his approval.

*To not have his disapproval—*

Is better than nothing.

*But it would be nice to have a conversation with him about what you do. You would probably have to assume that—given your upbringing—he would object to it.*

My father's not incredibly confrontational about things like that.

*He gave you loud advice. He gave you orders.*

My father has had a lot of tragedies in his life. I have some very crazy brothers who really keep my father busy.

*So you're a success story, despite the fact that some of what you do flies in the face of his religion.*

Absolutely.

*At least you're not in rehab.*

I'm not in rehab, and he's not still supporting me.

*Is he still supporting them?*

Well, if they could spend a couple of months out of rehab they could get jobs.

*How many of them are doing that?*

There are two of them that sort of go in and out. They have problems. One's just an older version of the other.

*And one of them was in "Truth or Dare."*

Yeah.

*Do you get along with him?*

Yeah, I do.

*Has he seen the movie?*

No, he hasn't. I know he's looking forward to it because he really wants to be a star in his own right.

*A star at what?*

Anything. He's a real con artist. He's got this great deep voice, so for a while he was a disc jockey for black radio stations. He thinks he's a black person, I think. He's hysterically funny.

*It's that gallows humor. You better be funny if you're going to be a big problem.*

Oh, he *is* funny. That boy can make you laugh. I'd like to see him have a stable life.

*Do you get along with your brother Christopher?*

I get along with him fabulously, famously.

*And he works.*

Many of my brothers and sisters work. It's just that Christopher really understands what happens to me in my life from day to day.

*He's the only family member who has that experience.*

Yeah.

[*My friend Julian died of AIDS on Saturday at 4:45 P.M. in Sherman Oaks Hospital, in Los Angeles. He had been staying with me for a month. Madonna and I resumed this interview on Tuesday evening. I described some of the particulars of his death to her off the record. I tend to joke about things that are awkward or painful for me. So if some of what follows seems offhand or flippant in any way, I apologize.*

*Being with someone while they die is a very intense and inspiring process. It hardly seems like something to cover in a Madonna interview. After all, we were there to shed some light on a glaringly illuminated individual and to talk about her new film. Death is intimate. Real. Big Real. This interview worked out to be a kind of truth or death for me. But as they say, the truth will out, or "Yea, though I walk through the valley of the shadow of death, I found myself humming 'Vogue.' "*]

I heard your friend died, and I can't believe you'd even want to do an interview today. I don't want the gory details, but what happened? Was it sudden?

*Yeah. He went to the emergency room Friday morning, and he died Saturday. I got the "Vanity Fair" with the story about you when I was at the hospital, so he saw your pictures. He wanted me to hold them up. He liked them very much.*

Oh, that breaks my heart. How old was he?

*Thirty-one. I'd never seen anything like that.*

It's a very cruel, gruesome death.

*He was a real shtarker about it. "This is so silly" and "My slippers
are under the bed" were, I believe, his last complete phrases. He was
delirious at the end.*

It's confusing to talk about other people dying.

*But when you see somebody doing it, they're very busy doing it—
so it's not as bad as you think. He was Catholic.*

I didn't have such a pleasant experience. It was the ugliest, most
horrible thing I've ever seen. I was in the room with my best friend
when he died. I was absolutely, positively horrified. He didn't have the
same sense of humor your friend had. I wish he would have. It was
very "Why me?" He felt persecuted to the end.

*Everybody has their own idea about death. Do you have any death
thoughts that you'd like to share with the group?*

Death thoughts. That's funny because I was thinking about dying
the other day. You get so preoccupied with thinking about being eter-
nally youthful, but every once in a while a death thought comes upon
you.

*That's what is so scary about being a woman in this business. Not
only can you not age gracefully, you can't age at all.*

Yeah. The death thought came while I was sitting on my toilet pee-
ing—that's where I have my most contemplative moments. I like sitting on the toilet, period—number one or number two. I was thinking
about dying. I'm obsessed with it because my mother died of breast
cancer when she was thirty.

*So you check all that regularly.*

Yes, I go to the mammogram vault on a regular basis. It's the most
horrifying thing in the world. You go in and you feel like you're getting your death sentence. First of all it's painful because they smash
your breasts into this thing. Then you put a robe on and go into this
room where everybody scatters because of the radiation. You're lying
alone on this table and the radiation is coming in and you're thinking,
"Well, they're giving me cancer while they're looking for cancer." You
just feel really creepy. My mother was a radiation technologist—I always thought maybe they didn't make her wear lead aprons. Anyway,
I turned thirty and didn't die, so I felt really good about that.

*Where do you see yourself in ten years?*

I don't think I'll be dead.

*But in terms of your career, won't you have to stop being as sex-
ual at a certain point before it becomes weird?*

Why?

*That's the law. Not at forty-two.*

Sexy in what way? Marlene Dietrich is still sexy.

*My father slept with her.*

Really? I wish I had slept with her.

*With her?*

Yeah, she's gorgeous. She had a very masculine thing about her, but I think she maintained a sexual allure. You just do it in a different way. I'm absolutely not afraid of whether I'll find work or not in ten years. What is going to be tougher for me, I'm sure, is just the emotional idea of being older.

*Marilyn Monroe died at thirty-six, before she had to deal with all that.*

I think it would have been pretty tough on her.

*There aren't that many women who were sex objects who have survived. There are a couple of them, but when you see them interviewed, they don't look very good.*

Why do you think that is? Is it just a state of mind?

*I think when you're valued for something that you didn't have much business in acquiring—like your looks—you're more out of control. As your looks diminish with age, you feel your value is diminishing and you get afraid.*

But do you think that I'm valued for my looks?

*Partly.*

Because I have never considered myself a conventionally pretty person. I look at girls and go, *"They're* perfect." I have to work at it.

*But your beauty is part of your impact—like Marilyn and Jayne Mansfield. And there's one whose name I can't remember—*

Mamie Van Doren?

*That's the one. She's alive.*

But they didn't cultivate anything else.

*And you are creatively involved in your career. It's not simply your looks, although they help. You do get very involved in keeping yourself attractive. But you're not as self-destructive as Marilyn. She was very male identified; she went from one male to the next and was constantly disappointed.*

I know that feeling.

*It's interesting that you identify with Marilyn, because she's somebody who didn't survive the fire.*

I identify with her to a certain extent, but then I have to draw the line. I mean, I don't look at her and go, "Ooh, her life is just like mine." No way.

*That's why I think it's better to focus on a part of your image that*

*you have more control over—which would be your songwriting or pro-*
*ducing—and get involved in a way that you don't have to be young*
*and beautiful forever.*

You won't hear me disagreeing with you on that.

*What about your whole spanking thing? I don't get that.*

It's a joke. I despise being spanked. I absolutely detest it. It's play.
I say I want to be spanked, but it's like "Try it and I'll knock your fucking head off." It's a joke!

*But I saw you on Arsenio and you said—*

I was just playing with Arsenio.

*This is a very important piece of news.*

I certainly punish myself in lots of ways but not by having people
hit me. I hate it. And if someone tries to spank me, like before sex or
something—

*But if kids hear some of that stuff and think it's cute, it could be*
*misinterpreted.*

I suppose so.

*You could be a little bit clearer about that, to my mind.*

I thought it would be obvious—because of my image as a person
who wants to be domineering and take charge—that there was no way
I would actually want somebody to spank me.

*I didn't get it or that stuff on the "Express Yourself" video with*
*you in a dog collar.*

But it's all the same thing. These are traditional roles that women
play, and here I am doing them, but that's not really what I'm doing.

*I thought perhaps you felt that you had so much control that you*
*had some berserk fantasy about having some of it removed.*

I didn't mean it that way. I think it was just my sick little sense of
humor, or not-so-little sense of humor. The spanking thing started because I believed that my character in *Dick Tracy* liked to get smacked
around and that's why she hung around with people like Al Pacino's
character. Warren [Beatty] asked me to write some songs, and one of
them—the hanky-panky song—was about that. I say in the song,
"Nothing like a good spanky," and in the middle I say, "Ooh, my bottom hurts just thinking about it." When it came out, everybody started
asking, "Do you like to get spanked?" and I said: "Yeah. Yeah, I do."

*And on "Nightline" you talked about putting a dog collar on your-*
*self and all. I thought, "Well, why would somebody in her position*
*choose to put a collar on herself?" So I thought maybe it was a way*
*to punish yourself for all the rewards you had gotten.*

It is, I'm sure. I can't entirely explain it. It's just an image I thought was powerful, and I chose to use it in my video. It showed an extreme. First you see me chained to a bed, then you see me on top of a stairway with these working men below, and I'm wearing a suit and grabbing my crotch. Extreme images of women: One is in charge, in control, dominating; the other is chained to a bed, taking care of the procreation responsibilities.

*You're more known through your videos and songs, so perhaps your sense of humor isn't as obvious to people.*

It will be soon, though.

*If you do a lot of press and people understand that you're kidding—*

Then the real me will be revealed.

*I don't think there's any such thing.*

No, I'm being sarcastic.

*What would be a good way for someone to woo you?*

If I knew, I'd call them right away and tell them.

*No, I think you should leave that to me. I think it would be better if I told them and they approached you. It would be bad if you just thought they were following your instructions.*

I like letters.

*So, you'd like to go out with a writer.*

Oh, God, I would love to.

*I'm telling you, I can set you up with one! He has tattoos and a brain.*

That's worth at least a hard-on.

*And what else?*

I like it if I haven't seen somebody in a while and he remembers my favorite thing to eat or my favorite flower.

*You like someone to be considerate.*

Yeah. A considerate good writer.

*Good-looking is not essential? It seems to have been a factor. The last one was a model.*

Yeah, but you haven't seen everybody I've gone out with.

*How do you know? Do you think I'm too busy to follow you around and know all about your life?*

I suppose looks are important, but I've certainly found myself attracted to men who aren't conventionally attractive. Painters are good, too. There are two things that I can't do and wish that I could—write and paint.

*But you do write.*

I know, but to sit down and write a novel is mind-boggling to me. I just can't imagine sitting down and applying yourself to that much paper. How do you sit still for so long? My attention span isn't that long.

*I read you write songs in fifteen minutes.*

Yeah, but pop songs are really easy to write. Michael Jackson's been working on his album for something like three years. I can't imagine doing that! I'd go insane.

*Has anyone written a song about you?*

Pat Leonard, this guy that I write music with, wrote a song about me called "Queen of Misery."

*Are you like that? Do you get depressed?*

I have been. I write all my sad songs with Pat.

*What are your sad songs?*

You want me to name *all* of them?

*No, just a smattering.*

"Live to Tell," "Oh Father," "Promise to Try."

*Do you play any instrument?*

No. When I was really little I played piano and then decided I didn't want to. Then in New York, after I decided that dancing was a big waste of time as a career, I asked this guy to teach me to play the guitar. I started writing immediately. For a couple years I practiced the guitar two hours a day and the drums four hours a day. But as I got more involved in the things you have to do to make records and videos and go on tour, I just stopped playing. On my first album, I wrote almost every song myself. Then I guess I got lazy.

*I would hardly characterize you as lazy. What's the song you're proudest of?*

That's like saying which child do I like best in my large family. There are different things that are great about each one. There are certainly plenty that I don't really give a shit about. I don't like listening to my music. I listen to all those weird tapes you get at Bodhi Tree [a New Age bookstore in Los Angeles]. Chimes. My masseuse has one amazing tape that just keeps playing Pachelbel's Canon over and over.

*Do you write when you're upset?*

Yeah, a lot. Words just come spewing forth. I've written my best things when I'm upset, but then who hasn't? What's the point of sitting down and notating your happiness?

*No, generally you don't have that kind of concentration. And it's not that interesting unless it's psychotic. When it's a manic high you*

*can have a skewed sensibility. Someone told me it's called dysphoria—
elation with a limit. You become aware of the limit, and you're notating it before it ends.*

I've never done that, I don't think. No, I have written songs in that
state.

*"Cherish."*

Yeah, in a super-hyper-positive state of mind that I knew was not
going to last.

*Do you like gifts? What's the best gift you've ever gotten?*

Letters. And I've gotten some *really beautiful* jewelry from Warren. He has excellent taste in jewelry: necklaces, rings, earrings,
bracelets, pins, beautiful brooches—antique stuff. It's rare that a guy
will give you really good jewelry. I was shocked, pleasantly. Most people just go out and use their own bad taste.

*Do you get gifts for men?*

Oh, yeah. My gift giving comes in the first few weeks of dating.

*That's when you give head.*

They're not getting head from me, they're getting gifts from Max-
field.

*I want to go back to your perfect date. This is your version of an
ad. What's the ideal? We know about letters and a good memory.*

Gotta smell good.

*Their own body smell or do you like a particular after-shave?*

I'm not crazy about colognes. Some people just smell good, and it
doesn't have anything to do with something they put on. Smell good
and be clean, those are really important things. Another essential thing
about a guy is that he's got to be able to pay his own rent. Not the rent
on my house, just his own rent.

*What's a good date—movies, dinner?*

Both. Dinner is really good.

*What kind of restaurant?*

Where they have good margaritas.

*So a Mexican restaurant.*

No, I hate Mexican food. But Muse [in L.A.] has great margaritas. The lighting is really good there; you can't see the zits that I always have.

*I don't see them.*

I'm dying to meet someone who knows more than me. I keep meeting guys who know less.

*It's not going to be easy to find somebody who knows more than you and is more powerful. In every situation you have to compromise. What are you willing to compromise?*

Okay, he doesn't have to have a good memory.

*So you'd rather go for smarter.*

Smarter over sweeter. When you have a conversation and then a week later you say, "You said you were going to do this," and the other person says, "I never said that"—that drives me crazy.

*Do you get to say everything that you want to say when you get in those arguments?*

Yes, because I always go: "Shut up! Just shut up! Let me say what I have to say!" And they shut up.

*I let mine build up, and then I come out with this hairball of observation.*

And it's so forceful that whoever is standing in the room has to shut up. I save up lines. I save up what I consider to be really incredible things to say to somebody to really wound them.

*And does it?*

Yeah.

*Do you imagine getting married again like you got married before?*

No, Carrie, no, no. You don't make those kind of mistakes twice.

*So, next time you'll just do it off to one side, like a salad?*

Yeah, it'll be a side-dish kind of thing.

*Just do it and get it over with, and it'll be like something that just happened. "Oh, by the way—I got married."*

No, I don't want to do it like that. I wouldn't want to treat it like coleslaw or anything. I guess I'd just like to think of it as spa cuisine versus a full twelve-course meal.

*Would you have to be with someone who you couldn't ask for a prenuptial agreement?*

No, I'd have to be with somebody who I could ask for one. They'd have to be not insulted if I asked for one—bottom line.

*So you just have to have someone who is really confident.*

Confident, smells good, smart.

*Is that the order?*

No. Smart, confident, smells good, sense of humor, likes to write letters, likes antique jewelry. The three toppers are smart, smells good, confident.

*Sense of humor—can't take that out.*

Carrie, do you have anything *really* important left to ask me?

*No, I think we've covered it. We talked about your movie.*

I explained the spanking issue.

*That was very good for me.*

We discussed growing old, having children, getting married and what I'm going to do with my life.

*And breast cancer and skin.*

What else is there?

*We just have to get that information for the blind date. Muse, margaritas, letters. I think we're done.*

■ **RANDOM NOTES** (June 27, 1991)

Continuing to push the outer envelope of overexposure, Madonna attended premières for her new movie, *Truth or Dare,* on both coasts. In New York, a small gathering of the sleazy and semifamous hovered in the aura of the pop icon at a party before viewing the movie and then celebrating its importance at the downtown disco of the moment, Shelter. The United States was finally able to catch its collective breath when the self-promotion mogul set her sights on the land of Jerry Lewis fans—France—and her film's première at the Cannes Film Festival.

■ **NOTABLE NEWS** (August 8, 1991)

Madonna and Time Warner are holding preliminary discussions for a new contract that could put the pop star at the head of a new multimedia entertainment company. "I assume she's trying to get a deal as big as Michael Jackson, or at least Janet," says a Time Warner record executive. Not likely, says one record-biz insider.

■ **NOTABLE NEWS** (September 5, 1991)

Prince protégée Ingrid Chavez (she appeared in *Graffiti Bridge,* and her new album, coproduced by Prince, is due out soon) has sued Lenny Kravitz for "fraudulently inducing" her to sign a contract that gave him all of the publishing and 75 percent of the writer's royalties for *Madonna's* hit song "Justify My Love." In the complaint, filed in a Minnesota district court, Chavez alleges that Kravitz told her he didn't want her to receive credit for co-writing the song, because he "feared that his wife, Lisa Bonet, a television actress, and the public, would learn of their relationship if Chavez took credit."

## PETER TRAVERS

# MADONNA: *TRUTH OR DARE* VIDEO REVIEW

T HERE ARE FEW better self-promoters than Madonna, and this shrewd mix of onstage-and-off coverage—directed by Alek Keshishian—shows why. Family, friends and lovers all figure in the stew, with the insults flying faster than the tortured self-revelations. It's all hugely entertaining, even if you don't buy a word of it.

■ **YEAR-END RANDOM NOTES:** (December 12–26, 1991)

**March**

Did she see him naked? The most bizarre report to surface after Madonna and Michael Jackson took in the Oscars was that the stars had later stripped and given each other the once-over. Madonna's take on their relationship? "We exchange powder puffs, we powder each other's noses, and we compare bank accounts."

**May**

After all is said and done, *Truth or Dare* probably did as much for Evian water as it did for Madonna's career. The singer, got up in one of her umpteen get-ups, appeared at premières for the docu-psychodrama on both coasts. In general, we have to wait until a legend dies before we see footage of her lounging around in a white bathrobe and waxing about Me, Myself and I. Probably we could have stood the wait.

# 1992 MUSIC AWARDS

MARCH 5, 1992

## READERS PICKS

### BEST FEMALE SINGER

Mariah Carey
Bonnie Raitt
Siouxsie Sioux
**Madonna**
Amy Grant

### WORST FEMALE SINGER

Paula Abdul
Mariah Carey
**Madonna**
Sinéad O'Connor
Amy Grant

### SEXIEST FEMALE ARTIST

Mariah Carey
Paula Abdul
**Madonna**
Lita Ford
Janet Jackson

### BEST-DRESSED FEMALE ARTIST

**Madonna**
Paula Abdul
Mariah Carey
Amy Grant
Cher

# ARTISTS PICKS

**SCOTT IAN of Anthrax**

1. Public Enemy, *Apocalypse 91 . . . The Enemy Strikes Black:* A PE release is always a major event in my life because it'll basically rule my disc and tape players until the next PE release. They never disappoint. Since 1986 they've been my favorite group, and *Apocalypse* is another level above all of their previous releases. It's so immediate. "Lost at Birth" is the heaviest intro ever. What can I say, they fuckin' rule. I'm an unabashed fan, and nothing else even comes close. PE in effect . . . boyeee!!!

2. Alice in Chains, *Facelift:* Simplicity at its heaviest. 'Nuff said.

3. Andrew "Dice" Clay, *Dice Rules:* The album title says it all. I can see all of you Dice bashers sitting in your closets late at night with headphones on, laughing.

4. **Madonna,** *The Immaculate Collection:* Our sound man, George, who hates Madonna, loved this record. I already love Madonna, so my feelings about the record are, are, are . . . words cannot describe.

5. Fishbone, *The Reality of My Surroundings:* This record was not as immediately appealing to me as *Truth and Soul.* I actually didn't listen to this album for about three months, but I always found myself humming bits and pieces until I finally played the record again, and man, now I can't stop.

6. Urban Dance Squad, *Mental Relapse:* The Dancetaria version of "Fastlane" really, really makes me move.

7. James Brown, *Star Time:* Some things never get old. This collection is missing one song; where's "The Grunt"?!

8. "Diane, The *Twin Peaks* Tapes of Agent Cooper," *Soundtrack From Twin Peaks:* It's mandatory to drink a lot of coffee while listening to this as long as it hasn't been anywhere near fish.

9. Slayer, *Decade of Aggression:* The best live album since *Kiss Alive.*

10. Anthrax, *Attack of the Killer B's:* Normally, I wouldn't put one of our own records, but "Bring the Noise" was one of my best—if not *the* best—times I've had being in Anthrax.

## PETER TRAVERS

# BAT GIRLS ON THE LINE

*A League of Their Own*

Film Review

SOMETHING REFRESHINGLY different is up with this summer's movies: Women, usually the forgotten sex in a season dominated by male stars, are muscling in on macho turf. And you can't dismiss them as babes, either, as the following film shows.

*A League of Their Own* is based on the true story of the All-American Girls Baseball League, begun in 1943 to sub for the men at war. Though the teams continued playing ball until 1954, the girls mostly marched back into the kitchen when their Johnnies came marching home. It wasn't until 1988 that they were honored by the Baseball Hall of Fame.

Seen from a Nineties perspective, the story has the makings of a stinging feminist manifesto. That, however, is not what director Penny Marshall delivers. Marshall's take is uniquely her own—lots of laughs, lots of heart and very little sermonizing. Writers Lowell Ganz and Babaloo Mandel *(City Slickers)* and the actors are also known for their light touch.

Geena Davis stars as Dottie, a dairy worker recruited by a caustic baseball scout (Jon Lovitz is pure joy in too brief a role) who wants players to be lookers. Dottie agrees to try out for the Rockford Peaches if he'll bring along her jealous sister, Kit (Lori Petty). A slugger dubbed All-the-Way-Mae also makes the team; Madonna plays her with scrappy wit, especially in tandem with Rosie O'Donnell as another player fond of ball jokes.

At first the girls are shaken by the jeering, leering male fans and by Jimmy Dugan, their boozing manager. But since Tom Hanks plays Dugan, you know there's a softie under the stubble. Dugan's hands-off flirtation with the married Dottie and his grudging respect for the team redeem him. Despite reports that the actresses trained hard for the baseball scenes, none should quit their day jobs. Still, their spirit enlivens the tired plot. Sentiment mars the film, as it did Marshall's otherwise admirable *Awakenings*.

At her best, Marshall captures the camaraderie of these women in ways that rip the film out of its clichéd roots. Davis, who is terrific, subtly shows us the conflicting emotions of a Forties woman torn between ambition and duty, without patronizing Dottie or her choices. In these moments it seems fair to stop razzing *League* and let rip with a "Go, Peaches!"

## ELIZABETH TIPPENS

# MASTERING MADONNA

NO FEMALE POP-MUSIC FIGURE has ever infiltrated the halls of academia as Madonna has. Scholars like Susan McClary, E. Ann Kaplan and Camille Paglia have taken up the Material Girl as a postmodern icon, making her the subject of study at Harvard, Princeton and UCLA. Naturally, Madonna is at the center of the raging debate between high and pop culture. Those who teach her are often called upon to defend her place in their syllabuses.

Harvard University's Lynne Layton, whose course includes a day on Madonna, says: "Teaching students how to read popular culture critically is as important as teaching them to read high art. Madonna is dedicated to breaking down hierarchies of race, class and gender."

Roger Kimball, author of *Tenured Radicals,* charges Madonna's presence in the classroom with nothing short of "defrauding students of a liberal-arts education."

"Here are four years in which students have an opportunity to immerse themselves in the history of their culture," Kimball says, "and to spend time dealing with things that they are bombarded with every day is a waste of time and money. Madonna is entertainment."

Ironically, it is Camille Paglia of the University of the Arts in Philadelphia, herself something of a lightning rod of controversy, who emerges as a voice for coexistence. "We do not need a *whole course* in Madonna," Paglia says, "but within a big course like mine, it is absolutely legitimate to show how images of the present inherit the meanings of the past."

Given the fact that Madonna's songs, videos and movies have only occupied our consciousness for a mere ten years, it may be fair to ask, is it art yet? Do we wait another fifty years before we dare to deconstruct Madonna? To ask what she is teaching us about ourselves and our culture?

There will be those to whom a soup can will always be just a soup can and a pop phenomenon just a Midwestern girl in a bustier. But for those who seek some measure of meaning with their Madonna, here is a course of study.

*Humanities 427: Women and Sex Roles, the University of the Arts, Philadelphia*

The course follows images of women throughout the history of art and religion, from the cave period to modern popular culture, including historical references to the biblical Madonna up to the twentieth-century Hollywood Madonna, who is used as an example of "new" feminism.

*Madonna text:* "Open Your Heart" video to examine the similarities between pornography and art and to address the issue of performer as sex object in control; "Vogue" to examine the worship of art, beauty and glamour and to examine the New York drag-queen origins of voguing.

*Instructor:* Camille Paglia, professor of humanities, author of *Sexual Personae,* is nothing less than passionate on the subject. "Madonna has cured all the ills of feminism," she says. With her "prosex, take-charge, streetwise, rock & roll, in-your-face, kick-the-door-down feminism," says Paglia, "Madonna, like me, rejects the victim-centered view of the universe. Madonna *is* modern American womanhood."

*Women's Studies 102: Women and Popular Culture, Harvard University, Cambridge, Massachusetts*

An examination of women's roles in production and reception of pop culture, audience dynamics and women's representation in various mediums.

*Madonna text:* "Oh Father," "Keep It Together" and "Till Death Do Us Part" to examine elements of the dysfunctional-family discourse; "Lucky Star" to examine Madonna's appropriation of the male "gaze" (meaning viewpoint); "Like a Virgin" to examine Madonna's deconstruction of fixed female identities.

*Instructor:* Lynne Layton, associate of the Committee on Degrees in Women's Studies, a clinical psychologist at Harvard Medical School and author of "Like a Virgin" in *Desperately Seeking Madonna,* has a "measured like for Madonna." She says: "My students say, 'Almost

everywhere men are on top, and I like seeing a woman on top sometimes.' "

*Musicology 13: Twentieth Century Music, University of California,
Los Angeles*
   A history of music from 1900 to the present in Europe and America.
   *Madonna text:* "Like a Prayer" to analyze Madonna's fusing of
Catholic music and gospel; "Vogue" to examine Madonna's connec-
tion to African-American musical dimensions and gay culture.
   *Instructor:* Susan McClary, professor of musicology, author of
*Feminine Endings: Music, Gender and Sexuality,* likes Madonna's
"unparalleled willingness to take very strong positions and get shot at
for taking them." "Madonna makes possible good discussions," says
McClary. "There is a great deal at stake there, much more than when
you're talking about Stravinsky."

*Popular Culture 350:367, developed at Rutgers University, New
Brunswick, New Jersey*
   This course gives students a theoretical framework before exam-
ining detective fiction, soap operas and rock videos.
   *Madonna text:* "Material Girl" to show the video's link with the
film *Gentlemen Prefer Blondes;* "Like a Prayer" and "Papa Don't
Preach" to examine Madonna's willingness to take on issues of the day.
   *Instructor:* E. Ann Kaplan, professor of English and Comparative
Studies, director of the Humanities Institute at State University of New
York at Stony Brook and author of *Rocking Around the Clock: Music
Television, Post Modernism and Consumer Culture,* says she admires
Madonna's "brave way of exhibiting sexuality with a kind of auton-
omy." "Some women students feel threatened by Madonna and don't
like her," says Kaplan. "Others think she's really groovy."

*English 370: Feminism and Mass Culture, University of Texas, Austin*
   An examination of mass culture targeted to a female audience, including pop novels, movies of the Forties, fashion magazines and
Madonna.
   *Madonna text:* "Vogue" to examine images of glamour in mass culture; "Like a Virgin"—live version—to examine images of gender-
bending and self-pleasuring female sexuality.
   *Instructor:* Ann Cvetkovich, assistant professor of English and author of "The Powers of Seeing and Being Seen: *Truth or Dare* and *Paris*

*Is Burning,"* finds herself "a dedicated but somewhat ambivalent follower of Madonna." "Students are excited by Madonna," Cvetkovich says. "It's an eye-opener for them to realize serious issues of consumption and feminism are at stake when discussing Madonna."

*English 377: Post-Modernism and Contemporary Culture, Princeton University, Princeton, New Jersey*
This survey course of film, music, literature and fashion of the last twenty years uses Madonna as a reference point in lectures and seminar discussions.

*Madonna text:* "Papa Don't Preach" to analyze the teenage persona and how it negotiates the question of choice on abortion issues and to compare the rebel persona of Madonna's teenage girl with that of Public Enemy's hard-core rapper in its song "Rebel Without a Pause."

*Instructor:* Andrew Ross, associate professor of English and author of *No Respect: Intellectuals and Popular Culture,* says, "Students will talk about Madonna till the cows come home." Ross also notes students' particular willingness to "write papers about her at the drop of a hat."

*Music 5: American Popular Song, Dartmouth College, Hanover, New Hampshire*
This survey course introduces students to composers and performers from the mid-eighteenth century to the present.

*Madonna text:* "Living to Tell: Madonna's Resurrection of the Fleshly," an article by musicologist Susan McClary, to examine Madonna's musical vision, as well as her mode of collaboration; "Live to Tell"—music only—to analyze the arguments put forth in the McClary article.

*Instructor:* Robert Walser, assistant professor of music, author of *Running With the Devil: Power, Gender and Madness in Heavy Metal Music.* Walser finds students are skeptical when it comes to Madonna. "They haven't thought about her in certain ways," he says, "because they've been trained not to imagine that there could be anything important going on in popular culture, especially in popular culture produced by women."

## ARION BERGER

# *EROTICA* ALBUM REVIEW

★ ★ ★ ★

IT TOOK MADONNA ten years, but she finally made the record everyone has accused her of making all along. Chilly, deliberate, relentlessly posturing, *Erotica* is a post-AIDS album about romance—it doesn't so much evoke sex as provide a fetishistic abstraction of it. She may have intended to rattle America with hot talk about oral gratification and role switching, but sensuality is the last thing on the album's mind. Moving claustrophobically within the schematic confines of dominance and submission, *Erotica* plays out its fantasies with astringent aloofness, unhumid and uninviting. The production choices suggest not a celebration of the physical but a critique of commercial representations of sex—whether Paul Verhoeven's, Bruce Weber's or Madonna's—that by definition should not be mistaken for the real thing. It succeeds in a way the innocent post-punk diva of *Madonna* and the thoughtful songwriter of *Like a Prayer* could not have imagined. Its cold, remote sound systematically undoes every one of the singer's intimate promises.

Clinical enough on its own terms when compared with the lushness and romanticism of Madonna's past grooves, *Erotica* is stunningly reined in; even when it achieves disco greatness, it's never heady. Madonna, along with coproducers Andre Betts and Shep Pettibone, tamps down every opportunity to let loose—moments ripe for a crescendo, a soaring instrumental break, a chance for the listener to dance along, are over the instant they are heard. *Erotica* is Madonna's show (the music leaves no room for audience participation), and her production teases and then denies with the grim control of a dominatrix.

Against maraca beats and a shimmying horn riff, "Erotica" introduces Madonna as "Mistress Dita," whose husky invocations of "do
as I say" promise a smorgasbord of sexual experimentation, like the
one portrayed in the video for "Justify My Love." But the sensibility
of "Erotica" is miles removed from the warm come-ons of "Justify,"
which got its heat from privacy and romance—the singer's exhorta-
tions to "tell me your dreams." The Madonna of "Erotica" is in no
way interested in your dreams; she's after compliance, and not merely
physical compliance either. The song demands the passivity of a listener, not a sexual partner. It's insistently self-absorbed—"Vogue"
with a dirty mouth, where all the real action's on the dance floor.

Look (or listen) but don't touch sexuality isn't the only peep-show
aspect of this album; *Erotica* strives for anonymity the way *True Blue*
strove for intimacy. With the exception of the riveting "Bad Girl," in
which the singer teases out shades of ambiguity in the mind of a girl
who'd rather mess herself up than end a relationship she's too neurotic
to handle, the characters remain faceless. It's as if Madonna recognizes
the discomfort we feel when sensing the human character of a woman
whose function is purely sexual. A sex symbol herself, she coolly re-
moves the threat of her own personality.

Pure disco moments like the whirligig "Deeper and Deeper" don't
need emotional resonance to make them race. But the record sustains
its icy tone throughout the yearning ballads ("Rain," "Waiting") and
confessional moods ("Secret Garden"). Relieved of Madonna's
celebrity baggage, they're abstract nearly to the point of nonexistence—
ideas of love songs posing as the real thing. Even when Madonna
draws from her own life, she's all reaction, no feeling: The snippy
"Thief of Hearts" takes swipes at a man stealer but not out of love or
loyalty toward the purloined boyfriend, who isn't even mentioned.

By depersonalizing herself to a mocking extreme, the Madonna of
*Erotica* is sexy in only the most objectified terms, just as the album is
only in the most literal sense what it claims to be. Like erotica, *Erotica* is a tool rather than an experience. Its stridency at once refutes and
justifies what her detractors have always said: Every persona is a fake,
the self-actualized amazon of "Express Yourself" no less than the
breathless baby doll of "Material Girl." *Erotica* continually subverts
this posing to expose its function as pop playacting. The narrator of
"Bye Bye Baby" ostensibly dumps the creep who's been mistreating her,
but Madonna's infantile vocal and flat delivery are anything but as-

sertive—she could be a drag queen toying with a pop hit of the past. *Erotica* is everything Madonna has been denounced for being—meticulous, calculated, domineering and artificial. It accepts those charges and answers with a brilliant record to prove them.

■ **YEAR-END RANDOM NOTES** (December 10-24, 1992)

**January**
Madonna was sued by three dancers.

**April**
Ask and you shall receive. In April, Madonna signed a $60 million deal with Time Warner—a deal that meant the singer could launch her own record label, dabble in books, movies and TV and collect a staggering 20 percent royalty rate. Take that, Janet.

**October**
The entertainment juggernaut known as Madonna celebrated the release of her naughty-picture book, *Sex,* with a bash at Manhattan's Industries SuperStudio. The party—a heavy-petting zoo that featured black leather, S&M high jinks and a preponderance of outsized dildos—found the ever-pensive Billy Idol telling reporters: "I don't have to think. I mean, just look at those boobs!"

# 1992 BOOKS OF THE YEAR

*Sex*

**D**EAR DITA: I must tell you what happened to Ingrid and me back in October. Our pierced nipples were getting hard, and our loins were moist in eager anticipation of buying *Sex,* Madonna's full-metal-jacketed paean to porno. For weeks the media whipped us both into a frenzy with front-page headlines and TV news segments about the Forbidden Book. Finally, we snatched up a copy for fifty bucks, tore open the sealed Mylar bag with our teeth and explored the singer's most secret fantasies.

Here's what we found: Thanks to its cheapo, spiral-notebook-style binding, just getting the cover of *Sex* open can be a frustrating, sado-masochistic struggle itself. Inside, the campy fashion-ad photos, by Robert Mapplethorpe–wanna-be Steven Meisel, reveal Madonna's fondness for Vanilla Ice, lesbian skinheads, Latin males, black rubber, group gropes, golden retrievers and pizza. Talk about cheesy—the book's erotic text is so dumb (e.g., "My pussy has nine lives") that it makes the dialogue from an X-rated Ginger Lynn movie sound like vintage Anaïs Nin. Restrain yourself, Dita, but *Sex* is, forgive the expression, an anticlimax.

Love and switchblades, Johnny.

JEFFREY RESSNER

# THE MADONNA MACHINE

Think Madonna Does It All by Herself?

Think Again. Here's a Rundown of the Circle

That Surrounds the Star.

FORGET ABOUT *SEX.* If you really want to read Madonna's dirty little secrets, take a peek at her personal appointment journal. "I'm not sure if it's a Day Runner or a Filofax," says producer Shep Pettibone, who describes the daily diary as a depository of hot phone numbers, important deals and other valuable info. "It's filled with thousands of these Post-it notes piled on top of each other. She'll get an idea, scribble it down in pencil and stick it in there."

Pettibone, the dance-music knob-twirler who remixed "True Blue" and produced "Vogue," is a trusted member of the Madonna Machine, most recently cowriting and coproducing ten of the fourteen tracks on *Erotica.* He is also one of the select few who wasn't asked to sign a "nondisclosure contract," that legally dubious document requiring employees to keep their yaps shut about her private life. "Everyone that is employed by me signs a privacy contract, from my maid to a backup singer," Madonna has said. "It's a way of protecting myself before I get to know people and know that I can trust them."

Pettibone is so inside she has even asked him to be a part of a bizarre endurance test. "Hit me! Hit me!" pleaded Madonna. The world's most famous fetishist was standing in Pettibone's apartment on the Upper East Side. Her slender body tensed up, she gritted her teeth in steely submission as she implored him to give her solar plexus a solid wallop. "It was weird," says Pettibone, recalling the masochistic moment that took place at his home studio last year during sessions for *Erotica.* "You know, she works out constantly and does these stomach exercises that make her abdominal muscles really tight. She wanted to show me how strong she was, so she asked me to hit her. I did and she said, 'That's it, now harder!' so I hit her harder. It was like a brick wall."

Madonna can take a licking because she commands strict discipline over her body as well as every other facet of her life, from her movies and music to her friendships and business deals.

"She's the opposite of calm," says Pettibone. "Her patience level is incredibly low, so you have to make things run smoothly. It's better to bring out the angel in her, because the beast ain't that much fun."

"She's a powerful lady," says director Uli Edel, whose *Body of Evidence* stars Madonna as a woman on trial for murdering her lover with rough sex. "Sometimes you feel like a tamer with a she-lion in a cage. You have to force her to jump through this burning hoop, and there are just two possibilities. Either she'll jump though the ring of fire . . . or she'll kill you."

"When she's in New York, I usually get a hold of her right after her morning workout, which is about 10:30 my time," says Freddy De-Mann, the suave, smooth-talking music industry vet who has served as Madonna's manager for the last nine years, following a stint co-managing Michael Jackson. DeMann heads Madonna's new L.A. multimedia company, Maverick Entertainment, and is the key man in her tightly knit gang of advisers, friends and associates who carry out her commands, support her with slavish devotion and endure her high-voltage tirades.

Power cronies like Creative Artists Agency chief Mike Ovitz and heavyweight attorney Allen Grubman may step in when there's negotiating, but Madonna's allies cover the showbiz spectrum: There's supermogul David Geffen, high-paid fashion photographer Steven Meisel, famous auteur's daughter Sofia Coppola, *A League of Their Own* costar Rosie O'Donnell, androgynous country singer k.d. lang, music video director Bobby Woods and design wizard Fabien Baron.

The youngest member of the retinue is Maverick A&R man Guy Oseary. "I'm, like, the most fortunate kid in the world," bubbles the gangly twenty-year-old who frequently escorts Madonna to underground clubs. "Madonna and I go over everything," says Oseary, discussing how he sorts through artists' demo tapes for her to approve as possible signings. And his boss? "She's into breaking rules."

Though Madonna has often spoken of "traveling through people"—a euphemism referring to the high turnover rate of her close friends—the core of her inner circle has remained largely unbroken. While Madonna is daring us to pounce on her, these are the faithful who stand by with the bottles of Evian water, the fluffy towels and the sponge baths to cool her down between rounds:

• Younger brother Christopher Ciccone, nicknamed "the Pope" for his powerful position of authority in the Madonna organization, designs her concert sets and homes in Manhattan, Los Angeles and Miami. "He has the best taste of anyone I know," said Madonna.

• Art expert Darlene Lutz squires Madonna to antique shops and auction houses the world over for treasures ranging from Picasso paintings to Persian rugs. Madonna, who made *Art & Antiques* magazine's list of the 100 biggest collectors last year, favors modern works by Salvador Dali, Tamara de Lempicka, Fernand Léger and Man Ray.

• Personal assistants Melissa Crow and Missy Coggiola take notes, do grocery shopping, field calls, schedule meetings and go through the nonstop stream of faxes, among other duties.

• Former background singer Niki Harris bailed from the "Like a Prayer" video because "burning crosses meant something to me as a black woman," but didn't squawk when Madonna supposedly lifted her song idea "Express Yourself" for her own hit.

• Background singer Donna DeLory, currently embarking on a solo career with MCA Records, is said to have been hired by former tour manager and record producer Pat Leonard to sweeten Madonna's vocals.

• Former beautician Debi Mazar, before her acting break in *Goodfellas* and TV's *Civil Wars,* helped create several Madonna personas and later served as the model for the Blonde Ambition "contessa" look.

One of Madonna's closest advisers is Warner Bros. Records publicist Liz Rosenberg. When there's a gossip item issued, a posed photo to be placed, a magazine cover to be negotiated, Rosenberg is the one who makes the call. "My job is more casual than people might think," she says. "Madonna does not wake up in the morning and plan her media campaign, nor do I. We don't think, 'Who are we going to fuck over today?' There's no 'master plan,' no army of press agents and tanks."

Perhaps the most intimate of Madonna's newest initiates is Alek Keshishian, the young filmmaker who graduated from making rock videos to directing the 1991 rockumentary *Truth or Dare.* Keshishian says that behind the bondage mask, Madonna is a regular sort who enjoys driving herself around without a chauffeur and always finds time to catch a matinee at the Beverly Center mall.

"She just likes to eat Caesar salads with her friends and lead a normal life," says Keshishian. "I remember last Halloween, she served pasta to about eight of us and fastforwarded to the juicy parts of this Marilyn Monroe movie *Don't Bother to Knock.* There were probably forty

Madonna impersonators on Santa Monica Boulevard that night, but she wore jeans and a blouse at home. No costume. She wears enough costumes every other day of the year; Halloween is like her day off."

Some souls who pass too close to Madonna's orbit find the heat unbearable. Famed gal pal Sandra Bernhard, for example, parted ways when the singer appropriated her lesbian lover, a Cuban model named Ingrid Casaras. Adding insult to injury, on her new album, Madonna recorded an updated version of Peggy Lee's old pop classic "Fever," a song Bernhard had been using for years in her nightclub act. ("These people that disappoint, they hurt me," said Sandra.)

Rocker Lenny Kravitz, the cowriter of "Justify My Love" who introduced Madonna to the breathy, spoken-word style of then-girlfriend Ingrid Chavez, was also humiliated. Seeking her involvement for his update of John Lennon's "Give Peace a Chance," he was refused a meeting with Madonna unless he rode an exercise bike while he talked. After suffering through a painful, hour-long workout, he left her apartment thoroughly exhausted. She blew him off anyway.

Perhaps the most highly charged defection involved Oliver Crumes, Gabriel Trupin and Kevin Stea, the three dancers who sued Madonna over their appearance in *Truth or Dare*. The suit, which hadn't been settled or given a trial date at press time, alleges that Madonna's director promised he would cut anything out of the film they wanted but later rebuffed their pleas to remove scenes, including some that exposed Trupin's homosexuality. "Get over it, I don't care," Madonna is supposed to have screamed during a screening when Trupin asked her to delete the revealing footage. After the lawsuit was filed last year, Crumes ran into Madonna at a party, where he claims she hissed, "If you want money, why don't you sell that Cartier watch I bought for you."

These days, Crumes seems ambivalent. During a conversation with him in a small office as he recalls life on the road with Madonna, he glances toward his two attorneys who shake their heads or use sign language to hush him whenever he strays into dubious legal areas. Curiously, he takes time to praise his former employer, not to bury her. "I still want to thank her for hiring me. It was fun. I don't think there will ever be a tour like that again. . . . We were all part of her life for almost a year and there was nothing bad. Everybody was so close, we always partied, we always was together. I just wonder and hope that she, you know, that she thinks about us. . . . I wish it wasn't like this, and I would love to work for her again. I really would."

## PETER TRAVERS

# MADONNA'S COME-ON
# *BODY OF EVIDENCE* (THE TRAILER)
# FILM REVIEW

WHEN IT COMES TO the come-on, nobody does it better than Madonna. In the last few months alone, she's hustled an album, *Erotica,* that wasn't erotic and a $49.95 picture book, *Sex,* that wasn't sexy. The suckers may howl, but her steely sales savvy has envious marketeers breathing hard. So, on the theory that Madonna is a turbo-tease with a major follow-through problem, let's skip her two-hour movie *Body of Evidence* and jump to what really matters—the film's two-minute trailer.

Trailers, also known as previews or coming attractions, have become the movie art form of the Nineties—or con game, depending on your point of view. A stylish trailer can help even a bad movie, such as *Dracula,* open big. It can use original material—to plug *Toys,* Robin Williams was filmed doing shtick in a wheat field ("I'm back, wind me")—or a hit song (Whitney Houston's MTV-friendly "I Will Always Love You," from *The Bodyguard*). Trailers even have a life outside of theaters—TV stations such as E! Entertainment Television run them as regular programming. No wonder studios will pay as much as $500,000 per trailer to the companies that produce them. An effective one is money in the bank. The *Body of Evidence* trailer, whipped up by Fattal & Collins in Santa Monica, provides a useful peek into how it's done.

Things begin with a roar. Not Madonna's but the MGM lion's. It's a clever touch, associating Madonna with the classy studio that spawned Greta Garbo and Jean Harlow. Maybe *Body of Evidence* won't be the lurid thriller its title suggests. Still, this glitzy star package hardly seems a step up for German director Uli Edel after his arthouse hit *Last Exit to Brooklyn.* And producer Dino de Laurentiis once worked with Federico Fellini. Only writer Brad Mirman seems to be making a wise move; he used to be in real estate. Anyway, miracles can happen.

Madonna needs one. She hasn't been impressive onscreen since *Desperately Seeking Susan,* except when she played herself in *Truth or Dare.* The trailer introduces her dressed dowdily in a dark coat and scarf and looking stricken as costar Willem Dafoe approaches her in a cemetery. Just when you fear the worst—Ms. Blond Ambition turns Master Thespian—the trailer cuts to Madonna leaning over Dafoe in bed. You can't tell for sure if they're completely naked, since genitals are a no-no in trailers. But even Macaulay Culkin would catch the drift as Madonna, holding a lighted candle of prodigious width, drips hot wax on Dafoe's nipples and heads south while he writhes in what passes for ecstasy. Madonna lets her upper lip protrude wickedly as she blows out the candle. Just when we're all het up, three words, accompanied by a drumroll, are spelled out: BODY OF EVIDENCE.

Next come flashes of scenes that let us in on what's happening. Madonna is someone named Rebecca Carlson. You can tell she's a babe with bucks by her killer wardrobe: silk pj's with fuck-me pumps to match her mood in the boudoir and pearl earrings and necklace to match her innocent expression in court. The DA, played by Joe Mantegna, doesn't buy her act. "She's a killer and the worst kind," he says. Dafoe, playing her lawyer, Frank Dulaney, insists that "the state's case is built on fantasy, not fact."

What's the case? Says the DA, "You have a weakness for rich, older men with bad hearts, don't you, Miss Carlson?" Says the orally fixated Rebecca, sucking on a strawberry, "He was a sixty-three-year-old man—he couldn't handle it." Frank sums it up best: "It's not a crime to be a great lay." There you have it. Madonna in the role of a woman accused of using her body to kill. She's a lethal sex weapon. Hell, Sharon Stone needed an ice pick to dispatch her bed mates in Paul Verhoeven's *Basic Instinct.*

Other *Basic Instinct* parallels include the Germanic directors and the convenient battles to get an NC-17 rating changed to an R and reap lots of free press. But let's stick to the trailers. Fattal & Collins, no fools they, know that *Basic Instinct* grossed $330 million worldwide. So they milk the *Basic* trailer shamelessly. Stone is a blonde suspected of multiple murder; ditto Madonna. Stone uses a handkerchief for bedtime bondage; Madonna uses handcuffs. Stone seduces Nick (Michael Douglas), the cop who protects her; Madonna seduces Frank, the lawyer who defends her. Douglas has a jealous girlfriend (Jeanne Tripplehorn) who warns him about Stone; Dafoe has a jealous wife (Julianne Moore) who slaps Madonna in a rage.

These *femmes fatales* even sound alike. Stone: "Have you ever fucked on cocaine, Nick? It's nice." Madonna: "Have you ever seen animals making love, Frank? It's intense." The dialogue is interchangeable. When Dafoe says to Madonna, "I must have been out of my mind to get involved with you," we don't hear her retort. But Stone's line to Douglas in *Basic* would fit just fine: "Nicky got too close to the flame. Nicky liked it."

The *Body* trailer trades on associations with other hit thrillers that *Body* would desperately like to be. Anne Archer turns up for a close-up that seems purposeless except to remind viewers that she was the cheated-on wife in *Fatal Attraction*. Likewise, Moore appeared as the sassy friend in *The Hand That Rocks the Cradle,* for which *Body*'s composer, Graeme Revell, did the score. As the images add up—hands being tied, clothes being ripped, the smirking Madonna being forced to act—you have to marvel at the energy being expended to sell the same old sadism. But the job gets done. Anyone who wants to see more of *Body of Evidence* after this trailer is a glutton for punishment.

## PETER TRAVERS

# *BODY OF EVIDENCE*
# FILM REVIEW

L AST ISSUE, I reviewed the trailer for this Madonna S&M flick, which made the film look like a trash rehash of the worst of every fatal-attraction thriller from *Body Heat* to *Basic Instinct*. I was misled. The trailer underestimated the film's vile ineptitude. Madonna plays an Oregon art-gallery owner accused of killing a rich man with a bad heart. Sex is her weapon. It's not just that Madonna doesn't make an effective Sharon Stone; she doesn't make an effective Madonna. There is no sign of her stage charisma. Her character is a stunning nonentity. Instead of emoting, Madonna strikes poses and delivers stilted lines that sound like captions from her book *Sex* read aloud in a voice of nerve-jangling stridency: "I fuck—that's what I do."

Indeed, she does, showing off her no-flab body and no-talent acting. Director Uli Edel *(Last Exit to Brooklyn)* favors foggy lighting, perhaps to protect the identity of the cast. No such luck. Willem Dafoe gives his first boo-worthy performance as Madonna's lawyer and sex slave. All the actors should sue their agents for sticking them in this career crusher. It's early, but *Body* seems unbeatable as the worst movie of 1993. Anyone want to give me odds for the decade?

# 1993 MUSIC AWARDS

MARCH 4, 1993

## READERS PICKS

### BEST FEMALE SINGER

Annie Lennox

**Madonna**

Mariah Carey

Natalie Merchant of 10,000 Maniacs

Sinéad O'Connor

### WORST ALBUM

*Some Gave All*, Billy Ray Cyrus

*Totally Krossed Out*, Kris Kross

*Erotica*, **Madonna**

*Am I Not Your Girl?*, Sinéad O'Connor

*Adrenalize*, Def Leppard

### WORST SINGLE

"Achy Breaky Heart," Billy Ray Cyrus

"How Do You Talk to an Angel," the Heights

"Erotica," **Madonna**

"Smells Like Teen Spirit," Nirvana

"Make Love Like a Man," Def Leppard

### WORST VIDEO

"Erotica," **Madonna**

"November Rain," Guns n' Roses

"Baby Got Back," Sir Mix-a-Lot

"Achy Breaky Heart," Billy Ray Cyrus

"How Do You Talk to an Angel," the Heights

### WORST ALBUM COVER

*Erotica*, **Madonna**

*Metallica*

*Am I Not Your Girl?*, Sinéad O'Connor

*The Chase*, Garth Brooks

*Bobby*, Bobby Brown

### SEXIEST FEMALE ARTIST

**Madonna**

Mariah Carey

Vanessa Williams

En Vogue

Annie Lennox

## CRITICS PICKS

### HYPE OF THE YEAR

**Madonna**

# THE 100 TOP MUSIC VIDEOS

NOT SURPRISINGLY, when the editors of ROLLING STONE chose the best videos of all time, six of Madonna's videos rated in the top 100—more than any other artist or band.

# #10

### "EXPRESS YOURSELF"
Madonna
1989

Since her career began at roughly the same time as the behemoth network, Madonna and MTV are forever intertwined: They've courted (the 1983 premiere of "Holiday"), they've quarreled (1990's "Justify My Love" was banned), and they've compromised (1992's "Erotica" was shown—but after midnight). As our girl morphed from gum-snapping street urchin to the world's most famous woman, so, too, did MTV evolve into a sleek superpower.

No video is sleeker or more superpowered than "Express Yourself," which was inspired by Fritz Lang's 1924 silent-film opus, *Metropolis.* "I think lots of Madonna's videos are done more like films," says veteran costume designer Marlene Stewart. To dress Madonna for her gender-swapping scenarios, Stewart took her cue from *Metropolis'* bleak and sinister cityscape. As to Madonna's menswear-and-lingerie look: "I know Jean Paul Gaultier has gotten all the credit," says Stewart, "but from the early days, we've been using those bras." Stewart chose Madonna's shrink-wrapped rubber dress (worn as she crawls across the floor) "because it worked for that bondage kind of vibe." As for the extras, a coterie of studly factory workers, "We cross-pollinated your local grease monkey with a military factory look."

# #20

**"LIKE A PRAYER"**
Madonna
1989

"Life is a mystery, everyone must stand alone . . . ," opens the title song of Madonna's fifth studio album, but the video shows a world where no one but Madonna can afford to stand alone. Dancing unabashedly in front of a field of burning crosses, kissing to life a black saint's statue and finally freeing a wrongly imprisoned brother accused of a stabbing actually committed by wilding whites, her world appears to be anything but the "home" she sings about.

Moments after its debut, the video outraged viewers around the world. A newly struck promotional deal with Pepsi was squashed. For many the video's most controversial image was Madonna singing before the field of burning crosses. "The burning crosses," says director Mary Lambert, "are a reference to the Ku Klux Klan and things they do to black people. But the image isn't exclusive to the Klan; it crops up throughout Renaissance painting." While the crosses got the most attention, Lambert believes that the hints of eroticism among Madonna, the black saint and the black prisoner pushed America's deepest buttons.

"Interracial unions are still controversial in this country," Lambert says, "especially within the broad demographic of MTV and national television. In 'Like a Prayer,' it's not just Madonna having an affair with a black man. The religious imagery makes it much deeper than that."

# #24

**"BORDERLINE"**
Madonna
1983

This Mary Lambert–directed video was notable for being one of the first to tell a coherent story successfully: Boy and girl enjoy simple pleasures of barrio love, girl is tempted by fame (in the person of a British photographer), boy gets huffy, girl gets famous, but her new beau's out-of-line reaction to a behavioral trifle (all she did was spray-paint his expensive sports car) drives her back to her true love, with whom she plays a game of pool. Seems pretty straight-forward, but according to Cathy Schwichtenborg, editor of the fascinating academic essay anthology *The Madonna Connection,* "Borderline," like many other Madonna videos, is a "reflexive [commentary] on male 'looking' countered by her feminine 'look.' " Madonna's not inclined to talk about her early videos these days, and why should she be, since everybody else is only too happy to.

# #28 "VOGUE"
Madonna
1990

*Paris Is Burning,* Jennie Livingston's stirring documentary on the Harlem drag balls, may have introduced voguing to the masses, but it got a big push from Madonna's "Vogue" (directed by David Fincher). "I remember being in a drugstore," says Livingston, "and there was a white woman with two children, and one of the kids said, 'Look, Mommy, Johnny's voguing!' I was shocked, and that was really all because of Madonna." Although the black-and-white video perfectly showcases the dance, it's also a gorgeous tribute to Forties style glamour, complete with flawless close-ups borrowed from fashion photographer Horst P. Horst. "What impressed me was how many people from the ball world loved it and embraced it," says Livingston.

# #43 "JUSTIFY MY LOVE"
Madonna
1990

Two years before setting a new, um, standard for public display of sexuality with her book, *Sex,* Madonna led us through a house of (her) erotic fantasies—including scenarios of bondage, submission, domination, voyeurism and lesbianism. While "Justify" ended up as one of the most controversial videos of all time, its origins were banal enough.

"When Madonna called me," says director Jean Baptiste Mondino, "about filming 'Justify,' I said, 'Why don't you come over here [to Paris]? It would be nice to do something simple.' We locked ourselves in the Royal Monceau [a Paris hotel] for two days and one night without any idea of what we were going to do. The only idea I had was for her to come with a suitcase, like she was going for a fantasy. We rented the whole floor and shot everyone in their own room; there was no set. That's why the video shocked people. You could see it was not a fake.

"We didn't think we were going to do something wild," he says. "None of what you see was planned. But when I started to edit, I said, 'This is never gonna be shown.' " Sure enough, MTV refused to air it, unwittingly paying Madonna a favor: She got to play the clip on *Nightline* and made a bundle off it on home video.

# #66

**"OH FATHER"**
Madonna
1989

Inspired by Madonna's tumultuous marriage to actor Sean Penn, *Like a Prayer* was an emotionally pivotal album of dark and desperate tracks, not the least of which was the ballad "Oh Father," which touched on physical abuse, betrayal in parental love and Madonna's ongoing conflict with her Catholic upbringing. Director David Fincher's accompanying black-and-white video is severely beautiful and bleak. References to *Citizen Kane* abound—odd angles and threatening shadows, distorted faces and the image of a small girl twirling on her mother's grave in a blinding snowstorm.

Cinematographer Jordan Cronenweth says that though he and Fincher had the Orson Welles *oeuvre* in mind, it didn't dominate the direction of the video. "The song was somewhat autobiographical and had a sense of melancholy and loss," says Cronenweth. "The setting, a graveyard in winter, was appropriate to that feeling." He recalls that Madonna was quite involved in the creative evolution of the piece "not only in her own performance but in getting good performances out of the children." In fact, Fincher allowed Madonna to direct the sequences in the snow with her young alter ego. "David stood back and let it all happen," theorizes Cronenweth. "Because that [little girl] was Madonna."

## THOM DUFFY

# PERFORMANCE REVIEW

Wembley Stadium, London, September 25, 1993

**M**ADONNA HAS DISCOVERED that life is not just a cabaret or dance club, old chum, but a sexy circus as well, one in which the singer plays a refreshing new role as a clown princess of dance pop. Opening night of the Girlie Show tour, before 72,000 fans at Wembley Stadium, offered enough titillation for the excitable British press, but the real "shock" was the humor and warmth Madonna brought to her production, with its big-top staging, Broadway choreography and nods to numerous pop icons of the past.

Smokey Robinson's recording of "Tears of a Clown" gave way to a tooting calliope as a red, shirred curtain rose. A bare-breasted female dancer in a G-string slid down a silver pole as a masked Madonna, riding crop between her legs, issued the hushed invitation of "Erotica" to a low, pulsing synth beat. For "Fever," she stripped shirts from—and straddled—two male dancers (a move made early to virtually assure a tabloid splash the next morning).

But the upbeat, bell-bottomed romps with her eight-member dance troupe through "Express Yourself," "Deeper and Deeper" and "Why's It So Hard" were about as shocking as a *Hair* revival. Ditto her adoption of a Marlene Dietrich pose to sing, with self-mocking seriousness, "Like a *wirgin.*"

And just like Pagliacci did, this clown had other feelings hid. Her ballad "Rain," with a touch of "Just My Imagination" and choreography from *Singin' in the Rain,* was an elegant delight. "Justify My Love" paid cool, costumed homage to *My Fair Lady.* And "In This Life," her AIDS-cure plea set to a somber piano solo, held the stadium crowd absolutely rapt.

Throughout, Madonna's live vocals were augmented by two backup singers, while her seven-piece band faultlessly re-created her multilayered club grooves. But, like a pit orchestra, they seldom drew attention from the visual production. Not until the encores of "Holiday" and an organ-fired blend of "Everybody" and Sly Stone's "Dance to the Music" did the boys in the band get to cut loose as freely as Madonna had done all night.

**PETER TRAVERS**

# *DANGEROUS GAME* FILM REVIEW

S AY WHAT TRASH you will about Madonna's acting (it's more like voguing), she doesn't work with hacks. *Body of Evidence,* her most recent fiasco, was directed by Uli Edel (*Last Exit to Brooklyn*). Now the torch passes to Abel Ferrara, a street fighter when it comes to making movies his way (*Bad Lieutenant*). In *Dangerous Game* (originally *Snake Eyes*), Madonna plays Sarah Jennings, a TV bimbo who wants to act in a serious movie, *Mother of Mirrors,* about the breakup of a hedonistic marriage. The director is the very intense and Ferrara-like Eddie Israel, played to the manner born by the superb Harvey Keitel. Israel is skeptical, but hiring the babe gets his arty film financed. (*Dangerous Game* is financed in part by Madonna's Maverick productions.)

Art and life imitate each other with a vengeance in this mesmerizing jigsaw, especially when Ferrara's real wife, Nancy, shows up as Israel's wife. She berates Israel for fucking Jennings, who is also fucking leading man Francis Burns (the able James Russo). Israel tries to coax tears and a performance from Jennings by viciously insulting her off camera. Did Ferrara use the same method? No matter. Madonna's take on an emotional crackup comes up snake eyes either way, and Ferrara's *Dangerous Game* stops being worth the playing.

**YEAR-END RANDOM NOTES** (December 23, 1993–January 6, 1994)

### January

The *Titanic*. The *Hindenburg*. *Body of Evidence*. Madonna. Babe. There isn't a person alive on the planet who hasn't seen your boobies, so why don't you show us some acting, okay? Yes, the disastrous "film" starring Madonna (her eleventh) and Willem Dafoe was flayed by critics and drew unintentional belly laughs from audience members, despite frantically publicized scenes in which Ms. Ciccone dripped hot candle wax on Dafoe's naked stomach. "She makes a fool of herself as does everyone else involved," said *New York* magazine critic David Denby.

### September

We give up! Uncle! We surrender! Madonna continued her assault with her Girlie Show tour, which was unveiled at London's Wembley Stadium. The show, which promised to "put a lump in your throat and perhaps in your trousers," was the usual cavalcade of costume changes and half-naked dancers.

# 1994 MUSIC AWARDS

### JANUARY 27, 1994

### READERS PICKS

| BEST FEMALE SINGER | FEMALE SEX SYMBOL |
|---|---|
| Janet Jackson | Janet Jackson |
| Natalie Merchant | **Madonna** |
| Mariah Carey | Cindy Crawford |
| **Madonna** | RuPaul |
| Björk | Mariah Carey |

**MIM UDOVITCH**

# MOTHERS OF INVENTION

THERE ARE SOME THINGS you can't cover up with lipstick and powder, and one of them is that if there is a subject female musicians do not want to discuss, it is, precisely, their condition as female musicians. Some, like L7, dislike it so very, very much that they decline to be interviewed on the topic at all. Others, such as Luscious Jackson drummer Kate Schellenbach, are willing but equivocal. "Sometimes it's almost like you should be 'And don't forget to write that we're an all-female band!' " says Schellenbach. "We get a lot of questions about the women-in-rock thing, whatever that thing is that everyone asks about, and I'm trying to think who they're talking about. And then I'm thinking further back, and I'm thinking, 'God, there were so many more bands when I was growing up.' There were the Slits, the Raincoats, Delta 5, the Mo-Dettes, Kleenex. It's a marketing ploy; the trend of women in rock is just a piece of shit." In short, the mere existence of their ovaries does not necessarily unite these artists in other ways. Some, like Tori Amos, feel that they write from the womb rather than the head. Others, like Me'Shell Ndegéocello, wonder, "If you write from the womb, where do you put the pen exactly?" Some, like Schellenbach, Courtney Love, Sonic Youth's Kim Gordon and Kat Bjelland of Babes in Toyland, were inspired by the anarchic integration of punk; others, like Velvet Underground drummer Moe Tucker, Chrissie Hynde and Joan Jett, were raised in the less gender-categorical age of Sixties flat-out rock & roll. Still others, like the incomparable Madonna, are simply unprecedented.

The fact of the matter is that there has always been an enormous female presence in popular music: lyrically, in the work of male artists, as any girl who grew up with the Springsteenian ideal of leaving ghosts in the eyes of all the boys she sent away can tell you; artistically, as girl groups from the Supremes to Bananarama could attest; and culturally, as muses from Anita Pallenberg to the GTO's to Britt Ekland.

Although there are currently more women with guitars, there have always been some of those, too, ever since the Duchess played guitar for Bo Diddley. Nevertheless, in rock as in life, what is male continues to be perceived as known, normal and natural, whereas what is female is taken to be a mystery in need of explication. In other words, to most of these female artists, to be classified as women in rock is not so much recognition as a cleverly disguised attempt to prevent them from speaking for themselves as themselves.

"Life has always been divided into what's a man's job and what's a woman's job," says Madonna. "And rock music has always been a man's world. And now women are coming up, and they're calling the shots—they're people and artists in their own right, and that's very frightening because it affects everything."

Herewith, ten of today's notable female artists take back the talk.

## ADDRESSING THE WOMEN-IN-ROCK THING, WHATEVER THAT IS

HYNDE: I speak for forty-two-year-old ex-cocktail waitresses, divorcees and single parents. And if anyone else is interested, they're welcome to listen.

BJELLAND: I remember reading "Midol rock" once, and it was kind of funny, but it's also like "Okay, just because we're screaming, they think we're bitches, and we're on our periods twenty-four-seven, thirty days."

GORDON: I would be interested, but nobody writes any real intellectual, semiotic overviews of it. I used to study—sort of—masculinity when I was writing articles about art. And when I started getting involved with music, I was in the audience, and I was drawn to the male guitarist. I was a voyeur in a way, just fascinated by the power of the sexuality. And I have always thought if you wanted to find out about female sexuality in rock, you had to first look at male sexuality in rock.

TUCKER: Actually, ironically, things were more open thirty years ago.

AMOS: I don't really feel labeled. I don't respond to it—let's put it that way. When you get a letter from a fourteen-year-old girl that says to you, "I'm coming to your show tonight, can I just come by and say hi, because I know that when I'm finished here, I know I have to go home to my stepfather. He molested me last night, he's gonna molest me tonight." When you read this stuff, you don't think about labels anymore, you just think, "Get her backstage, and put on the kettle."

## SUGAR AND SPICE, ET CETERA

MADONNA: No one talks about the sex lives of these rock stars with twenty groupies lined up to give them blow jobs after a show, and they have a wife and kids and a mistress in every town, but my sex life is absolutely the centerpiece of everything that's ever written about me, and I probably have a lot less sex than other people—that's the final irony of it all. Does anyone talk about the women that Prince has sex with, you know, his harem that he makes records with and then puts in prison somewhere, and you never hear from them again? I'm serious.

NDEGÉOCELLO: To say that because you're a woman you are more sensitive is bullshit. Because I can be an asshole, I am an egomaniac. If I dated a woman, I wouldn't want her to work. I have my own misogyny.

BJELLAND: I don't think about male-female, I think assholes/cool people or closed-minded/open-minded people.

GORDON: There aren't any all-female bands in the mainstream, and maybe to go Top Forty, you do have to be more like Heart. It's just too extreme, contentwise. People really don't want to hear women talking about their scars and stuff.

SCHELLENBACH: Being gay—it's the same thing as being a woman musician: You'll always be tagged, and you are that and don't want to deny it. But I would say it's more of a challenge being a woman musician than being gay, so far. Yeah, we are four girls, but we don't want to be models, whether you believe it or not. Some guy bands must enjoy getting dressed up, but I can't see them telling Helmet to wear a Gianni Versace miniskirt.

## PROGRESS, NOT PERFECTION

MADONNA: Maybe it's easier for people now because they are more used to hearing about [female musicians], or maybe it's because I have more power, and when someone has more power, they're more of a threat. Or maybe it's because my titties are bigger. I fucking don't know.

HYNDE: I've been resisting this idea of women in rock for a long time, and I've always been like "No, leave it out," but I suppose . . . let's face it, it is a phenomenon. I no longer want to be the anti-feminist, because I love people, I'm not one of these animal people who doesn't like people. It's easy to love animals. It's much harder to love people. And I like to rise to the challenge.

BJELLAND: I think the press is coming around in general after three or four years of all the girl bands saying, "Hey, shut the fuck up."

## AND SPEAKING OF THE PRESS . . .

SCHELLENBACH: We've had some bad experiences with female rock journalists, where the interviews have been really, you know, "Your keyboardist is a bimbo," which is a really odd thing to say, especially to another woman.

AMOS: Look, no bullshit: The worst are the women journalists, because they are much harder than any other women that I've ever run into in my life. If you don't get into your heart place for ten minutes, then you are cutting out a part of yourself. It's about the balance of the head, the heart and the spirit and all that stuff. And I can be very hard-ass. Do you think I can't push your ass against the wall right now? Of course I can. But we're talking about vulnerability here.

JETT: I'm not directing this, obviously, at you, but I just have to say it: It's the media that always tries to pigeonhole.

LOVE: Excuse me, but the last three women on the cover of ROLLING STONE have had their tits out. And I can practically see Winona Ryder's nipples on her cover.

## MUSIC AND SELF-IMAGE, IN WHICH THE SUBTEXT OF A BILLY JOEL SONG IS REVEALED, AND ROBERT PLANT LEARNS OF A MISSED OPPORTUNITY

MADONNA: I used to dance in front of my mirror to the Isley Brothers, to "Who's that lady, beautiful lady, sexy lady," but I just assumed I was that sexy lady. Of course, I was desperate for that to be the truth.

SCHELLENBACH: The only song that comes to mind is Billy Joel: "She's Only a Woman to Me" or "Always a Woman" or whatever it is.

AMOS: Well, Zeppelin are my biggest influence. I wanted to give my virginity to Robert Plant when I was ten years old. I was bleeding, babe, I was bleeding. When I would listen to their music, I would feel passionate. I would get wet, and then it all dried up as I got older. It made me feel like a hot girl. "Black Dog." Yummy. Put it on, throw that head back. Rrrrowwww. But my commitment is to being wet.

## WHEN DO YOU FEEL THE MOST WOMANLY?

MADONNA: When I'm around a real man.

NDEGÉOCELLO: Uh, I guess when I take a bath, a nice bubble bath. You know, you're washing your body, it's a sensual act.

SCHELLENBACH: Every time I start PMS-ing, and my breasts start killing me. It's a kick in the ass constantly, or a kick in the breasts—like a reminder: *You are a woman.* Maybe it's a drummer thing because you're always throwing yourself around.

BJELLAND: Right before my period, when nature makes you really aware of your breasts. Most of the time, I don't think of myself as a woman. I mean, I don't go around saying, "Oh, I can't do this, and I *just know* it's because you're *oppressing* me." I think I can do whatever the fuck I put my mind to. Sorry.

AMOS: When I'm playing.

TUCKER: I guess when I'm doing the damn dishes.

GORDON: Now that I'm a mother.

JETT: I don't ever think of it like that. I always just feel human.

GORDON'S PERFUME: When I wear it, I wear Joy. But most perfumes give me a headache.

## GIRLS TOGETHER OUTRAGEOUSLY, OR SISTERHOOD IS HARDER THAN YOU MIGHT THINK

MADONNA: I'm forever finding myself in this position where I'm a fan of somebody's, and I'm rooting for them, and I'm thinking that we're, like, in this sort of mutual agreement about life, and then I'll read something they wrote about me, and it'll be the biggest slap in the face. Much more so than some old fart writing about me and saying shit—I could care less about that, and I expect it. But it happens to me all the time, where I think I have a solidarity with somebody, and then they think I'm an idiot.

SCHELLENBACH: I hate to say it's coming from women, but it's almost turning out that way, although we've also met so many cool women. But coming from women, it's just that much more upsetting, because it's like "My God, this is another woman who's putting you down."

AMOS: I run into women who can't handle it as much as guys. It's much more gutting from the women—it just is. Because I think there's that sense of betrayal when you look at another woman going, "Okay, hang on a minute, how can you not be supportive of healing?"

HYNDE: I have to admit I met this band in Cleveland called the Vivians. I never heard them, but I could tell they could rock just by meeting them. They were out of their minds, and it was obvious they were a rock band. And they were real badass girls, and they said, "Chrissie, we wouldn't have been in a band if it weren't for you." And I said,

"Aw, bullshit, what the hell else would you have done?" And they all kind of stopped and looked at each other and said, "No, you're right, we would have." But you know, I took it as a compliment.

LOVE: I wore this gown at a video shoot—like a prom gown—and I got some tits in it. And there was like this whole PC contingent, this riot-grrrl contingent, that was there, and I was like "Oh, my God, one of these falsies is gonna pop out in front of one of these PC feminists."

TUCKER: In the mid-Seventies women's songs were usually pretty sappy. Like, oh, God, what was that horrible song that was No. 1 by Whitney Houston? Oh, God, give me a break. I haven't listened to Hole or L7 or Babes in Toyland, and this is a bad thing to say, but from their pictures I assume they're not singing sappy songs.

BJELLAND'S PERFUME: Just oil stuff like frangipani.

## BORN ROBERTA JOAN ANDERSON

HYNDE: And what about Joni? Why is everybody forgetting about Joni? Hell, she's a fuckin' excellent guitar player, excellent. I don't know any guitar player, any of the real greats, who don't rate Joni Mitchell up there with the best of them. And I hope to God you talk to her and encourage her to do some shows. Because we *want* her. We want you, Joni. Get out there. Put down your paintbrush for five minutes, please.

NDEGÉOCELLO: It's just I'm tired of being, like, betted against one another. Like a woman in rock, a woman in music—I mean, Joni Mitchell is a hell of a guitar player, but she's not known for that, it's her sensitivity.

AMOS: Joni Mitchell. How great was she? What a great musician, and, you know, Zeppelin, all those guys listened to her. Jimmy Page told me. What an influence, what a musical genius she is.

LOVE'S PERFUME: Fracas.

## CHILD'S PLAY, WITHOUT CHUCKY

NDEGÉOCELLO: I was fifteen when I started playing bass guitar—a friend of my brother's left it over at the house. I started fiddling with it, and it was love at first sight. Music was like "I walk, I talk, I breathe, I play music." And I don't talk very much. I just would hang in the house and play music. That was pretty much my life.

BJELLAND: I have a picture of me in second grade with a guitar, and that was when I wanted to start playing, but it was too big. It was like a classical guitar, and no second-grader could get their little fingers around the neck. And then when I saw the Cramps, I thought, "Easy guitar. I could do that."

TUCKER'S PERFUME: What the hell is it called? Ambush.

SCHELLENBACH: I was terrified to go to Manny's or Sam Ash. I resisted buying drumsticks for the first four years that I played. I would just find them on the stage or under the stage, or if somebody threw them in the audience, I'd make sure to get them because I just couldn't deal. I think part of my fear was that they would find out that I didn't know what I was doing, because, you know, you're constantly feeling defensive as a woman about your craft, especially if it's something male dominated. I taught myself to play drums, and all these guys could do, like, heavy-metal arpeggios for hours, and sometimes the worst thing you can get is "Oh, are *you* in a band? That's *cute.*" Plus I was fifteen, and it probably was pretty cute when I went up there to buy drumsticks.

JETT: I got a guitar for Christmas when I was thirteen, and I went to go take guitar lessons, and I remember, vividly, walking into this guitar shop where this guy taught lessons and saying to him, "Teach me how to play rock & roll." You know, I had that thirteen-year-old thing. I was so into it, and he looked at me like I was out of my mind, like I ate heads or something. And we went back, and he taught me "On Top of Old Smokey," and I thought, "Man, forget about this, this is not it." So I bought one of those learn-how-to-play-guitar books, and I just basically learned how to play by ear. I listened to a lot of Black Sabbath stuff because the chords were very slow.

LOVE: Play chords with two fingers like a bass player. As a teen girl, your hands are too small to do it another way. And it's like this big Masonic secret or something. No one would tell me. I'd be like "Why can you do this, and I can't? I'm smarter than you."

MADONNA'S PERFUME: Tuberose by Creed.

## SEXISM AND ROCK & ROLL. NO DRUGS.
## AND, AGAIN, NO CHUCKY

NDEGÉOCELLO: I like Snoop Doggy Dogg. He's misogynist as hell, but you can't tell me he doesn't have a flow. Sometimes you just put on music to hear it, and it's rocking—it makes you want to move, makes you want to dance, makes you want to fuck.

BJELLAND: I think being open, honest and baring your soul onstage is more sexy than wearing a miniskirt. And I don't think I'm ever gonna wear another baby barrette for the rest of my life if I have to keep seeing that everywhere.

JETT: You never hear two women or two all-female bands played on the radio back to back. It just won't happen. They just won't do it unless the *Billboard* Top Ten is at least half female—then they're basically forced to, but that's really the only situation.

SCHELLENBACH: I mean, I was talking about what an easy time I've had of it as a female musician, but I was kicked out of the Beastie Boys for being a woman because they changed from punk to rap, and Rick Rubin said he didn't like the sound of female rappers. I mean it's not like I was a great rapper, but neither were they.

LOVE: When that guy at *Time* magazine wrote that Pearl Jam cover story, he used, describing Babes in Toyland, the word *punkette*. Punkette! Do you say poetette? Do you say astronautette? It was so disgusting. It's like "Hey, *down here*, we don't use *punkette.*" Fucker. And it said alternative-band members shun dating models and groupies. That was the first paragraph. He was definitely coming from this perspective that all models and groupies are female. And this is *Time*.

GORDON: The bands that are the most interesting, malewise, are bands that express some kind of vulnerability—like Pavement, at least to me. And from Little Richard to Mick Jagger, what's made them interesting onstage is them expressing their female side. So maybe in a way the stage isn't about gender, it's about power. And power isn't gender specific. Maybe onstage, men feel enough power to put on a dress and pout.

JETT'S PERFUME: I wear Nahema by Guerlain. If that's how you pronounce it. Made from passion fruit.

## SO WHY DOES THE MEDIA FIXATE ON GENDER?

NDEGÉOCELLO: I don't know. That's just the most frustrating thing about all this. Someone has an agenda for you, or they want you to give what you may not have. I may be seen as a role model, but often you're given a job you may not be ready for or a job that you may not want. But I went to barber school. So I will always have something to do.

AMOS: Because they're so desperately trying to find an answer to something that I don't think has an answer.

GORDON: Because people like to look at pictures of girls, and they're slow to pick up on things. It's good copy, it's good picture, it's like how supermodels are good copy.

SCHELLENBACH: Maybe it's like "Well, we have to make it up to women for Anita Hill and Tailhook and William Kennedy Smith and all this crazy stuff. Let's give them something. We'll make Courtney Love the patron saint of rock."

AMOS' PERFUME: I don't wear it, but I do use grapefruit soap. Everywhere. And can I ask you a favor? No exclamation points, please!

## CLOSING COMMENTS

MADONNA: I think progress is being made, but it's very, very slow. But it's being made.

HYNDE: For a long time I thought that an all-girl band was a peculiar thing—like a band of Jews—but I don't know, maybe it is different. I like the idea anyway. I'm glad there's a lot of babes doing this shit because it's kind of lonely out there. Just bring on the bands, you know?

SCHELLENBACH: For a song like "Under My Thumb," even for people who really freak out about it, the reality is that in all relationships there are dynamics that would put somebody under somebody's thumb. But what do I know? I'm just a drummer.

GORDON: I don't really have a position except that for some reason it's more fun to watch girls playing music at this point. When you see women playing, you kind of don't know what's going to happen, and maybe that is because they're more willing to make themselves vulnerable. Or not. It can be like "Fuck you, you expect us to be vulnerable, and we're not." But still, the context for vulnerability is set up, merely because you're looking at girls onstage.

BJELLAND: The one nice thing is that girls will say they're starting up bands.

NDEGÉOCELLO: If I play a show, and it goes well, and people are calling out my name, it feels great. I feel like a rock star, and after that I go to my room, and I sit there lost, and I don't know where I fit in. And I think, "Is this the way my life is gonna be? This isn't where I want it." That's why I get so jaded when people ask me about being a woman. Don't just assess me as a woman, there are other things, there are so many other things.

LOVE: This is the thing with women, this is the issue: We all want to be in *Musician*. It's a common thing, you know why? Because, like, all the grungy guys are like "Why would you want to be in that fucking fascist magazine?" And it's because there's some kind of weird validation in the question "What kind of bass strings do you use?"

JETT: I just go out and tour my ass off and try to prove that it's rock & roll, no matter what gender is onstage.

TUCKER: What spurred me on to play drums was I just loved the Stones, and to just sit and listen to them was unacceptable. And the only thing that's ever surprised me or made me curious is that it's so much fun. And why aren't more women having some fun?

## BARBARA O'DAIR

# *BEDTIME STORIES* ALBUM REVIEW

★ ★ ★1/2

AFTER THE DRUBBING she has taken in the last few years, Madonna deserves to be mighty mad. And wounded anger is shot through her new album, *Bedtime Stories,* as she works out survival strategies. While always a feminist more by example than by word or deed, Madonna seems genuinely shocked at the hypocritical prudishness of her former fans, leading one to expect a set of biting screeds. But instead of reveling in raised consciousness, *Bedtime Stories* demonstrates a desire to get unconscious. Madonna still wants to go to bed, but this time it's to pull the covers over her head.

Still, in so doing, Madonna has come up with some awfully compelling sounds. In her retreat from sex to romance, she has enlisted four top R&B producers: Atlanta whiz kid Dallas Austin, Kenneth "Baby-face" Edmonds, Dave "Jam" Hall and Britisher Nellee Hooper (Soul II Soul), who add lush soul and creamy balladry. With this awesome collection of talent, the record verily shimmers. Bass-heavy grooves push it along when more conventional sentiments threaten to bog it down. Both aspects put it on chart-smart terrain.

A number of songs—"Survival," "Secret," "I'd Rather Be Your Lover" (to which Me'Shell Ndegéocello brings a bumping bass line and a jazzy rap)—are infectiously funky. And Madonna does a drive-by on her critics, complete with a keening synth line straight outta Dre, on "Human Nature": "Did I say something wrong?/Oops, I didn't know I couldn't talk about sex (I musta been crazy)."

But you don't need her to tell you that she's "drawn to sadness" or that "loneliness has never been a stranger," as she sings on the sorrowful "Love Tried to Welcome Me." The downbeat restraint in her vocals says it, from the tremulously tender "Inside of Me" to the sob in "Happiness lies in your own hand/It took me much too long to understand" from "Secret."

The record ultimately moves from grief to oblivion with the seductive techno pull of "Sanctuary." The pulsating drone of the title track (co-written by Björk and Hooper), with its murmured refrain of "Let's get unconscious, honey," renounces language for numbness.

Twirled in a gauze of (unrequited) love songs, *Bedtime Stories* says, "Fuck off, I'm not done yet." You have to listen hard to hear that, though. Madonna's message is still "Express yourself, don't repress yourself." This time, however, it comes not with a bang but a whisper.

■ **YEAR-END RANDOM NOTES** (December 29, 1994–January 12, 1995)

**March**

In case you missed Madonna's now-infamous appearance on *Late Show with David Letterman,* may we offer a summary: fuck, fuck, fuck, fuck, fuck. There, that about does it. Oh, yeah, the world's most famous nude model also revealed that urinating in the shower helps prevent athlete's foot. Chuck Berry could not be reached for comment.

## ARION BERGER

# OUR MADONNA COMPLEX

**M**ADONNA'S BEEN HAVING a rough time of it. Starting with 1992's seemingly nonstop Madonnathon of Her Nakedness, she's been renounced by the press and public in a hurt, angry way, like someone we once loved but whose singular charms are now irritants. It's a peculiarly American need, to personally like the celebrity of the moment.

We also like our stars to know their place, and it's a measure of Madonna's savvy that she pretends not to. She refuses to act like an Eighties relic, instead putting out albums as if she had a perfect right, and aging—albeit slowly—in front of the world. Madonna's mutations, once hailed as her greatest strength, have lately been perceived as offenses; her piquant pansexual hi-jinks are called crude exhibitionism; her jokey forthrightness is dismissed as vulgar self-parody. All of which, not coincidentally, happened about the time she stopped dressing like a saucy boy toy and took up the sexual whip hand. It looks like Madonna's pushed some buttons she wasn't even aiming for.

The scandals and disappointments are actually irrelevant to her talents. Madonna is primarily a musician—a point that gets lost amid the range of star projects she keeps simmering—and her critics let themselves forget that. But the chart numbers don't: *Erotica* spun off single after hit single, effortlessly. And now, with the dreamy, womanly *Bedtime Stories* staking its claim everywhere the national unconscious is sold, Madonna has proved once again that she's not going away. She's too great a pop singer.

It's no crime. In fact, it's a rarity to find someone with as sure a sense of craft, melody, hook and insight whose gifts don't diminish over time. Madonna's writing gets, if anything, more complex, more in line with her mature priorities. Her audience, however, has dwindled— Madonna's records have been selling about a million fewer each release since 1984's *Like a Virgin*. The fact is, she would have lost that number of fans anyway; the chilly, conceptual post-techno soul found on *Bedtime Stories* isn't as crowd-pleasing as her carefree downtown disco.

The postmodern mania for finding significance in every speck of pop effluvium burdened Madonna with more "meaning" than she cared to haul. She proved so quick and smart about sniffing out the next moment that she became a touchstone for all our secret attitudes and fears. (There's a small cult of theorists who maintain she's actually a human being, but let that pass.) If we take her at her word, Madonna considers herself to be a mere instigator, and what we do with her subversive proddings is our hang-up. The quibble over *Sex* was that her fantasies were so dull, juvenile, obvious. Of course, those might actually *be* her fantasies, meaning that their only fault was in not living up to our fantasies about her fantasies.

Since the release of *Bedtime Stories,* even virulent backlashers have calmed down. At worst, the attitude toward this soulful, meditative new Madonna is one of wariness. Skepticism plays a part—no one wants to be caught buying wholesale another of Madonna's temporary personas.

But the album's low-key genuineness doesn't allow for pushy questions. Here's a thirty-six-year-old lapsed Catholic yearning for a baby, a vulnerable woman whose loneliness informs every note. It would be coarse to equate that woman with the toy personalities of her butterfly years. The only real continuity between that time and this is that Madonna's still making great singles, great enough to hush dissenting voices.

■ **RANDOM NOTES** (July 13–27, 1995)

"You might think it strange that a girl who does what I do would be interested in a guy who does what he does," said Madonna at New York's Marriott Marquis, where Muhammad Ali was being honored by the Parkinson's Disease Foundation. Yes, indeedy! "It's not so strange. We are both survivors. We do not mince words. And most of all, we both love having our picture taken."

■ **RANDOM NOTES** (August 24, 1995)

Madonna was clutching her Chee Wa Wa, Chiquita, as she made her way to the stage at a KISS-FM concert at Irvine Meadows, in California. She was there to introduce UNV, an act on her Maverick label.

## PETER TRAVERS

# *BLUE IN THE FACE*
# FILM REVIEW

WHAT A BOLD NOTION for a movie, and what a bust in terms of execution. Writer Paul Auster and his codirector Wayne Wang had such a fine time filming *Smoke*, the summer arthouse hit that revolved around the eccentric characters in a Brooklyn, New York, tobacco shop run by Auggie Wren (Harvey Keitel), that they prevailed upon Miramax Films to let them make a second movie using the same setup.

The deal was they'd shoot it cheap and in five days. Keitel would be back with some of the original cast (Mel Gorham, Giancarlo Esposito, the great Victor Argo) and name newcomers such as Roseanne, Lily Tomlin, Michael J. Fox, Lou Reed, Jim Jarmusch, RuPaul and Madonna. Oh, yeah, there would be no script this time. Auster and Wang would provide comic situations around which the actors could improvise until they were blue in the face. You get the drift.

Great, huh? Try grating. It takes about ten minutes for the novelty to wear off. Then you start grabbing for fleeting moments of pleasure: Gorham practicing being sexy in the mirror, Argo warbling a country song, Jarmusch enjoying one last cigarette before he quits, Lou Reed being Lou Reed. *Fleeting* is the operative word. When these characters start talking at length without the benefit of Auster, the novelist *(The Music of Chance, Mr. Vertigo)* whose script for *Smoke* was a model of artful construction, you want to run for the nearest exit. Tomlin is a whiz at improv, but her role as the Belgian Waffle Man, complete with facial and chest hair, is a hand-me-down conceit. Fox has an extended monologue that defines the word *strained*. Then there's Roseanne. My admiration for her TV show remains undimmed after seven seasons—its writing has the toughest core of wit and intelligence on the tube. But *Blue* leaves Roseanne rudderless. She plays a wronged wife who harangues her husband with a crass invective that grows more shrill with each "fuck you."

Reportedly the directors held up cards that read BORING or FASTER or LIGHTEN UP or GET TO THE POINT. It's too bad the actors didn't pay attention. Look for Madonna, though, who turns up to deliver a singing telegram. Her performance is nothing to shout about, but her appearance marks the end of the movie and the audience's misery.

■ **RANDOM NOTES** (October 19, 1995)

Shall we push our way backstage for the 1995 MTV Video Music Awards at New York's Radio City Music Hall? Let's. There's Madonna, who didn't perform ("I'm too busy getting ready for *Evita* right now") but acted the part of the kvelling mother to Alanis Morissette, one of the artists signed to Madonna's label, Maverick. "Watching her gave me goose bumps," Madonna gushed. "I felt really proud."

■ **YEAR-END RANDOM NOTES:** (December 28, 1995–January 11, 1996)

**September**

The MTV Video Music Awards, held at New York's Radio City Music Hall, proved once again to be a heck of a lot more fun than the Grammys (although it did lead off with a ghastly performance by Michael Jackson, comprising an endless medley—*gaaahhh!* not "Billie Jean" again!—of his hits). TLC and Alanis Morissette turned in good performances, Tom Petty copped Best Male Video for "You Don't Know How It Feels," and Madonna picked up Best Female Video for her girl-meets-matador, girl-loses-matador opus, "Take a Bow."

■ **NOTABLE NEWS** (February 22, 1996)

The nut accused of harassing Madonna, Robert Dewey Hoskins, was found guilty of stalking and assault. The Los Angeles jury deliberated only four hours. (Sound familiar?) Hoskins, who was shot and wounded by bodyguards as he scaled Madonna's fence, faces up to ten years in prison.

■ **RANDOM NOTES** (March 7, 1996)

Madonna riled things up in Argentina when she arrived for the filming of *Evita*. Residents were irked that she'll portray Eva Perón, who is practically a saint there. Expertise in handling candle wax and crucifixes—what more do they want?

■ **RANDOM NOTES** (May 2, 1996)

Due out on June 25 is *Sweet Relief II: Songs of Vic Chesnutt.* Participants include R.E.M., Soul Asylum, Cracker, Indigo Girls and Joe Henry, who's teaming up with his sister-in-law, Madonna. Proceeds will aid musicians with medical hardships.

■ **RANDOM NOTES** (June 13, 1996)

Frontman in a prom dress. Drummer in green plastic overalls. Dancers in business suits. And Mike Watt in a full mouse costume on bass, blasting Madonna tunes before a slightly confused audience at Sacred Grounds Coffee House, in San Pedro, Calif. Ladies and gents, the world debut of the Madonnabes. "Hey, I'm thirty-eight, I've got to play every day—I can't let the meat loaf," says Watt. "The Madonnabes are Pedro dudes who've always been there for me." Er, the mouse suit? "It's a side mouse. Like if you and a buddy are at a restaurant and he gets served first—you start mousin' his chow. In a way, I'm side-mousin' Madonna. But this was a tribute."

## MIM UDOVITCH

# MADONNA

MADONNA IS EXPLAINING the better-known and more controversial of the two Frida Kahlos in her then not-yet-on-the-market home in the Hollywood Hills. "It depicts her birth and the relationship she had with her mother," she says. "That's the Virgin of Sorrows with her neck being pierced above the bed, and that's the mother saying, 'I want nothing to do with you.' And it's got a scroll on the bottom, which a lot of Latin painters used when they painted on tin; but she never filled that in, which is kind of strange, like: No comment. And she paid attention to the details. You know, she was a girl."

Of course, Madonna, wearing a nice white sleeveless maternity dress and Prada pony-skin-print pumps, is herself a girl who pays attention to the details. "When we were recording the album for *Evita*," says her co-star Antonio Banderas, "she was quite ritual in the way she prepared the studio. She put candles there and flowers and little things like that; the light was very, very down. She tried to create an environment, and she did; it was good."

Needless to say, the details Madonna is paying attention to (her life in the context of the birth, impending at the time we spoke, of her daughter, Lourdes Maria; her bicoastal relationship with beau and co-parent, the trainer and actor Carlos Leon; and the completion and release of her most ambitious movie project to date), and the details the world is paying attention to (posed naked! wore a cone bra onstage! likes sex! likes success! dyes her unmarried hair whatever color she feels like!) are not always exactly in sync.

In fact, if for some reason you were struck with total aphasia and had to relearn the fundamental truths of our social ways based solely on their representation in a Madonna-maniacal world press, you might well assume that liking sex and success was so aberrant that any woman admitting to it was pretty much divorced from the common bonds of human experience altogether. ("Talk about a good career move," opined one article written shortly after Lourdes Maria's birth, which I like to think even most hard-bitten cynics would concede to be, if not a blessed event, at least within the personal rather than the professional realm.)

With *Evita*—a risky project by even non-Madonnalogical standards, seeing as the movie musical as a form has only rarely found an audience since the days of *West Side Story*—Madonna, thirty-seven, is again venturing into the one professional realm where her liking for success has been the least gratified. Nevertheless, "that the level of her celebrity would get in the way of people seeing her as an actress playing a role was my only negative," says *Evita* director Alan Parker of the casting process. "Which no one would even worry about if it was Meryl Streep or Michelle Pfeiffer or whoever. But I always thought she would be able to do it; obviously, she could sing it better than either of those two women, for instance. And it's her finest performance, there is no doubt. And it's in a genre that plays to her strengths; she's very comfortable singing and acting together." And, in fact, early response to the soundtrack has been respectful and positive.

So don't cry for Madonna, who on this point, anyway, is not crying for herself. "After years of seeing me get the shit kicked out of me, people might be starting to . . . I don't know, not feel sorry for me, because I don't think they do, and I don't want them to," she says of the pendulum of public sentiment that tends to swing through the mass-culture commentary on her work without regard to its reception by the consumer. "I guess it's like if you keep spraying Raid on a cockroach and it won't die, after a while you just say, 'Oh, well, I'll let you live; there's your little space in the corner.' And I think also with *Evita,* you can't ignore that it's a great piece of work, not just that I've done, but of itself."

"When we were in Argentina," says Banderas, "half of the people were hating her and half of the people were loving her. It was really the story all over again of Eva Duarte. There is a famous saying of hers before she died, when she said something like, 'I'll be back and I'll be millions.' And here we go, she is now millions. It's something magic, I think, especially for Madonna. I know how much heart she risked in this project, and I really, really wish for her to be beautiful and powerful on the big screen so that someday I can tell my little grandchildren: 'Hey, I did the movie with Madonna, superstar.' "

*How often does the press get to you personally?*

I suppose it depends on the subject. I pretty much can let most stuff roll off. One thing I read that really, really, *really* irked me, where I did have to take a couple of deep breaths, was a little blurb during that minute there when everybody was making a big deal about the Clintons and their maybe wanting to adopt a baby. It said something like: "Hillary wants to adopt a baby; Madonna has one available." You know, implying that I was completely and utterly disconnected from my pregnancy and could care less about my baby. I really got upset.

*Did you see the piece by Jonathan Alter in "Newsweek"?*

No, but I heard about it. Was that where they were saying I was a bad role model for kids, or something, because I wasn't married? He must have been talking to Camille Paglia, who thinks that the reason I'm not married is that I can't bond with a man.

*Really? What happened to all that stuff you guys had in common? You didn't used to be able to turn on "Charlie Rose" without seeing Camille Paglia explain that you and she were soul mates in every way.*

I think I never paid her any mind, so she decided we didn't have anything in common after all. But about the press, you do obviously get better and better at accepting it over the years.

*It's odd how the cycle of bashing and building up works with you. Was the turning point the "Sex" book?*

Probably in the couple of years after, where my skin grew at least six inches thicker. I do think that society tends to root for you to win or lose. It's kind of tragic, in a way, because what goes up must come down. Anyone who attains an enormous popularity is about to see what the bottom of a boot looks like.

*You seem very serene about it.*

I think it's probably the hormones.

*Oh. I thought they were supposed to work the other way.*

They do. They work both ways. They give you an incredible sense of calmness and serenity and the ability to wait peacefully, because you have no other choice, and then the tiniest things can set you off. It's the most unbelievable thing to go through. I went to a concert the other night and this stranger came up to me and said, "Um, please let me touch your stomach, I know you're Madonna and everything, but I really believe that it will bring me good luck, and I'm going to the racetrack tomorrow." And he just looked really sincere, so I let him.

*The thing being that with you, that whole story could have happened even without the pregnancy.*

Yes. Though I'm not sure it's my stomach they want to touch.

*Were you trying to get pregnant?*

No. I certainly entertained the idea, but I was offered the movie and it kept going from being six months away to seven months away to seven and a half months away, but never a feasible time; and when I actually did get pregnant, I wasn't trying.

*You did it the old-fashioned way?*

By mistake? Basically, yeah.

*Well, way to go!*

Well, you know, it wasn't something I was trying to do; but after I got over the shock of knowing it, I felt that it was kind of poetic that it happened while I was trying to give birth to another sort of baby. And it just seemed like the right moment, though there were days. Really, it felt like we couldn't acknowledge too much that I was pregnant, because then you start worrying about everything: about the temperature, and how long I was on my feet, and all the dancing. I think we all went around, or I went around, in and out of pretending that I wasn't pregnant, because it was really difficult to focus on the character *and* worry about whether I was getting the right kind of rest. So, I don't know, I think I thought about it as if it were some sort of a gift, and I thought if it's happening in this way, then nothing will get in the way of it—this baby's coming no matter how many hours I stand on my feet.

*What are your feelings about Dennis Rodman's book? I guess it's unlikely that you've dreamed since girlhood of being characterized sexually not as an acrobat but not a dead fish, either.*

Well, I somehow think he had some help with the writing, because to tell you the truth, I don't think even he would say that. But you never know.

*You do never know. I like to watch him in interviews and wonder what it is he thinks he's saying. What he's actually saying makes so delightfully little sense.*

Well . . . it's hard for me to pay him any compliments because I thought what he did was really low, but there is some truth about people who don't fit into categories or are rebellious or defy convention or whatever, though not at the expense of hurting people. I do think that is one of the things I found interesting about him. I also fantasized somehow that there was a great mind behind all that rebellion, and I think there's actually just a scrambled brain; so it was sort of disappointing.

*How did the material in "Evita" change from the stage to the movie version?*

A lot of lyrics changed that were too abstract, because some of the rhyming that [*Evita* lyricist] Tim Rice did had a little bit of crossword-puzzle thing going on—it sounded good, but it didn't make any sense. Alan [Parker] went through everything and made sure that the songs were telling a story. And they expanded certain musical themes; the one new song that was written is a love song between [Juan] Perón and Eva, so that adds a dimension of their love versus just two people who are using each other.

*I ask because, to me, the original version is kind of misogynist.*

It's beyond misogynist. The funny thing is when I was cast in the movie, I was psyched to play the part; then, the more research I did, the more I hated the point of view. I thought, this is unfair, it's so sexist, this is so awful. And I came to realize that it was the typical reaction that all the aristocrats and most men had toward her; they were completely frightened by the kind of power that she had. And it's always easy, it's the most obvious and predictable way out, to call a woman a whore and imply that she has no morals and no integrity and no talent. And God knows, I can relate to that. It's the oldest trick in the book. And Sir Andrew Lloyd Webber and Sir Tim Rice fell for it, and . . . well, it was extremely popular, that story. But it was popular because it was anti-fascist as well. [The Peróns] were considered to be fascists, and you know, there was a time when we were against all that.

*So how do you feel you changed the character?*

I just tried to make her a human being. I certainly don't see her as a saint. But what I tried to do was flesh her out and show her humanity and her sadness and pain, and give it some connection, you know? She came from a big family; she was an illegitimate child; she came from extreme poverty. And I think this really disturbed her. I think that her whole life was that, really. But who knows? I could say the same thing about myself. Why did I emerge from my family and say, I'm getting the fuck out of here, I'm going to New York? I think it would be foolish to paint her one way or the other, and I think that a person who attained the kind of power she attained and accomplished what she accomplished could not be stupid or *just* opportunistic. You know? You've got to have something going on up there.

*What are your happiest expectations about motherhood?*

I think it will be a very healing experience because I didn't grow up with a mother and I envision hugging and tactile pleasure and the happiness of that. And I think how amazing to have someone in my life who's a part of me in a way that no one else can be, no matter how much you love them. There's also the feeling of responsibility that's different from any other love. People would always say, "If you have a baby, you'd better pray that it's a boy," because they think that a daughter would be some sort of competition. But it doesn't feel that way.

*And with a girl you get to play dress up.*

Oh, my God, yes. That gets me through my worst moments.

## ELYSA GARDNER

# *EVITA: THE COMPLETE MOTION PICTURE MUSIC SOUNDTRACK*

### Album Review

★ ★1/2

A YOUNG WOMAN from humble stock, desperately seeking fame and adulation, sweats and seduces her way to the top of the world, only to be forced to come to terms with her mortality. It's no wonder that Madonna was so attracted to the story of Argentina's legendary first lady, Eva Perón, the subject of Andrew Lloyd Webber and Tim Rice's 1978 musical, *Evita*. Nearly twenty years later, the stage production makes it to the big screen, and Ms. Ciccone has the starring role. As you can hear on the film's two-hour-long soundtrack album, the result has all the earmarks of a Big Hollywood Event—from the lush orchestration and thundering vocal choruses to the lusty singing of Madonna's co-star Antonio Banderas, who plays the narrator, Che. (The verdict on Banderas' vocal abilities: not awful, but he shouldn't give up his day job.)

*Evita* is, above all else, a vehicle for its leading lady. As a composer for the musical theater, Webber is slick and banal. But for the part of Eva Perón, he and lyricist Rice crafted songs that are undeniably rich in dramatic potential. Madonna, however, does not always rise to the occasion. She is hindered by the thin tone and limited range of her voice and seems at times to be intimidated by her material. Webber and Rice's hit ballad "Don't Cry for Me Argentina" could have been an ideal showcase for the plucky tenderness and unabashed yearning that distinguish Madonna's best pop singles, yet her delivery is curiously tentative. Likewise, her rendition of "Buenos Aires" has little of the fire and grace that Patti LuPone brought to this percolating number on Broadway.

Madonna is more effective in moments of vulnerability. In the stage version of *Evita*, the bittersweet "Another Suitcase in Another Hall" is sung by Juan Perón's previous mistress. Madonna reclaims the song for Eva, revealing a hidden loneliness in her character's *femme fatale* façade. In "You Must Love Me," a new song written by Webber and Rice specifically for the movie, Madonna captures with trembling intensity the dying Eva's need for constant affirmation. That no amount of money and celebrity can satisfy such a basic craving is one of life's bitter ironies. That Madonna can explore this issue in song with such personal conviction is part of what makes her, for all of her foibles, utterly fascinating.

# DISCOGRAPHY

**MADONNA**
Sire (July 1983)
**Produced by:** Reggie Lucas
**Singles:** Holiday (produced by John "Jellybean" Benitez); Borderline; Lucky Star
**Additional Tracks:** Burning Up; I Know It; Think of Me; Physical Attraction; Every-
body (produced by Mark Kamins)

**LIKE A VIRGIN**
Sire (November 1984)
**Produced by:** Nile Rodgers
**Singles:** Like a Virgin; Material Girl; Angel; Dress You Up
**Additional Tracks:** Over and Over; Love Don't Live Here Anymore; Shoo-Bee-Do;
Pretender; Stay

**TRUE BLUE**
Sire (June 1986)
**Produced by:** Madonna, Patrick Leonard and Stephen Bray
**Singles:** Live to Tell; Papa Don't Preach; True Blue; Open Your Heart; La Isla Bonita
**Additional Tracks:** White Heat; Where's the Party; Jimmy Jimmy; Love Makes the
World Go Round

**WHO'S THAT GIRL**
Sire (August 1987)
**Singles by Madonna:** Who's That Girl (produced by Madonna and Patrick Leonard);
Causing a Commotion (produced by Madonna and Stephen Bray)
**Additional Tracks by Madonna:** The Look of Love (produced by Madonna and
Patrick Leonard); Can't Stop (produced by Madonna and Stephen Bray)

**YOU CAN DANCE**
Sire (November 1987)
No singles; all dance remixes.
**Tracks:** Spotlight (produced by Stephen Bray); Holiday (produced by John "Jelly-
bean" Benitez); Everybody (produced by Mark Kamins); Physical Attraction (pro-
duced by Reggie Lucas); Over and Over (produced by Nile Rodgers); Into the
Groove (produced by Madonna and Stephen Bray); Where's the Party (produced

by Madonna, Patrick Leonard and Steven Bray); Holiday (dub version) (produced by John "Jellybean" Benitez); Into the Groove (produced by Madonna and Stephen Bray); Where's the Party (produced by Madonna, Patrick Leonard and Steven Bray)

## LIKE A PRAYER
Sire (March 1989)

**Singles:** Like a Prayer (produced by Madonna and Patrick Leonard); Express Your-self (produced by Madonna and Stephen Bray); Cherish (produced by Madonna and Patrick Leonard); Oh Father (produced by Madonna and Patrick Leonard); Keep It Together (produced by Madonna and Stephen Bray)

**Additional Tracks:** Love Song (produced by Madonna and Prince); Till Death Do Us Part (produced by Madonna and Patrick Leonard); Promise to Try (produced by Madonna and Patrick Leonard); Dear Jessie (produced by Madonna and Patrick Leonard); Pray for Spanish Eyes (produced by Madonna and Patrick Leonard); Act of Contrition (produced by Madonna and Patrick Leonard)

## I'M BREATHLESS
Sire (May 1990)

**Singles:** Vogue (produced by Madonna and Shep Pettibone); Hanky Panky (pro-duced by Madonna and Patrick Leonard)

**Additional Tracks:** He's a Man (produced by Madonna and Patrick Leonard); Sooner or Later (produced by Madonna and Bill Bottrell); I'm Going Bananas (pro-duced by Madonna and Patrick Leonard); Cry Baby (produced by Madonna and Patrick Leonard); Something to Remember (produced by Madonna and Patrick Leonard); Back in Business (produced by Madonna and Patrick Leonard); More (produced by Madonna and Bill Bottrell); What Can You Lose (produced by Madonna and Bill Bottrell); Now I'm Following You (Part I) (produced by Madonna and Patrick Leonard); Now I'm Following You (Part II) (produced by Madonna, Patrick Leonard and Kevin Gilbert)

## THE IMMACULATE COLLECTION
Sire (November 1990)

**Singles:** Justify My Love (produced by Lenny Kravitz); Rescue Me (produced by Madonna and Shep Pettibone); Crazy for You (produced by John "Jellybean" Ben-itez) [originally released as a single in 1985 from the *Vision Quest* soundtrack]

**Additional Tracks:** Holiday (produced by John "Jellybean" Benitez); Lucky Star (pro-duced by Reggie Lucas); Borderline (produced by Reggie Lucas and John "Jelly-bean" Benitez); Like a Virgin (produced by Nile Rodgers); Material Girl (produced by Nile Rodgers); Into the Groove (produced by Madonna and Stephen Bray); Live to Tell (produced by Madonna and Patrick Leonard); Papa Don't Preach (produced by Madonna and Stephen Bray); Open Your Heart (produced by Madonna and

Patrick Leonard); La Isla Bonita (produced by Madonna and Patrick Leonard); Like a Prayer (produced by Madonna and Patrick Leonard); Express Yourself (produced by Madonna and Stephen Bray); Cherish (produced by Madonna and Patrick Leonard); Vogue (produced by Madonna and Shep Pettibone)

## EROTICA
Maverick (October 1992)

**Singles:** Erotica; Deeper and Deeper; Bad Girl; Rain (all singles produced by Madonna and Shep Pettibone)

**Additional Tracks:** Fever (produced by Madonna and Shep Pettibone); Bye Bye Baby (produced by Madonna and Shep Pettibone); Where Life Begins (produced by Madonna and Andre Betts); Waiting (produced by Madonna and Andre Betts); Thief of Hearts (produced by Madonna and Shep Pettibone); Words (produced by Madonna and Shep Pettibone); Why's It So Hard (produced by Madonna and Shep Pettibone); In This Life (produced by Madonna and Shep Pettibone); Did You Do It? (produced by Madonna and Andre Betts); Secret Garden (produced by Madonna and Andre Betts)

## BEDTIME STORIES
Maverick (October 1994)

**Produced by:** Madonna, Nellee Hooper, Babyface, Dallas Austin and Dave "Jam" Hall

**Singles:** Secret; Take a Bow; Bedtime Story; Human Nature

**Additional Tracks:** Survival; I'd Rather Be Your Lover; Don't Stop; Inside of Me; Forbidden Love; Love Tried to Welcome Me; Sanctuary

## SOMETHING TO REMEMBER
Maverick (November 1995)

**Singles:** You'll See (produced by Madonna and David Foster)

**Additional Tracks:** I Want You (with Massive Attack) (produced by Nellee Hooper); Take a Bow (produced by Babyface and Madonna); Crazy for You (produced by John "Jellybean" Benitez); Live to Tell (produced by Madonna and Patrick Leonard); Love Don't Live Here Anymore (remix) (produced by David Reitzos); Something to Remember (produced by Madonna and Patrick Leonard); Forbidden Love (produced by Nellee Hooper and Madonna); One More Chance (produced by Madonna and David Foster); Rain (produced by Madonna and Shep Pettibone); Oh Father (produced by Madonna and Patrick Leonard); I Want You (orchestral, with Massive Attack) (produced by Nellee Hooper); This Used to Be My Playground (produced by Madonna and Shep Pettibone) [originally released as a single in 1992 from *A League of Their Own,* but not on soundtrack album]; I'll Remember (produced by Patrick Leonard) [originally released as a single in 1994 from *With Honors* soundtrack]

## EVITA: THE COMPLETE MOTION PICTURE MUSIC SOUNDTRACK

Warner Bros. (November 1996; 2 CDs)

**Principle Vocals:** Madonna, Antonio Banderas, Jonathan Pryce, Jimmy Nail

**Produced by:** Nigel Wright, Alan Parker, Andrew Lloyd Webber, David Caddick

**Singles:** You Must Love Me; Don't Cry for Me Argentina (remixed single with additional producer Emilio Estefan)

**Additional Tracks:** A Cinema in Buenos Aires, 26 July 1952; Requiem for Evita; Oh What a Circus; On This Night of a Thousand Stars; Eva and Magaldi/Eva Beware of the City; Buenos Aires; Another Suitcase in Another Hall; Goodnight and Thank You; The Lady's Got Potential; Charity Concert/The Art of the Possible; I'd Be Surprisingly Good for You; Hello and Goodbye; Peron's Latest Flame; A New Argentina; On the Balcony of the Casa Rosada 1; On the Balcony of the Casa Rosada 2; High Flying, Adored; Rainbow High; Rainbow Tour; The Actress Hasn't Learned the Lines (You'd Like to Hear); And the Money Kept Rolling In (and Out); Partido Feminista; She Is a Diamond; Santa Evita; Waltz for Eva and Che; Your Little Body's Slowly Breaking Down; Eva's Final Broadcast; Latin Chant; Lament

# VIDEOGRAPHY

**Selective Full-Length Videos**

**MADONNA**
(1984)
**SONGS:** Burning Up; Borderline; Lucky Star; Like a Virgin

**MADONNA: THE VIRGIN TOUR LIVE**
(1985)
**SONGS:** Dress You Up; Holiday; Into the Groove; Everybody; Gambler; Lucky Star; Crazy for You; Over and Over; Like a Virgin; Material Girl

**CIAO ITALIA: LIVE FROM ITALY**
(1988)
**SONGS:** Open Your Heart; Lucky Star; True Blue; Papa Don't Preach; White Heat; Causing a Commotion; The Look of Love; Medley: Dress You Up/Material Girl/Like a Virgin; Where's the Party; Live to Tell; Into the Groove; La Isla Bonita; Who's That Girl; Holiday

**THE IMMACULATE COLLECTION**
(1990)
**SONGS:** Lucky Star; Borderline; Like a Virgin; Material Girl; Papa Don't Preach; Open Your Heart; La Isla Bonita; Like a Prayer; Express Yourself; Cherish; Oh Father; Vogue; Vogue (from 1990 MTV Awards)

**THE GIRLIE SHOW: LIVE DOWN UNDER**
(1993)
**SONGS:** Erotica; Fever; Vogue; Rain; Express Yourself; Deeper and Deeper; Why's It So Hard; In This Life; The Beast Within; Like a Virgin; Bye Bye Baby; I'm Going Bananas; La Isla Bonita; Holiday; Justify My Love; Everybody Is a Star/Everybody

**Single-Song Videos**

**"EVERYBODY"**
(1982)
**Director:** Ed Steinberg
**Location:** New York City

**"BURNING UP"**
(1983)
**Director:** Steve Barron
**Location:** Castaic Lake and Angeles National Forest, California

**"BORDERLINE"**
(1984)
**Director:** Mary Lambert
**Location:** Los Angeles

**"LUCKY STAR"**
(1984)
**Director:** Arthur Pierson
**Location:** Los Angeles

**"LIKE A VIRGIN"**
(1984)
**Director:** Mary Lambert
**Location:** Venice, Italy and New York City

**"MATERIAL GIRL"**
(1985)
**Director:** Mary Lambert
**Location:** Los Angeles

**"CRAZY FOR YOU"**
(1985)
**Director:** Harold Becker
**Location:** New York City [clips from *Vision Quest*]

**"INTO THE GROOVE"**
(1985)
**Director:** Susan Seidelman
**Location:** New York City [clips from *Desperately Seeking Susan*]

**"DRESS YOU UP"**
(1985)
**Director:** Danny Kleinman
**Location:** Live footage from the Virgin Tour in Detroit

**"GAMBLER"**
(1985)
**Film Director:** Danny Kleinman
**Location:** Live footage from the Virgin Tour in Detroit

**"LIKE A VIRGIN"** (*Madonna: The Virgin Tour Live* version)
(1985)
**Director:** Danny Kleinman
**Location:** Detroit

**"LIVE TO TELL"**
(1986)
**Director:** James Foley
**Location:** Los Angeles

**"PAPA DON'T PREACH"**
(1986)
**Director:** James Foley
**Location:** Staten Island, New York

**"TRUE BLUE"**
(Note: Two versions—U.S. and European; U.S. version created by winners of an MTV
    contest, and Madonna is not in video)
(1986)
**Director:** Angel Gracia and Cliff Guest (U.S.); James Foley (European)
**Location:** New York City (European)

**"OPEN YOUR HEART"**
(1986)
**Director:** Jean Baptiste Mondino
**Location:** Downtown Los Angeles

**"LA ISLA BONITA"**
(1987)
**Director:** Mary Lambert
**Location:** Los Angeles

**"WHO'S THAT GIRL"**
(1987)
**Director:** Peter Rosenthal
**Location:** Los Angeles

**"LIKE A PRAYER"**
(1989)
**Director:** Mary Lambert
**Location:** Los Angeles

**"EXPRESS YOURSELF"**
(1989)
**Director:** David Fincher
**Location:** Los Angeles

**"CHERISH"**
(1989)
**Director:** Herb Ritts
**Location:** Los Angeles

**"OH FATHER"**
(1989)
**Director:** David Fincher
**Location:** Los Angeles

**"DEAR JESSIE"** (European)
(1989)
**Director** (animated)

**"VOGUE"**
(1990)
**Director:** David Fincher
**Location:** Los Angeles

**"JUSTIFY MY LOVE"**
(1990)
**Director:** Jean Baptiste Mondino
**Location:** Royal Monceau Hotel, Paris

**"LIKE A VIRGIN"** (*Truth or Dare* version; includes footage from tour and film)
(1991)
**Director:** Alek Keshishian
**Location:** Various

**"THIS USED TO BE MY PLAYGROUND"**
(1992)
**Director:** Alek Keshishian
**Location:** Los Angeles

**"EROTICA"**
(1992)
**Director:** Fabien Baron
**Location:** New York City

**"DEEPER AND DEEPER"**
(1992)
**Director:** Bobby Woods
**Location:** Los Angeles

**"BAD GIRL"**
(1993)
**Director:** David Fincher
**Location:** New York City

**"FEVER"**
(1993)
**Director:** Stephane Sednaoui
**Location:** Miami

**"RAIN"**
(1993)
**Director:** Mark Romanek
**Location:** Los Angeles

**"I'LL REMEMBER"**
(1994)
**Director:** Alek Keshishian
**Location:** Los Angeles

**"SECRET"**
(1994)
**Director:** Melodie McDaniel
**Location:** Harlem, New York

**"TAKE A BOW"**
(1994)
**Director:** Michael Haussman
**Location:** Ronda, Spain

**"BEDTIME STORY"**
(1995)
**Director:** Mark Romanek
**Location:** Los Angeles

**"HUMAN NATURE"**
(1995)
**Director:** Jean Baptiste Mondino
**Location:** Los Angeles

**"I WANT YOU"**
(1995)
**Director:** Earle Sebastian

**"YOU'LL SEE"**
(1995)
**Director:** Michael Haussman
**Location:** Spain and London

**"LOVE DON'T LIVE HERE ANYMORE"**
(1996)
**Director:** Jean Baptiste Mondino

**"YOU MUST LOVE ME"**
(1996)
**Director:** Alan Parker
**Location:** Los Angeles

**"DON'T CRY FOR ME ARGENTINA"**
(1996)
**Director:** Alan Parker
**Location:** Los Angeles

# FILMOGRAPHY

**A CERTAIN SACRIFICE**
**Release Year:** Released on video in 1985 (filmed in Super 8 in 1979 and never released theatrically)
**Company:** Worldvision
**Director:** Stephen Jon Lewicki
**Character:** Bruna

**VISION QUEST**
**Release Year:** 1985
**Company:** Warner Bros.
**Director:** Harold Becker
**Character:** Performs "Crazy for You" and "Gambler" in a club scene

**DESPERATELY SEEKING SUSAN**
**Release Year:** 1985
**Company:** Orion
**Director:** Susan Seidelman
**Character:** Susan

**SHANGHAI SURPRISE**
**Release Year:** 1986
**Company:** Metro-Goldwyn-Mayer
**Director:** Jim Goddard
**Character:** Gloria Tatlock

**WHO'S THAT GIRL**
**Release Year:** 1987
**Company:** Warner Bros.
**Director:** James Foley
**Character:** Nikki Finn

**BLOODHOUNDS OF BROADWAY**
**Release Year:** 1989
**Company:** Vestron
**Director:** Howard Brookner
**Character:** Hortense Hathaway

**DICK TRACY**
**Release Year:** 1990
**Company:** Touchstone
**Director:** Warren Beatty
**Character:** Breathless Mahoney

**TRUTH OR DARE**
**Release Year:** 1991
**Company:** Miramax
**Director:** Alek Keshishian
(Documentary)

**A LEAGUE OF THEIR OWN**
**Release Year:** 1992
**Company:** Columbia
**Director:** Penny Marshall
**Character:** Mae Mordabito

**SHADOWS AND FOG**
**Release Year:** 1992
**Company:** Orion
**Director:** Woody Allen
**Character:** Marie

**BODY OF EVIDENCE**
**Release Year:** 1993
**Company:** Metro-Goldwyn-Mayer/United Artists
**Director:** Uli Edel
**Character:** Rebecca Carlson

**DANGEROUS GAME**
**Release Year:** 1993
**Company:** Metro-Goldwyn-Mayer
**Director:** Abel Ferrara
**Character:** Sarah Jennings

**BLUE IN THE FACE**
**Release Year:** 1995
**Company:** Miramax
**Directors:** Wayne Wang and Paul Auster
**Character:** Cameo delivering a singing telegram

**FOUR ROOMS**
**Release Year:** 1995
**Company:** Miramax
**Directors:** Allison Anders; Alexandre Rockwell; Robert Rodriguez; Quentin
Tarantino
**Character:** A witch in Allison Anders' segment "The Missing Ingredient"

**EVITA**
**Release Year:** 1996
**Company:** Hollywood
**Director:** Alan Parker
**Character:** Eva Perón/Evita

# ABOUT THE CONTRIBUTORS

**Vince Aletti** was a regular early contributor to ROLLING STONE and other music magazines on the subjects of black music and disco. His "Disco File" column ran for four years in *Record World*. He is currently a senior editor and the photography critic for the *Village Voice*.

**Arion Berger** is a freelance writer who lives in Washington, D.C.

**Debby Bull,** a former contributing editor for ROLLING STONE, has a master's degree in American Studies. As a rock critic and popular-culture observer, her writing has appeared in many magazines. She is the author of *Blue Jelly* (Hyperion) and lives in Livingston, Montana, and St. Croix Falls, Wisconsin.

Californian **Keith Cahoon** has worked in various capacities in the music business, since 1984 for Tower Records in Tokyo. His writings on music have appeared in *Big O* (Singapore), *Bounce* (Japan), *Rip It Up* (New Zealand) and *Pulse* (U.S.A.), among others.

**Mark Coleman,** a former ROLLING STONE senior editor, is currently a freelance writer.

**Christopher Connelly,** a former associate editor at ROLLING STONE and former editor-in-chief of *Premiere*, is currently an *MTV News* correspondent.

**J.D. Considine** has been writing about music since 1977. In addition to his duties as pop music critic at the *Baltimore Sun* and *Evening Sun,* he is a contributing editor at *Musician* and writes regularly for ROLLING STONE; his work has also appeared in a variety of other publications, including *Playboy,* the *Village Voice,* the *Washington Post* and *Request*. He also contributed to *The ROLLING STONE Illustrated History of Rock & Roll*, third edition, and *The ROLLING STONE Album Guide*.

**Anthony DeCurtis** is a writer and contributing editor at ROLLING STONE. He is the editor of *Present Tense: Rock & Roll and Culture* and coeditor of *The ROLLING STONE Illustrated History of Rock & Roll* and *The ROLLING STONE Album Guide*. He won a Grammy for his liner notes for the Eric Clapton retrospective *Crossroads* and has twice won ASCAP Deems Taylor Awards for excellence in writing about music. The author of the introduction to *R.E.M.: The ROLLING STONE Files*, he is currently at work on a biography of R.E.M.

**Adrian Deevoy** is a contributing editor for the U.K. music magazine *Q*.

**Thom Duffy** is international deputy editor of *Billboard* in London. He was previously talent editor of *Billboard* in New York and pop music writer for the *Orlando Sentinel* and the *New Haven Register*. His work has appeared in ROLLING STONE, *US, People, Entertainment Weekly, Musician, Rock & Rap Confidential* and other publications.

**Paul Evans** has contributed his writing to *The ROLLING STONE Album Guide, The ROLLING STONE Encyclopedia of Rock & Roll* and the forthcoming ROLLING STONE *Jazz and Blues Album Guide*.

**Jim Farber** is the pop music critic of the *New York Daily News*. His work has appeared in ROLLING STONE, the *Village Voice, Entertainment Weekly, New York* magazine and many other publications.

**Carrie Fisher** is an actress *(Shampoo, Star Wars, When Harry Met Sally)* and author *(Surrender the Pink, Postcards From the Edge, Delusions of Grandma)*.

**David Fricke** is a senior editor of ROLLING STONE. He joined the magazine in 1985 as a senior writer. He is also the American correspondent for the English weekly *Melody Maker* and has written about music for *Musician, People* and the *New York Times*. He is the author of *Animal Instinct*, a biography of Def Leppard, and wrote the liner notes for major CD reissues of the Byrds, Moby Grape, John Prine, Led Zeppelin and the Velvet Underground.

**Mikal Gilmore** is a ROLLING STONE contributing editor and author of *Shot in the Heart*.

**Michael Goldberg** is the editor and publisher of *Addicted to Noise* (www.addict.com), an online music magazine. In 1996 he was named by *Newsweek* to their "Net 50" group of Internet visionaries; the Music Journalism Awards judges voted him "Music Journalist of the Year" for 1995. Between July 1993 and 1994, he was an associate editor and senior writer at ROLLING STONE. His writing has also appeared in *Esquire*, the *New Musical Express* and *Wired*.

**Kurt Loder** was an editor at ROLLING STONE from 1979 to 1988 and is still a contributing editor. He is the author of *I, Tina*, a best-selling biography of Tina Turner. He is currently an anchor of *MTV News*.

**Barbara O'Dair** is the editor of *US: The Entertainment Magazine*. Formerly the deputy music editor of ROLLING STONE, she has also worked as a senior editor at *Entertainment Weekly* and the *Village Voice*. She has written for ROLLING STONE, *Spin*, the *Village Voice*, and other publications. She is the recipient of the 1996 Mudfish Poetry Prize, the coeditor of a book of feminist essays, *Caught Looking: Women, Pornography and Censorship*, and the editor of *The ROLLING STONE Book of Women in Rock: Trouble Girls*.

**Jeffrey Ressner** was a senior writer at ROLLING STONE and West Coast bureau chief for *US*. He currently covers the entertainment industry for *Time* in Los Angeles. His favorite Madonna song is "Like a Virgin."

**Jean Rosenbluth** is a music critic for the *Los Angeles Times*.

**Anita Sarko** is a freelance writer and world-renowned DJ.

**Fred Schruers** is a contributing editor at ROLLING STONE.

**Don Shewey** has written for ROLLING STONE, *Esquire, American Theater*, the *Village Voice* and the *New York Times*, among other publications. He has also written three books about theater, including the biography *Sam Shepard* and *Out Front: Contemporary Gay and Lesbian Plays*. He studied classic languages at Rice University and acting at Boston University. Born in Denver, Colorado, he grew up in a trailer park on a dirt road in Waco, Texas, and currently resides in midtown Manhattan one block from Carnegie Hall.

**Davitt Sigerson** has been a music journalist, songwriter, producer (Tori Amos, David & David, the Bangles) and recording artist (on Island Records). He is currently president and chief executive of EMI Records.

**Lauren Spencer,** formerly a senior editor at *Spin* and ROLLING STONE, is a freelance writer living in New York City. She was recently senior director of video promotions at Elektra Records.

**Elizabeth Tippens** is the author of *Winging It,* a novel published by Riverhead Books. Her writing has appeared in a number of magazines including ROLLING STONE, *Cosmopolitan, Playboy* and *Mademoiselle,* and in anthologies including *Voices of the Xiled.* She is at work completing her second novel, *Sleeping Beauty Takes a Nap.* She lives in New York City with her husband.

**Peter Travers** is the film editor and movie critic of ROLLING STONE.

**Mim Udovitch** is a New York–based writer.

**Peter Wilkinson** is a contributing editor at ROLLING STONE and *Men's Journal.*

**Bill Zehme,** currently a senior writer at Esquire, never slept with Madonna, but he has been naked with Sharon Stone. He is also author of *The ROLLING STONE Book of Comedy.*

# OTHER BOOKS IN *THE ROLLING STONE FILES* SERIES

**U2: *The* ROLLING STONE *Files***
By the Editors of ROLLING STONE
Introduction by Elysa Gardner
The ultimate compendium of articles, interviews and indispensable facts for the die-hard U2 fan. This book covers everything about the band, from the group's beginnings as a punk band in Dublin to superstardom and the Zoo TV Tour. From album reviews to fascinating snippets of trivia, learn all there is to know about one of the hottest bands of the past two decades, from the original rock & roll magazine.
[$12.95 (Canada $15.95); ISBN 0-7868-8001-5]

*Neil Young: The* ROLLING STONE *Files*
By the Editors of ROLLING STONE
Introduction by Holly George-Warren
Rock & roll will never die and neither will the amazing influence of Neil Young. ROLLING STONE has chronicled this rock icon since its third issue in 1967, covering his stint with Buffalo Springfield, his years of fame with Crosby, Stills, Nash and Young, his early solo successes and later years of commercial eclipse and his mainstream reemergence with songs like "Rockin' in the Free World."
[$12.95 (Canada $15.95); ISBN 0-7868-8043-0]

*R.E.M.: The* ROLLING STONE *Files*
By the Editors of ROLLING STONE
Introduction by Anthony DeCurtis
Unmatched in depth and information, this compendium covers everything from R.E.M.'s early days in Athens, Georgia, and years of nonstop touring to the band's commercial breakthrough in 1991 with *Out of Time* and the 1994 release of the guitar-blasting *Monster*. Incisive Q & A interviews with Michael Stipe and Peter Buck, in addition to

news stories, album reviews and performance critiques, make this a must-read for every true R.E.M. fan. [$12.95 (Canada $16.95); ISBN 0-7868-8054-6]

*Bruce Springsteen: The ROLLING STONE Files*
By the Editors of ROLLING STONE
Introduction by Parke Puterbaugh
Bruce Springsteen has remained one of the foremost artists of our time, and ROLLING STONE has been there from the beginning, documenting every detail surrounding his ascent to rock & roll superstardom. Part biography, part rock history, this compendium covers everything from Springsteen's early working-class years to his mid-Seventies break-through with the E Street Band, to his marriages and family life and his goals for the future.
[$12.95 (Canada $15.95); ISBN 0-7868-8153-4]

*IN BOOKSTORES EVERYWHERE FROM HYPERION*